BIOGRAPHY
AND
AUTOBIOGRAPHY

BIOGRAPHY
AND
AUTOBIOGRAPHY

*Essays on
Irish and Canadian
History and Literature*

Edited by
James Noonan

Carleton University Press
Ottawa
1993

©Carleton University Press Inc. 1993

Printed and bound in Canada
Carleton General List 24

Canadian Cataloguing in Publication Data
Main entry under title:

Biography and autobiography : essays on Irish and Canadian history and literature

Includes bibliographical references.

ISBN   0-88629-208-5 (casebound)
ISBN   0-88629-209-3 (paperback)

1. Ireland–Biography–History and criticism–Congresses.   2. Biography as a literary form–Congresses.   3. Authors, Irish–Biography–
History and criticism–Congresses.   4. Irish–Canada–History–Congresses.   I. Noonan, James.   II. Canadian Association for Irish
Studies. Conference (1991 : Carleton University).

CT21.B46 1993   809'.93592'00417   C93-090430-3

Carleton University Press   Distributed in Canada by:
160 Paterson Hall
Carleton University   Oxford University Press Canada
1125 Colonel By Drive   70 Wynford Drive
Ottawa, Ontario   Don Mills, Ontario
K1S 5B6   M3C 1J9
(613) 788-3740   (416) 441-2941

Cover design: Richard Karayanis
Typesetting: Carleton Production Centre

Acknowledgements

Carleton University Press gratefully acknowledges the support extended to its publishing programme by the Canada Council and the
Ontario Arts Council.

The Press would also like to thank the Department of Communications, Government of Canada, and the Government of Ontario
through the Ministry of Culture, Tourism and Recreation, for their
assistance.

Table of Contents

II
APPROACHES TO AUTOBIOGRAPHY

III
STORIES OF THE IRISH IN CANADA

Introduction

James Noonan

Biography and autobiography have always held an attraction for readers, whether they be readers of history or of literature. Even when there has been disagreement over the value of biography and autobiography to the study of both disciplines, ordinary readers have found the makers of history and literature endlessly interesting. And while the critical emphasis on the importance of these genres has fluctuated in recent times, publishers have continued to embrace works on Parnell, Burke, Coleridge, Shaw, Beckett, Lady Gregory, Maud Gonne, Virginia Woolf, Elizabeth Bowen, Tennessee Williams, Sylvia Plath, Irving Layton, E.J. Pratt, and many others; they have welcomed works by authors on themselves, for example, Yeats, Gogarty, Sean O'Casey, Morley Callaghan, John Glassco, Gabrielle Roy, Thomas Merton, George Woodcock, and Garret FitzGerald; and they have published whatever letters they could get their hands on by all of these. Memoirs of living politicians rank among the best sellers at any time.

The impulse behind the thirst for these books seems to be that we are getting close to the real truth of a person, whether written by that person or another, and that this is a closer connection with the mind and heart of the person than whatever he or she has written in another genre. The desire behind the impulse is that of knowing how other — usually famous — people have conducted their lives, and the readiness to learn from these lives how ordinary mortals might think or conduct their own.

The recent publication, or imminent publication, of biographies and autobiographies on and by Irish figures made this topic an appealing theme for the 1991 Conference of the Canadian Association for Irish Studies. There were, to name a few, books by Conor Cruise O'Brien on Edmund Burke, Brenda Maddox on Nora Joyce, Deirdre Bair on Samuel Beckett, Roy Foster on W.B. Yeats, Denis Donoghue on Yeats' memoirs, Ann Saddlemyer on George Yeats, Michael Holroyd's three volumes on Shaw, the continuing popularity of Peig Sayers and of writers of other island memoirs, Paul Bew on Parnell,

Jane Côté on the Parnell sisters, and Garret FitzGerald's autobiography.

Besides these primary works there has been much recent critical reflection on the nature of the two forms of writing. One of the aims of the Conference was to invite speakers who could address these changes as well as those who could speak from their own experience in writing biography or autobiography, in either the Irish or the Canadian context.

It was for this reason that the Conference was organized largely on the lines of the structure of this book, and speakers were sought who could discuss both the theoretical and the concrete approach to biography and autobiography. One day was devoted to biography, a second to autobiography, and a third to these forms as expressed by or about Canadians.

Ira Nadel began the Conference with his paper on 'Biography and Theory, or Beckett in the Bath,' a title which suggested both the theoretical and concrete nature of the conference. His paper emphasized the nature of biography, and would leave to others the task of showing how individual biographies were constructed. Paul Bew followed with 'The Nature of Irish Political Biography,' emphasizing the need for a revisionist approach by which 'we can now produce larger biographies in which a leader's contribution to a cause is evaluated but the cause itself is not.'

Bew was followed by Conor Cruise O'Brien speaking on his own 'Thematic Biography of Edmund Burke,' on which he worked for twenty years until its publication in 1992; the paper was his introduction to the long-awaited biography. Desmond Bowen's paper, 'Religion and Reticence: Paul Cardinal Cullen and the Problem of Religious Biography in Ireland', was given eight years after the publication of his book, *Paul Cardinal Cullen and the Shaping of Modern Irish Catholicism*, and reflected his view of the problems involved in writing a biography of a prominent religious figure.

Similarly, Jane Côté's essay, 'Writing Women into Irish History: The Biography of Fanny and Anna Parnell,' is a return to her 1991 book *Fanny and Anna Parnell: Ireland's Patriot Sisters*, and is another form of revisionist biography emphasizing the need to consider carefully the role and lives of Irish women in the country's history. Brenda Maddox gave her attention to another Irish woman — Nora Joyce — who was often forgotten in the shadow of her famous husband. The success and popularity of Maddox's award-winning book, *Nora: A Biography of Nora Joyce*, had preceded her, and she concentrated on the strenuous digging she had to do to discover the facts of her subject's life and to bring that book to the light of day.

S. Finn Gallagher's 'Bio as it Auto be: from the Letters of George Bernard Shaw' was one of two papers which showed how a life may be constructed from the letters of a famous person. Having sifted through the voluminous correspondence of Shaw, Gallagher revealed the many directives in Shaw's letters to his official biographer Archibald Henderson, author of *George Bernard Shaw: Man of the Century*. The other essay which used letters to reconstruct a life is Ronald Ayling's 'Sean O'Casey: A Life in the Letters,' which drew on the first three volumes of O'Casey's correspondence to bring out many facets of his life as a man of letters. These two essays found their way into different sections of the book: Gallagher's into biography, and Ayling's into autobiography. The different focus of each essay seemed to warrant a separation of the two: Gallagher deals with letters with directives from Shaw to his biographer, and Ayling with what O'Casey, as a letter writer, revealed about himself.

The final essay on biography is by James White, former director of the National Gallery of Ireland, who gave an illustrated lecture entitled 'Memories into Images in Modern Irish Painting' at the National Gallery of Canada during the Conference. White looked at paintings as a form of biography in the work of modern Irish painters, including John Butler Yeats, the father of W.B. Yeats, and Louis LeBrocquy. We are fortunate to be able to include in this book reproductions of several of the paintings White showed on slides to illustrate his lecture.

James Olney, one of the foremost critics of autobiography, opened the day of the Conference devoted to this topic with his essay 'On the Nature of Autobiography.' Reminding readers that 'autobiography has become the darling of literary critics and literary theorists in the past fifteen or twenty years,' he showed that several Irish writers — in particular, Yeats, Gogarty, and George Moore — anticipated the French theorists in theory and in practice by half a century. The most direct experience with the genre comes from Garret FitzGerald, Prime Minister of Ireland (Taoiseach) from 1981–1987, who published his memoirs in 1991 and graciously agreed to write of the experience for this volume after the Conference.

The other five papers on autobiography — besides Ayling's on O'Casey, already mentioned — are all devoted to literary figures. Cathal Ó Háinle writes of the Blaskett autobiographers — Tomás O Criomhthain, Muiris O Súilleabháin, and Peig Sayers — and how their much-loved tales often belie the facts of their islands' history. Dominic Manganiello, using St. Augustine as a foil, writes of the confessional imagination of James Joyce in his *Portrait of the Artist as a Young Man*. Ann Beer explores Beckett's alternating use of English and French throughout his career as a way of understanding the man himself. Laura O'Connor concentrates on a single work — Seamus Heaney's Station Island, which takes its title from an Irish place of pilgrimage and penance — to examine the nature of his self-probing imagination.

The day of the Conference devoted to the Irish-born or those of Irish background in Canada included many forms of biography — ranging from straightforward history through to poetry, fiction, drama, and anecdote. Robin Burns' paper examined some of the formative years — 1842–1849 — in the life of D'Arcy McGee, one of the fathers of Confederation, before he came to Canada. Hereward Senior explored the character and career of the founder of Orangeism in Canada, in 'Ogle Gowan: Aspiring Statesman and Stage Irishman.' D.M.R. Bentley analysed the influence of Isaac Weld, a Dublin-born Irishman, on Canadian poetry through his *Travels through the United States of North America, and the Provinces of Upper and Lower Canada, during the Years 1795, 1796, and 1797.*

Don Akenson and Roger Martin combined to discuss Akenson's 1990 work *At Face Value: The Life and Times of Eliza McCormack/ John White.* Akenson's historical fiction maintains that John White, Tory member of Parliament for the East Hastings riding in Ontario from 1871–1887, was in fact a woman, the first woman elected to the Canadian parliament. Martin prefers the recent term 'metafiction' and defends his predilection for the genre in 'Dressing Up History: A Critic Comments on Don Akenson's *At Face Value.'* *At Face Value* is also the only autobiography in the Canadian section of the Conference in which — one third of the way through the book — the speaker changes from third to first person.

James Reaney and Ken Mitchell are two of Canada's best dramatists, and both have written several works based on Canadian historical figures. These plays might be called 'biography as drama.' Reaney's paper took its title — 'They are treating us like mad dogs' — from a remark by the father of the famous Donnelly family of Lucan, Ontario, and his revisionist thesis is that the Donnellys have not been fairly treated by their biographers. His trilogy of plays *The Donnellys* made the same point in dramatic terms, as does his unpublished play *Sleigh without Bells,* a portion of which is published here. Ken Mitchell spoke of what inspired him to write his play *Davin, the Politician* about an Irishman whose 'contribution was his life, that ball of flame that blazed out of Kilfinane to Cork, Dublin and London, and finally to Canada where it crashed to ground once again.'

Much of the humour in the collection was provided by Joan Finnigan's 'Tracking Down the Irish "Entertainers" in the Ottawa Valley,' which was delivered at the conference banquet. As an oral historian she included many anecdotes from the countless men and women of Irish descent she interviewed in the course of gathering material for several books on the Ottawa Valley. She gave a final reminder that could be applied to the papers in this book as a whole: 'The storytellers' rewards were pride of recognition, personal fulfilment and an achieving of permanency for that part of their life story or autobiography when it was placed between the pages of a book.'

Some papers from the 1991 CAIS Conference are not included in this volume; those from the conference are supplemented by three that were not delivered but which fitted into the conference theme — those by Côté, FitzGerald, and Ayling. In many cases the informal tone of a conference paper has been retained to give readers a taste of the good will and lively exchange which prevailed throughout. Some speakers submitted a more formal paper for publication.

Besides the people whose papers appear in this volume, I wish to thank Michael Gnarowski, Director and General Editor, Steven Uriarte and David Lawrence, of Carleton University Press; S. Finn Gallagher of Trent University and Michael Kenneally of Marianopolis College, respectively President and Past-President of the Canadian Association for Irish Studies at the time of the Conference, who read the papers and who themselves have published books based on the CAIS conferences they organized; James Reaney, for permission to publish his four poems and the excerpt from his unpublished puppet play, *Sleigh without Bells*; and the members of the Finance Committee of the Conference, namely John O'Connor, Chair, Roydon Kealey, Jeffrey L.D. King, Charles Logue, Sheila O'Gorman, and Peter Rock.

I

APPROACHES
TO BIOGRAPHY

Louis Le Brocquy. *Drawing Towards An Image of Samuel Beckett.*

Biography and Theory
or
Beckett in the Bath

Ira B. Nadel

A few days after he moved into his first Parisian apartment on the seventh floor of 6 Rue des Favorites in April 1938, Samuel Beckett wrote the following to Gwynned Reavey: ' "having taken it furnished and having no furniture[,] I am promised at the corner store a bed, but not for a week, so I expect to sleep in the bath until then" ' (Bair 286). Did he? We don't know but, anecdotally, this amusing image of Beckett settling for the night in his bath satisfies our idea of what he — or one of his characters — *might likely* do. The key to the event, however, and its attraction, is its power to involve us narratologically with a moment of Beckett's life that we are unlikely to forget. The narrative activates our interest in his behaviour and from this incident we may search for parallels with other moments in his life or work — as seen perhaps in *Murphy*, Beckett's novel published that same year (1938), which begins with the hero sitting immobile and naked in his rocking chair in the corner of his West Brompton mew (*Murphy*, 1). And yet, only when so restricted can Murphy free his mind, as Beckett might have done in his tub. The biographical anecdote functions as a sign of Beckett's character and texts — inventive, isolationist, whimsical, and content with being alone.

But consider the reverse: a literary anecdote that finds later biographical confirmation. Molloy has a wall surrounding his garden with 'its top bristling with broken glass like fins' (*Molloy*, 52). Deirdre Bair reports in her biography of Beckett that when constructing the wall surrounding his summer home in Ussy near the Marne in 1954, Beckett had glass shards imbedded in the top to keep out intruders (Bair 443). In either case, anecdotes and their unique narrative expression create structures of memory for us, although Nietzsche's assertion that ' "three anecdotes may suffice to paint a picture of a man" ' (Fadiman xxi) hardly seems adequate.

The anecdote is the building block of biography, the morpheme of the language of biography that is both essential and satisfying. Regardless of their facticity, biographies absorb anecdotes for their narrative power, providing a vertical axis which competes with the horizontal axis of chronology. The fictionalizing element of the anecdote, a complete if brief tale, satisfies the need for the reader to observe the subject in an unguarded state, often exhibiting personality, while at the same time it supports the larger framework of discourse being constructed by the events and texts that externally measure the life of the subject.

Anecdote and narrative are the foundations for a theory of biography, the former demonstrating the New Historicist method of contextualizing, juxtaposing and enhancing the text, while the latter illustrates the pattern of tropes, structure of narrative units and role of diegesis. Anecdote, the ingredient of so many biographies we admire, is actually a fundamental element of biography's truth-value. Indeed, what the quotation is to a discursive text, the anecdote is to biography. As one theorist explains, anecdote

> determines the destiny of a specifically historiographic integration of event and context . . . as the narration of a singular event, [anecdote] is the literary form or genre that uniquely refers to the real...there is something about the anecdote that exceeds its literary status, and this excess is precisely that which gives the anecdote its pointed, referential access to the real. (Fineman 56)

In these New Historicist terms, enunciated by Joel Fineman, the anecdote becomes 'the smallest minimal unit of the historiographic fact' (57).

The textual agenda of New Historicism aids in the theoretical re-evaluation of biography by posing the following questions: (1) how do we establish the life of the biographical subject? (2) how do we choose what materials to include in the life? (3) what institutions and values shape or identify our representation of these materials? and (4) what influences affect the biographer in the construction of his narrative? The answers to these questions will necessarily reflect a functionalist view of language which presents the text as a process, mediating relationships 'not only of speech but of consciousness, ideology, role and class' (Fowler 80).

A sentence from Vladimir Nabokov identifies the narrative problem of biography: 'although there is plenty of space on a gravestone to contain, bound in moss, the abridged version of a man's life, detail is always welcome' (5). For biographers, this is a rallying cry; for critical readers, a warning. At issue is the presentation of that detail and why it is narratively needed. Biography is fundamentally a showing, not a telling, and values the quantity of narrative information at the same time that it seeks to remove the informer from the scene. A detailed narration without a narrator is its paradoxical goal. But showing is a way of telling and the presence of a narrator is inescapable since he is the source, authority, organizer, analyst, commentator, and stylist of the life.

Semioticians writing on narrative argue that biography is a form of prose discourse which aestheticizes a structure of interrelations. Such a position appropriately replaces the referential with the verbal as the primary constituent of biography. Genette expresses this view of non-fictional prose in *Narrative Discourse* when he writes that 'mimesis in words can only be mimesis of words. Other than that, all we have and can have is degrees of diegesis,' which for Genette means the abstracted succession of events or 'story' (164). In *The Order of Things*, Foucault concludes that, after Mallarmé, literature could only become a manifestation of language affirming no more than its own existence (300). From this point of view biography can exist only as a verbal artifact divorced from history and reality. Thus textualized, biography becomes a set of verbal features, not the record of a living historical object; its details become only elements of formal discourse demanded by convention.

Traditional critics and biographers react in horror to these claims, arguing that to shatter the distinction between the referential and the self-affirming is to destroy the historically accurate and factual basis of the language of biography. Post-structuralists respond that to limit biographical writing only to the referential prevents its entry into the broader field of prose discourse and that referentiality itself wrongly assumes an unambiguous correspondence between verbal sign and extra-verbal object. Yet the contribution of semioticians to narrative is to enlarge our critical response to biography, although for this view to be effective the following premises must be recognized:

1. Biography relies on language rather than fact to tell its story.
2. Biographical narration is not a neutral discourse, although biographers would have us believe otherwise.
3. The narrativity of biography gives real events the form of a story, imposing meaning and pattern on reality, which does not organize itself into either meaning or truth. 'Nothing puts up so much resistance to representation as the real,' notes Françoise Gaillard (73).
4. The assignment of meaning to life is the fundamental task of biography.
5. Non-fictional discourse performs and represents features of fictional discourse.

Through its narrative, biography provides a plot, and a means of interpretation for a life. It reassembles data so that it may take on meaning, but in so doing relies on narrative form to convey that truth. Or as A.J. Greimas writes, the 'generation of signification . . . [is relayed] by narrative structures, and these are the structures which produce meaningful discourse articulated in utterances' (24). Hayden White explain the production of 'meaningful discourse' as the result of our 'desire to have real events display the coherence, integrity, fullness and closure of an image of life that is . . . imaginary' (24). Annals and chronicles cannot do this because they lack the narrative elements to do so.

Samuel Johnson recognized these narrative demands in 1744, at the beginning of his life of Richard Savage. After three moralistic paragraphs on the 'miseries of the learned,' he turns in his own voice to the narrative of Savage 'whose misfortunes,' he announces, 'claim a degree of compassion not always due to the unhappy' (241). Unable to resist interpretation of the principal figures, the narrator constantly offers his assessment of Savage's mother, while also criticizing his own content, his placement of relevant information in the biography and the moral progress of his subject, famously and ironically summarized in thed words: 'thus had Savage perished by the evidence of a bawd, a strumpet, and his mother . . . .' (241–42, 246–47, 254–55). The combination of judgment and naïveté on the part of the narrator ('I know not whether he ever had for three months together, a settled habitation. . . . ' [259]) results in a narrative that does not require great detail, only responsible interpretation — and repetition, as Johnson repeats the principal misfortunes of his subject in an effort to project, in the diegetic elements of the narrative, the sympathy he feels for Savage (re 275, 280, 286–87).

This eighteenth-century example of an interpretative biographical narrative substitutes textual commentary for amplitude and emphasizes analysis rather than summary or scene. Furthermore, the narrative relies on analepsis (flashback) and prolepsis (anticipation), as when Johnson recounts Savage's unanticipated visit to his mother which resulted in her throwing him out of the house and accusing him of attempted murder (254–55), or his rejection of Lord Tyrconnel's admonitions to regulate his life (262). My purpose in citing these details is to show that in the mid-eighteenth century biography already displayed a narrative sophistication which narratological terms like order, duration, frequency, mood and voice (Genette's categories) illuminate. Metalepsis, a shift in the level of telling — in 'Savage' from third to first person — demonstrates, again, the self-conscious narrativity in the biography.

Ironically, in more recent times biography, while trying to limit experimentation and narrative disjunction, has developed the meta-diegetic possibilities of narrativity. This occurs when other voices, usually expressed through direct or indirect quotation, assume, if only temporarily, the narrative voice. A section entitled 'A Squalid Tragedy' in Leon Edel's revised, one-volume life of Henry James illustrates this practice. Focusing on the Oscar Wilde case, the reader confronts James in several voices as he writes to Gosse, his brother William, J.A. Symonds, himself, via a notebook entry, Mrs. Curtis, a Venetian friend, Paul Bourget and Alphonse Daudet. Other voices, who speak directly or indirectly through summary in the passage (a technique which always accelerates the pace), are Gosse, William James and Jonathan Sturges (437–39).

Richard Ellmann goes further in his revised biography of Joyce. The introduction of Pound into Joyce's life necessitates the full quotation of Pound's first letter to him (349–50); reference to Gertrude Stein in the passage requires quotation of her lengthy assessment of her literary position vis-à-vis Joyce in a paragraph that ends with the voice of Hemingway (528–29). In addition to Joyce, the major voices in the biography belong to Stanislaus, his brother, Lucia, his daughter, Sylvia Beach, his Paris publisher, Harriet Shaw Weaver, his patron, T.S. Eliot, his London publisher, Beckett, his Paris associate — and, of course, the narrator. Increasingly, biography since the nineteenth century foregrounds the voice of its subject rather than the biographer; or rather, the biographer, in seeking anonymity in order to sustain the objectivity prized by biographers, wishes to remove himself from the text and allow his subject, or his subject's actions, to speak for themselves.

But what does the biographical narrative provide? Primarily, coherence: the telling of the life should have a sustained voice which should maintain a constant tone, pattern of tropes and what Mieke Bal calls 'focalization' (100). The distance between the biographer and subject must be small; extended quotation from letters, for example, should be minimal in order not to dislocate the reader from the life being narrated. A further method of sustaining narrative coherence is the presence of the author in the narrative, not perhaps to the extent of J.A. Symonds in *The Quest for Corvo*, nor even Boswell in the Life of Johnson, but enough to allow the reader to feel that there exists a voice other than the subject's to provide guidance and direction. There must also be periodic remarks of a synchronic nature to establish both authority for, and trust in, the narrative voice.

The key to the process of selection and organization in a biography is the narrative. Its features establish what to include, exclude, emphasize or neglect. Factual reconstruction can never be the *raison d'être* of biography because it is impossible to achieve. It must be, rather, narrative desire, the urge to tell the story of the subject which in its telling establishes meaning. In a prescription for biography, those two atomists of reality, Bouvard and Pécuchet, conclude, as they try to reassemble the events of their day, that 'external facts are not everything. They must be completed by psychology. Without imagination history is defective' (129). In biography (and history) that imagination expresses itself through narrative. The contribution of narrative theory to the study of biography is a grounding in the narrative systemics of prose discourse, and one result will be the return of the narrator to biography (did he ever leave?) and the removal of his mislabelled mask of objectivity by the honesty of his narrative presence. But language, as a social discourse, and culture, as a communal process of negotiation and exchange, extend biography not in terms of defining individual achievement or narrative structures but as the participation in, and contributor to, the discourses of a culture.

Biography becomes a form of cultural discourse through its recovery of the past which refigures the encoded values, traditions, and desires of an earlier culture. The biographer, in recreating his subject and the context of his subject, not only re-presents that past and its culture, and not only transmits it to his readers, but re-orders it through its reconstruction. Biography re-imagines the past while recovering it and creates a work that exists in history and as history.

Marshall Sahlins, in his 1985 study *Islands of History*, is helpful. Arguing that history is culturally ordered 'according to a meaningful scheme of things,' he explains that the reverse is equally true: 'cultural schemes are historically ordered, since to a greater or lesser extent the meanings are revalued as they are practically enacted' (vii). For biographers this means that as they recover the society and culture of the subject in their narrative, they actually enact and transform those elements through their textualization of the events. In this way biography embodies the discourses of a culture, preserving (but also rewriting) a past culture while enacting a new one through certain choices of style, valuation, and presentation. A biography cannot isolate its subject from its culture; the conventions of birth, education, career and death prevent it from doing so, although these tropes of the *grand récit* may have lost their urgency, according to Jean-François Lyotard (Fineman 57). Furthermore, situating a subject in a culture encourages cultural analysis by the biographer, such as Deirdre Bair offers in a passage in her life of Beckett demonstrating Beckett's rejection of his identity as an 'Irish' writer (281–82).

Biography, however, is not only the centre of unity; it is also the site of difference. The implicit trope of wholeness for a life in a biographical text, with a clearly defined *terminus a quo* and *quid*, gratifies our desire for the aesthetic ordering of existence and satisfies the goal of unity imposed by the development and application of the genre (see Jameson 58). But to distinguish the life from others requires difference. This paradox creates a tension in the text between the need to celebrate uniqueness and the desire for unity. But these pulls reflect the larger cultural struggle between restrictive and expressive codes, while at the same time validating the authority of the biography to represent cultural realities.

Textualizing the experience of the subject alters the elements of the life and creates, in the terms of Michel Foucault, a site for the struggle of meaning. To clarify and confront those struggles, the biographer revisits the place of beginnings — either through reexamination of primary documents such as letters, diaries, memoirs or journals, or by literally retracing the experiences of his subject. Richard Holmes, author of biographies of Shelley and more recently Coleridge, makes a strong case for this in his 1985 narrative *Footsteps, Adventures of A Romantic Biographer*. Calling himself at one point the 'following shadow' (114), Holmes describes the necessity of experiencing the journeys, travels and even views of his subject because only in this way can the past retain a physical, palpable presence (67).

Genealogy, however, dominates biography, and openings repeatedly demonstrate its power. Whether it is the complicated background of Richard Savage in Johnson's account that orients the narrative, or the ambiguity of Beckett's birthday as narrated by Bair (Bair 3), 'beginnings' are the cornerstones of biography. Beckett himself encouraged the lies and legends of his origin, although Bair goes on to mark the geographical, religious, social and ancestral placement of her subject (4–13). This method, echoed by Ellmann in his life of Joyce and Jeffares in his life of Yeats (rev. 1988), demonstrates the Foucauldian notion of a 'body totally imprinted by history and the process of history's destruction of the body' (142). The site of biographical discourse must be genealogical because it establishes 'the beginnings' essential for the biographer so that he can express the difference of his subject. Such openings establish the 'accidents, the minute deviations — or conversely, the complete reversals — the errors, . . . the faulty calculations' that make the subject unique (Foucault 146). Genealogy is the method of individualization.

But focus on the genealogical method leads to a critical question for biography as cultural discourse: how is the individual produced within a social discourse and set of institutions, and how does he or she become the subject of the text? Genealogy can illuminate this process since it allows us to confront both origins and individuality. Discourse is a function of power, and biography is the distribution of an individualizing power that regulates the formation of ourselves. The discursive strategies of biography make us into subjects via the subject of biography by submitting readers to the power of a ruling set of disciplines: language, sex, economics, politics. In turn, the study of the discursive strategies of biography leads to the study of institutions, disciplines and thought of a time — in short, a culture. Genealogy unmasks the associations of discourse with power and materialities, while allowing for the full description of the complexly determined discursive practices it studies. Genealogy sets out to trace the actions that have coalesced under the systems of power that constitute the individual but which, fundamentally, exist in a contingent relation united only by narrative.

The genealogy of discourse for biography asks how the language of the work produces knowledge of the subject — and evaluates, through its narrative, which institutions operated to direct the shaping of the subject. Deirdre Bair, therefore, concludes her life of Beckett with the claim that writing for the theatre 'forced him to take an active role in society,' uniting an otherwise withdrawn individual with the world (640) through the institution of the theatre; Richard Ellmann concludes his life of Joyce with the statement that 'its central meaning was directed as consciously as his work' (744), establishing the institution of literature as the guide to Joyce's life. Both examples underscore the necessity of shaping the life of the subject into a completed whole and confirm the function of biography as a culturally determined narrative discourse evaluating and re-defining institutions as well as individuals.

Works Cited

Bair, Deirdre. *Samuel Beckett, A Biography*. NY: Harcourt Brace Jovanovich, 1978.

Bal, Mieke. *Narratology, Introduction to the Theory of Narrative*, 2nd ed. trans. Christine van Boheemen. Ithaca: Cornell UP, 1985.

Beckett, Samuel. *Molloy* in *Three Novels*. NY: Grove Press, 1965.

—— . *Murphy*. NY: Grove Press, 1957.

Boswell, James. *Life of Samuel Johnson*, ed. R.W. Chapman, rev. J.D. Fleeman, intro. Pat Rogers. Oxford: OUP, 1980.

Edel, Leon. *Henry James, A Life.* New York: Harper and Row, 1985.

Ellmann, Richard. *James Joyce,* rev. ed. New York: Oxford UP, 1982.

Fadiman, Clifton. 'Introduction,' *The Little Brown Book of Anecdotes,* ed. Clifton Fadiman. Boston: Little Brown, 1985.

Fineman, Joel. 'The History of the Anecdote,' *The New Historicism,* ed. H. Aram Veeser. New York: Routledge, 1989. 49–76.

Flaubert, Gustave. *Bouvard and Pécuchet,* trans. A.J. Krailsheimer. Harmondsworth: Penguin, 1986.

Foucault, Michel. *The Order of Things.* New York: Vintage, 1973.

———. 'Nietzsche, Genealogy, History,' *Language, Counter-Memory, Practice,* ed. and trans. Donald F. Bouchard. Ithaca: Cornell UP, 1977. 139–64.

Fowler, Roger. *Literature as Social Discourse, The Practice of Linguistic Criticism.* Bloomington: Indiana UP, 1981.

Gaillard, Françoise. 'The Great Illusion of Realism, or The Real as Representation,' *Poetics Today* 5 (1984): 746–60.

Genette, Gerard. *Narrative Discourse,* trans. Jane E. Lewin. Ithaca: Cornell UP, 1985.

Greimas, A.J. 'Elements of a Narrative Grammar,' trans. Catherine Porter, *Diacritics* 7 (1977): 23–40.

Holmes, Richard. *Footsteps, Adventures of a Romantic Biographer.* London: Hodder and Stoughton, 1985.

Jameson, Frederic. *The Political Unconscious: Narrative as a Socially Symbolic Act.* Ithaca: Cornell UP, 1981.

Jeffares, A. Norman. *W.B. Yeats, A New Biography.* 1988. London: Arena, 1990.

Johnson, Samuel. 'Richard Savage,' *Lives of the Poets,* ed. Edmund Fuller. New York: Avon, 1965.

Macherey, Pierre. *A Theory of Literary Production,* trans. G. Wall. London: Routledge and Kegan Paul, 1978.

Nabokov, Vladimir. *Laughter in the Dark.* London: Weidenfeld and Nicolson, 1969.

Sahlins, Marshall. *Islands in History.* Chicago: Univ. of Chicago Press, 1985.

White, Hayden. *The Content of the Form, Narrative Discourse and Historical Representation.* Baltimore: Johns Hopkins UP, 1987.

The Nature of
Irish Political Biography

Paul Bew

There is a definite tradition of Irish political biography. It is not to
be confused with Irish literary biography, which is often biography
with the politics left out. The three volumes of Michael Holroyd's
recent monumental *Bernard Shaw* (1988–1991) is a classic example:
Shaw's own account of his experience at the Central Model Boys'
School (which was attended by a significant number of Catholics) —
'I lost caste' is his phrase — is played down. Instead, his account is
presented as a displacement of Shaw's unusual domestic situation
as a child.[1] No real space is given to Shaw's interest in eugenics
or social Darwinism. Similarily, his public controversy with Arthur
Lynch, MP, over the role of Ireland in the First World War is omitted. Despite everything that has been written on Yeats or Joyce —
and Dominic Manganiello's book on Joyce's politics is of particular
value — do any of the eminent literary historians involved really ask
themselves the question: what was Parnellism as a political creed
in the 1890s? We know that Yeats and Joyce considered themselves
Parnellites, but what did that really mean? Is it just a matter of
the cult of the hero or anti-clericalism? I have tried to show in my
study of Parnell after Parnell that there is more to it than that.[2]

But, whatever about the conventions of Irish literary biography, there is no doubt that the Irish tradition of political biography
is alive and well. As Roy Foster has pointed out, biography will always be a most important part of the study of history in a country in
which political leaders have often employed national heroes as the
personification of the nation.[3] In fact, this tradition pre-dates the
use of popular Catholic nationalism in the nineteenth century — a
movement recently described by Brendan Clifford as being simultaneously committed to the values of the French Revolution of 1789
and medievalism.[4] The Irish Tory historians of the 1820s and 30s
followed closely the practice described by Foster. J.W. Croker described the purpose of the biography of eminent national figures
like Swift as that of affording 'justice to the dead, example to the
living; it is the debt we owe and the precept we should inculcate;

when such a man is emulated, his country is redeemed.'[5] This tradition of political biography has survived and is alive and well in Ireland today.

There is no doubt that currently the field in the modern period is dominated by what might be called the three great Trinity College biographies: F.S.L. Lyons's *John Dillon* (London: Routledge and Kegan Paul, 1968), Theo Moody's *Michael Davitt and Irish Revolution 1846–82* (Oxford: Oxford University Press, 1981) and Lyons's *Charles Stewart Parnell* (London: Collins, 1977). The term 'Trinity College biography' may be justified by the fact that the papers of Dillon and Davitt are housed in the manuscript room of Trinity College, Dublin; more profoundly by the fact that both Moody and Lyons spent decisive parts of their careers there; indeed Lyons was one of Moody's most distinguished pupils. There can be no question that the scholarly apparatus of all three works is highly impressive — Moody's *Davitt*, in particular, is also touched by a moral fervour which is in itself inspiring. Lyons's greatest work is his synthesis *Ireland Since the Famine* (1971), but in his *Dillon* and his *Parnell* he gave us magisterial portrayals. All three books deservedly won the highest praise when they were published. But there are difficulties with all of them, and it is to these difficulties that we must now turn.

Moody's picture of Michael Davitt in the Land League crisis (1879–82) is quite unambiguous. He shows us a man who left behind the ways of violent conspiracy which had marked his life hitherto — 'no one . . . more earnest in reprobating violence.'[6] Here is a politician leading a vigorous popular land reform movement with all the eloquence and energy at his command, who eschewed all form of illegality and violence. But there is one major empirical problem with such an interpretation: the survival of a letter from Michael Davitt to the Irish American revolutionary John Devoy in December 1880 which points in quite a different direction. A letter, moreover, which only came to light in Dublin after Moody had already formed his view of Davitt.

Let us place this letter in context. On 14 December 1880, Davitt issued a memorandum to the organizers and officers of the Land League which stated: 'Evidence is not wanting that numbers of men have formed and are joining the League who give but a half-hearted allegiance to the League programme . . . men who denounced the programme of the League but six months ago.' On 16 December, he wrote to Devoy:

> There is a danger, however, of this class and the priests coalescing
> and ousting the advanced men or gaining control of the whole

thing and turning it against us. I am taking every precaution, however, against this Whig dodge. Already I have carried a neat constitution by a *coup de main* and on Tuesday next I intend to carry the election of an executive council of fifteen in whose hands the entire government will be placed. The Council will consist of six or seven MPs, and the remainder men like Brennan, Egan and myself.

But, was such a manoeuvre adequate to deal with the serious problems faced by Davitt? These 'damned petty little outrages' gave the government grounds for coercion, while the offer of the 'three Fs' would, he believed, split the movement. Davitt outlined his solution to Devoy:

> I only see one way in which to combat it and neutralise the evil it would work upon the country—that is, by calling a Convention. The Delegates that would come from the country would be certain to support the No Partnership platform of the League against the compromise of the three Fs. If we could carry on this Movement for another year without being interfered with we could do almost anything we pleased in this country. The courage of the people is magnificent. *All classes are purchasing arms openly.*

It is certain that this letter disconcerted his biographer. Professor Moody's slightly po-faced but honest response to this letter is clear enough.

> The letter to Devoy which was published only in 1953 exposes Davitt to the imputation of lack of integrity more than any other surviving evidence for his life to this point. Its cynical tone, its mixture of flippancy and egotism, and its conspirator's jargon are a startling contrast with the passionate sincerity, the moral earnestness, the self-abandonment and the universal appeal conveyed by his public statements of this period to the central body of the league and its land demonstrations all over the country. The jubilation with which he tells Devoy that all classes are buying arms seems hardly compatible with his public reprobation of agrarian intrigues as not only inexpedient but morally wrong.[7]

If ever one is to hear the sound of a jaw dropping this is it. There is a possible explanation which would 'purify' Davitt: that is to blame John Devoy, the recipient of the letter. Moody says: 'Devoy, indeed, seems to have drawn out and encouraged Davitt's less admirable qualities — quickness of temper, irritability, suspicion of other men's motives, recklessness of judgement, a tendency to exaggeration, to wishful thinking, even to self-deception.'[8] More pointedly, it could be argued that Davitt wished to mislead John

Devoy, a key figure in Irish America, who helped to provide much of the funds for the Land League. Davitt laid stress on the revolutionary and violent aspects of the Land League in order to draw attention away from its reformist and legal substance. This is in itself a possible interpretation—though it does require perhaps a certain deafness to the tone of the letter. More importantly it involves a repression of the political context of the Land League crisis. Moody notes accurately, 'the ambivalence in Davitt's position was nothing new . . . and was noted in his commitment to what remained of the New Departure.'[9] But, what was the New Departure of 1878/79? In October 1878 Parnell was re-elected President of the Home Rule Confederation of Great Britain with Fenian support and against the wishes of moderates. Devoy, misjudging the importance of the moment and believing that a crisis had come, placed before Parnell the 'New Departure' package. He was offering Parnell the support of American nationalists on the following conditions:

1. Abandonment of the federal demand and substitution of a general declaration in favour of self-government.
2. Vigorous agitation of the land question on the basis of a peasant proprietary, while accepting concessions tending to abolish arbitrary eviction.
3. Exclusion of all sectarian issues from the platform.
4. Party members to vote together on all imperial and home questions, adopt an aggressive policy and energetically resist coercive legislation.
5. Advocacy on behalf of all struggling nationalities in the British Empire or elsewhere.

In his biography of Davitt, and elsewhere, Professor Moody attempts to draw a sharp distinction between the New Departure and the Land League which may not be sustainable. Dr. Moody has insisted that the Land League was an emergency organization arising out of a spontaneous reaction to distress. In fact, the agitation predated the onset of severe distress in 1879 by some months. The stress on the Land League as an emergency organization, arising out of a spontaneous reaction to the distress of 1879 has to be modified in the light of the fact that the agitation pre-dated the onset of this crisis by some months. It is perfectly true that the objectives of the Land League were attainable, and were eventually attained, within the structure of the United Kingdom. However, in 1879 hardly anyone of any political consequence on either side of the Irish Sea would have accepted this view. It is a consequence of the immense revolution achieved by the Land League that it later came to be so widely held. In 1879 the neo-Fenian leadership of the Land League certainly believed that the abolition of Irish land-lordism and the creation of a peasant proprietary could be achieved only when the British link was broken. In other words, the connections between the New Departure and the Land League, which Professor Moody allows, cannot be reduced to the matter of Devoy's probably genuine belief that Parnell was committed to the original New Departure. It lay at the very heart of the radical Land League leadership's conception of the role of their movement — to smash landlordism, certainly, but, by so doing, also to smash the British link. A land league of some kind is conceivable without the New Departure background, but it would have been a very different movement — characterized by an entirely different relationship between leadership and followers.[10]

To summarize this argument: our view of the Davitt-Devoy correspondence of December 1880 depends not simply on our reaction to the tone of the text. If one accepts a significant degree of connection between the New Departure and the Land League, then this view fits logically into a strategic discourse. There is no need to speculate about Davitt's state of 'excessive mental stimulation.' Davitt emerges as a coherent Irish neo-Fenian revolutionary of the period — albeit he appears as rather less of the humanitarian reformer who so inspired Theo Moody's warm heart. It is simply not possible to separate a social reformist Land League from its context of revolutionary Irish American plotting.

The most notable feature of Lyons's Dillon is the way in which the prospect of home rule nationalism is taken as a given, and a desirable given at that. There is no sustained discussion of agrarian radicalism — the ranch war of 1906-10 is not even mentioned, even though there is much discussion of it in the Dillon papers. We may surmise that this is because such a discussion would draw attention to serious divisions within the nationalist bloc. It would also raise doubts about the social ideals of Irish nationalism. Again, while Lyons does discuss — in a most interesting fashion — Dillon's opposition to compulsory Irish in 1909,[11] he does not discuss its *dénouement*. The proposals for school scholarships, which Dillon worked out with Augustine Birrell, the Chief Secretary for Ireland, floundered because the vast majority of nationalist county councils insisted on compulsory Irish in 1913. Dillon publicly denounced this as 'gross oppression . . . depriving Protestant boys of scholarships unless their parents compel them to learn Irish.'[12] Such problems — and they are fully reflected in the Dillon papers — raise fundamental problems about the project of constitutional nationalism, problems which — in the late sixties — Lyons was unwilling to raise.

When it came to attempting his *Parnell*, Lyons seems to have bent the stick the other way. It is clear from his private correspondence[13] that Lyons did not like Parnell, and this may be part of the problem. Having argued in his own *Dillon*[14] that the 'obstinate' resistance of Ulster Unionists to the 'moderate' proposal of home rule was 'one of the strangest mysteries of politics,' Lyons now castigated Parnell for sharing this view! Lyons notes with some acerbity: 'Parnell never seems to have asked himself what he meant by the Irish nation or the Irish race which he claimed to lead and the idea that Ireland might possibly contain two nations, not one, apparently never entered his head.' Even more acidly, Lyons observes: 'he never came remotely within reach of developing a constructive approach to the apparently lethal problem it [Ulster Unionism] presented.'[15] The difficulty with these firm statements lies in the fact that Lyons nowhere discusses (or mentions) Parnell's major attempt to deal with the problem presented by Ulster Unionism—his speech given in Belfast in May 1891.

> I have to say this, that it is the duty of the majority to leave no stone unturned, no means unused, to conciliate the reasonable or unreasonable prejudices of the minority. . . . (cheers) It has undoubtedly been true that every Irish patriot has always recognised . . . from the time of Wolfe Tone until now that until the religious prejudices of the minority, whether reasonable or unreasonable, are conciliated . . . Ireland can never enjoy perfect freedom, Ireland can never be united; and until Ireland is practically united, so long as there is the important minority who consider, rightly or wrongly—I believe and feel sure wrongly—that the concession of legitimate freedom to Ireland means harm and damage to them, either to their spiritual or temporal interests, the work of building up an independent Ireland will have upon it a fatal clog and a fatal drag.[16]

In making these critical observations, I have not been moved by a desire to 'knock' the status of these biographies. It is precisely because their status is unassailable, precisely because they are such important books, that it is worth drawing explicit attention to some of the defects. Biography increasingly plays a role in Anglo-American culture as the form of knowledge which, as it were, slips down easily. Early reviewing is often formal, perfunctory and ecstatic. By raising these difficulties, it is intended to sharpen our conception of the role of the political biographer. Personal details are always interesting, of course, but the 'political biographer must always give his or her prime commitment to political analysis and explanation in full view and focus attention accordingly.'[17] As

Gearóid Ó Tuatháigh pointed out in a recent historiographical essay, there is still plenty of work to be done: Sir James Craig, Sir Edward Carson, John Redmond and Joe Devlin are due for 'serious re-evaluation.'[18] In my view, this can only be done effectively if the categories of both unionism and nationalism are problematized; in the late twentieth century we can now produce larger biographies in which a leader's contribution to a cause is evaluated but the cause itself is not.

This is the seventy-fifth anniversary of the Easter Rising. Interestingly, the official celebrations in Dublin have been muted. Clearly, many Irish people are now uncomfortable with the notion of a revolutionary armed coup carried out by a small minority — its implications for the Ulster crisis are too painful. They also know that Pearse's nationalist philosophy led not to a population of twenty or thirty million, as he projected, but to only two or three million in the 1950s. The most sophisticated defence of the Easter Rising has, in effect, been an 'accidentalist' one; Garret FitzGerald has argued that it put Ireland in a better position to take advantage of the institutions of the EEC, but he admits that this was not, of course, the intention of the Rising.[19] Similarly, all the key leaders of Ulster Unionism now formally admit its contradictions — especially those that divide devolutionist and integrationist wings. Can historians and biographers afford to be less reflective?

Notes

1 Conor Cruise O'Brien was the first to make this point in his *New York Review of Books* review.

2 See my *Conflict and Conciliation in Ireland 1890–1910* (Oxford: Oxford University Press, 1987).

3 See R.F. Foster, History and the Irish Question, *Transactions of the Royal Historical Society*, fifth series, vol. xxx (1983), p. 170.

4 In his review of Foster's *Oxford Illustrated History of Ireland* in *Labour and Trade Union Review*, July/August 1991, no. 24, p. 16.

5 Joe Spence has demonstrated this in his fascinating thesis, *The Philosophy of Irish Toryism 1833–5* (University of London, 1991), p. 174.

6 Davitt, p. 326.

7 *Ibid.*, p. 440.

8 *Ibid.*, p. 441.

9 *Ibid.*

10 For an expanded version of this argument, see my *Land and the National Question in Ireland 1858–82* (Dublin: Gill and Macmillan, 1978).

11 Pp. 305–07.

12 *Leinster Leader*, 1 March 1913.

13 Quoted in Alan O'Day's essay on Lyons in W. Arnstein (ed.), *Recent Historians of Great Britain* (Ames, Iowa: Iowa State University Press, 1990).

14 *Dillon*, p. 483

15 *Parnell*, p. 619.

16 See my *C.S. Parnell* (Dublin: Gill and Macmillan, 1980), pp. 127–31. This work has recently been reissued in a revised format.

17 These are the words of Kenneth Morgan in his contribution to Eric Homberger (ed.), *The Troubled Face of Biography* (London: Macmillan, 1989).

18 'Irish historiography 1970–79', prepared for the Irish Committee of Historical Sciences and published under J.J. Lee's editorship in 1980.

19 *Irish Times*, 13 July 1991.

A Thematic Biography of Edmund Burke[*]

Conor Cruise O'Brien

American colonies, Ireland, France and India
Harried, and Burke's great melody against it.

Yeats, 'The Seven Sages.'

Is there such a thing as a thematic biography? I have to think there is, since I have just written one: *The Great Melody: A Thematic Biography of Edmund Burke.* It came about in this way. About twenty years ago, I set out to write a biography of Edmund Burke. That biography, had it been completed, would have been on conventional lines, emphasizing chronology, and without a sustained thematic dimension. The project soon got into difficulty. At first I ascribed this to the distraction of other concerns at the time, but these were not the root of the trouble. The real trouble was that the Burke that interested me — Burke's mind and heart, at grips with the great issues of his time — seemed to get further and further away, the more closely I studied his career along the lines I was then following. Also, and not merely through the usual effect of distance, Burke himself seemed to get smaller and smaller, until he became a quite inconsequential figure, hardly more significant than any of the other politicians of the time, and distinctly less significant than any of those who held major office.

This was largely due to the reductionist tendencies of most of the secondary sources I was consulting, influenced by Sir Lewis Namier. But the chronological method which I followed at the time, really as a matter of routine, had the effect of confirming those reductionist tendencies. Burke was an exceptionally diligent parliamentarian, and if you try to follow his political career, year by year, you will find that the exigencies of the parliamentary calendar, and the consequential frequent changes of theme, blur one's view of the person, seen within the parliamentary process.

---

[*]The Preface of Conor Cruise O'Brien's book *The Great Melody: A Thematic Biography of Edmund Burke* (Chicago: University of Chicago Press, 1992) is based on this essay.

So I got stuck, and I couldn't, at that time, understand why I got stuck. I had already done some work on Burke — as editor of the Penguin Classics edition (1968) of *Reflections on the Revolution in France* — and had experienced no such frustration: quite the contrary. I can see now that the reason why working on *Reflections* had been so satisfactory was that I was looking at Burke's mind at work on a single theme, whereas in the kind of biography I later successfully attempted the themes were being switched around all the time, resulting in a blur, and loss of contact. Amid that blur and loss, the reductionist perspective on him came to seem almost plausible for a time, though I could never really reconcile it with the Burke I had been able to see and hear while I worked on *Reflections*.

So I gave up on Burke, as I then thought, for good, and turned to an apparently quite unrelated subject. I wrote *The Siege: the Story of Israel and Zionism*. But while I was working on it, something kept nagging at me to go back to Burke once I had finished *The Siege*. The nagging took a precise form. The two lines of Yeats, quoted at the head of this essay, kept coming into my head and would not go away. At first my reaction was to wish that Yeats *would* go away, and his notion of the great melody along with him. I didn't treat Yeats seriously as an authority on Burke. Yeats, during the period of his greatest interest in Burke (around 1925), included him in a kind of Anglo-Irish Protestant aristocratic pantheon, along with Swift, Berkeley and Grattan. I knew Burke didn't really belong in that gallery, so I found it hard to believe that Yeats had a message for me, with a key to Burke.

After I had abandoned my original plan for a biography of Burke, I found myself being brought back to him, partly because of the incidence of relevant centenaries, and commemorations and partly (as I now realize) because my friend Owen Dudley Edwards, of Edinburgh University, was tactfully determined to keep my interest in Burke alive.

The first relevant commemoration was that of the bicentenary, in 1976, of the American Revolution. I read a paper on 'Edmund Burke and the American Revolution' at a Bicentennial Conference in Ennis, County Clare. Seen as part of the process that came to shape the present study, that paper is interesting because of the status accorded to those lines of Yeats. Clearly I felt their pull, but still wished to resist it. The paper opens:

Let us begin by considering two well-known lines from W.B. Yeats's poem 'The Seven Sages' (in *The Winding Stair and Other Poems*, 1933):

> American colonies, Ireland, France and India
> Harried, and Burke's great melody against it.

What was it? I shall come back to that question. For the moment, let us note the implied acknowledgement of Burke's 'consistency', a just acknowledgement of something that has been unjustly impugned. In other ways, I think Yeats's lines somewhat misleading. The key words, 'harried' and 'melody', suggest a Burke concerned to stir emotions by his eloquence on behalf of the persecuted. He could do that; he did it for the victims of the Irish Penal Laws, for the Begums of Oudh and, most famously, for Marie Antoinette of France. He knew well how to play on the emotions, but on the whole he used this skill sparingly. The great bulk of his writings and speeches consists of reasoned arguments. And nowhere is this more evident than in his speeches aimed at averting the conflict in America.

In all of Burke's great campaigns there was, as Yeats discerned, one constant target. That target—Yeats's 'it'—was the abuse of power. But the forms of the abuse of power differed in the different cases mentioned, and Burke's manner of approaching the different cases differs also.

That is fair enough as far as it goes. Later in the paper, my resistance became more querulous. Having stressed, and slightly overstressed, the rational character of Burke's writings and speeches on the American crisis, I went on:

> This commonsense, down-to-earth Burke, concerned with practical interests and assessment of forces, may perhaps seem, and indeed be, a less noble figure than the lamenting harpist of 'The Seven Sages.' Yet if one has come to distrust the plangent strain in politics, one turns with relief from that distorted Yeatsian Burke, recognisable though some of the features are, to the real Burke of the American Revolutionary period.

Yet the final reference, in that paper, to those lines, is one of acceptance: 'Burke, who had foreseen the disaster in America, in the closing years of his life foresaw disaster in Ireland. That disaster came in the year after his death, 1798. In that sense, Yeats was right.'

'Yeats was right.' I came to see that whatever reservations one might have about Yeats' general interpretation of Burke, and whatever qualifications one might add to his metaphor about the melody, Yeats was right about the main point. That is, he correctly identified, and isolated for attention, the main areas on which Burke's creative energies were concentrated throughout long and overlapping periods of his career. That was why those lines had been nagging at my mind. They were pointing me the way back, to find the Burke I had been looking for, and had lost.

I had accepted that, and was working accordingly, well before the next of the relevant centenary commemorations came round. These were the bicentenaries of the Impeachment of Warren Hastings (1988) and of the French Revolution (1989). I was invited by Owen Dudley Edwards, well ahead of time, to talk about Burke and Warren Hastings at a bicentenary commemorative conference on the Impeachment, held at Edinburgh University in February 1988. Up to now, I had done a certain amount of work in relation to Burke on America, on France, and on Ireland, but had not yet seriously tackled the apparently formidable volumes of Burke on India. The Edinburgh commitment therefore obliged me to complete the Yeatsian quadrilateral, and this finally determined the agenda for the present study. My contribution to the conference was entitled 'Warren Hastings in Burke's Great Melody,' and contained no word of reservation as to the propriety of that metaphor.

For the Bicentenary of the French Revolution, I reviewed for the *New York Review of Books* the great *Critical Dictionary of the French Revolution*, edited by François Fumet and Mona Ozouf. This enabled me to see Burke in the perspective of modern French scholarship, which is far more favourable to Burke than was the dominant French historiographical tradition of the nineteenth century and the first half of the twentieth. I also contributed an essay, 'Nationalism and the French Revolution,' to a collection entitled *The Permanent Revolution: The French Revolution and its Legacy*. This proved relevant to the consideration of Burke's struggle against what he continued to call 'Jacobinism', even after 1794. Finally, on the great day itself, 14 July 1989, I took part in a televised panel discussion in Paris, at the Invalides, set up by London Weekend Television. Through the great window we could see the gorgeous *défilé* organized by President Mitterrand, with all manner of songs and dances, ethnic spectacles, theatre and acrobatics. It was magnificent, but it wasn't the French Revolution. It was a wake. The tremendous thing that Edmund Burke had fought so fiercely, from a few months after its birth up to his own death, eight years later, was at last itself being laid to rest, in its own capital. On that same night in the same city, but away from the centre and the action, the true heirs of the French Revolution, the French Communist Party, in their own ceremonies in the Red *faubourg* of St. Denis, were doing their best to keep the tradition of the French Revolution alive. But nobody outside the dwindling and dispirited ranks of the faithful was paying attention any longer to the true heirs of the French Revolution.

When I resumed work on a book on Burke—those of you who may read *The Great Melody* will be able to judge for yourselves how far these claims are made good—I found that the thematic approach suggested by Yeats's lines worked well for me. The day-to-day clutter, which accumulates in the path of a strictly chronological approach, fell away. The reductionist interpretation, sometimes plausible enough in the dark corners of the day-to-day, is seen in its actual tawdriness, in the steady light of Burke's consistent and disinterested commitment to great causes, from the beginning to the end of his political career. Each trivializing or demeaning hypothesis successively collapses, when tested in the context of the history of his conduct, of the long pursuit of each one of the four causes, and of their interrelations. I shall not labour these points.

I should like to make two further observations about the propriety, respectively, of the title and the sub-title. The title, *The Great Melody*, should be understood primarily in a very broad sense, as implying the existence of a profound inner harmony within Burke's writings and speeches on the four themes. It should not be taken as implying passivity, merely elegant commentary, accompaniment. The melody is always 'against it' and is therefore a form of action, with varying fortunes. That action takes the form not only of rhetoric, but also of argument, aphorism, debate, logical and historical analysis; and all these are part of the Great Melody in the broad sense.

There is also a narrower sense, within the broad one, to which the poet's metaphor is felt to be peculiarly appropriate. In certain conditions, Burke's utterance, both in speech and in writing, attains a glowing eloquence, unique in English literature and in the annals of oratory. He reserves that vein for special occasions, and he never overworks it. These utterances form, therefore, only a relatively small part, in terms of statistical proportion, of Burke's total utterances as these have come down to us. But it is natural for us to think of these moments of highest eloquence as being also the highest expression of Burke's Great Melody.

To the Great Melody, in that special and restricted sense, belong certain speeches on America, and on India, and certain writings about the French Revolution. On America, we have 'On American Taxation' (1774), 'On Conciliation with America' (1775), and three other speeches of the same order. On India, we have 'On Fox's

East India Bill' (1783), 'On the Nabob of Arcot's Debts' (1785), two other speeches, and parts of the marathon eight-day speech opening (1788), and nine-day speech closing (1794), the Impeachment of Warren Hastings. On France, we have a number of passages in *Reflections on the Revolution in France* (1790); *An Appeal from the New to the Old Whigs* (1791); *Letter to a Member of the National Assembly* (1791); and *Letters on a Regicide Peace* (1796). *Letter to a Noble Lord* (1796) is in a special class of its own, but belongs in the general context of the French debate.

The attentive reader will have noticed that I have not proposed any of Burke's speeches or writings on Ireland as belonging to the highest category of the Great Melody. Burke attains his highest level of eloquence only in those conjunctures when he feels fully free to speak what he thinks and feels. For reasons examined in the present study, Burke never feels free with regard to Ireland. During most of his life, with one startling exception, Burke's public statements concerning Ireland were few, guarded, cryptic, sometimes evasive. The startling exception is supplied by a passage in the Bristol Guildhall Speech (1780) in which, at a moment of great stress, his real feelings about the Irish Penal Laws gush out in an almost trance-like manner. Ireland, in the Great Melody, is a brooding presence, expressed in haunted silences and transferred passions. Feelings which Burke represses over Ireland come out in other contexts, with regard to the French Revolution to some extent, but especially to India.

Those of you who read the book may feel that I have been too lavish in my use of inference, concerning Burke's relation to Ireland, and the connection of that relation to the other branches of the Great Melody. However, without some audacity in the use of inference, to which I plead guilty, no adequate understanding of Burke's relation to Ireland is attainable. And given the tremendous tensions of his upbringing, in the Ireland of the Penal Laws, if you can't understand Burke's relation to the land of his upbringing you can't understand Burke. All previous biographies of him skim that relationship and founder on that rock.

For adequate reasons, he did his best to cover his tracks where Ireland was concerned. The student of Burke must uncover those tracks as best he may, often relying on cryptic remarks, strained silences, perceived constraints, together with a scrutiny of the actual Irish context of positions that he took up, or avoided, over Ireland. A good example, in this study, of such an inquiry concerns his attitude towards the Irish Volunteers and legislative independence for Ireland, in the early 1780s. A good liberal 'friend of Ireland' would be expected to be strongly in favour, both of the Volunteers and of legislative independence. Burke hung back, with muffled but unmistakable expressions of distaste, from both.

The reason was — as Horace Walpole guessed at the time with the insistence of fascinated malice — Burke's emotional identification with the Irish Catholics, then governed by the Penal Laws. The Irish Volunteers were an overwhelmingly Protestant force, and legislative independence was for an exclusively Protestant parliament. Burke saw both as tending to perpetuate a stratified caste system, with the Catholics as permanent underdogs.

Can *The Great Melody* properly be described as a biography? It is certainly not a conventional biography, but it is a complete biography, extending from the circumstances — key Burkean word — of the subject's birth in Ireland to those of his death in Beaconsfield, and taking in, on the way, all the main events and circumstances of his education, career and compositions. His personal life, apart from politics, was uneventful, his family relations happy, until the untimely death of the only one of his children who lived to maturity, Richard, three years before his own death. The centre of Edmund Burke's interests was political, and any biography of him has to be mainly political. My own proceeds along the paths determined by its four themes, but it necessarily takes in, at every stage, the relation of his activities and utterances, concerning each theme, to their precise contexts in the British parliamentary politics of which he is part. British domestic politics are always seen, however, in their wider context of the momentous unrolling of international politics in the age of the American and French Revolutions. The idea is that British domestic politics must not be lost to view, but neither must Edmund Burke be lost to view, among the details of British domestic politics.

Within British politics, his relationships with major figures of the time are important and are explored in proportion to the perceived degree of their importance. His relationship with the Marquess of Rockingham and, through Rockingham, his growing influence on the Whig party, especially over American policy, are the main 'domestic' themes of the early part of his political career (1766–82). Between Rockingham's death in 1782, which roughly coincides with the end of the American War, and the outbreak of the French Revolution, seven years later, Burke's main preoccupation is with India. In British domestic politics, this meant that Burke had to carry with him, first Charles James Fox, and then William Pitt the Younger — against inclination in both cases — in order to obtain a majority in the House of Commons tthat would vote for the Impeachment of Warren Hastings at the bar of the House of Lords.

The French Revolution brought a complete break with Fox, and an alliance with Pitt. After some years, under Burke's influence, and as the French Revolution unfolds in the manner foreseen by him, a number of the Whigs, headed by the Duke of Portland and Earl Fitzwilliam, leave Fox and join Pitt's Administration. The expanded Administration is shaken from the outset by Irish Affairs, over which Burke and Pitt are opposed. Though deeply distressed by Pitt's handling of Ireland, Burke continues to support him, as indispensable to the conduct of the war against Revolutionary France. When, however, Pitt makes overtures towards peace with the Directory, Burke fiercely attacks this initiative in the last major political act of his political career, *Letters on a Regicide Peace* (1796). The peace initiative failed and the war continued, as Burke had insisted that it must until the restoration of the French Monarchy, completed eighteen years after his death.

At every stage of his career, the influence of George III was of central importance, and Burke's relations to the king went through many 'transmigrations', to use a Burkean expression. I argue that the concluding stages of the American War involved a battle of wills between George, who wished to continue that war even after Cornwallis's surrender at Yorktown, and Burke, whose influence caused Rockingham to dictate terms of accepting office, by which the king must be prepared to accept the independence of America. After drafting an instrument of abdication, George accepted Rockingham's terms, which were Burke's terms, and the way to peace was open.

I argue that Burke's influence over contemporary politics, both British and international, was more significant and pervasive, not merely in the above instances, but in several others, than many historians have supposed. I also argue that Burke's analysis of the workings of the contemporary British political system, and particularly his theory of a 'double Cabinet' (the method by which George III exercised personal power, bypassing Cabinet and Parliament), is far from being as wide of the mark as one influential school of historians has claimed.

The purpose of the above résumé of some of the domestic aspects explored in *The Great Melody* is to show that a thematic biography need not be as limited in scope, or as rarefied, as a mere enumeration of the principal themes might suggest. A thematic approach would probably not be productive for most biographies. In the case of Burke, I am convinced by experience, having tried the conventional approach and then turned to the thematic, that the thematic approach is far more flexible, and far more illuminating.

Then there is the 'commented anthology' aspect. The book's full sub-title is: *A Thematic Biography and Commented Anthology of Edmund Burke.* The commented anthology aspect follows necessarily from the choice of the Great Melody as governing concept. Under that sign, it is necessary that Burke's own voice, in all the variety of its inflections, be heard, frequently and at length. Summary and paraphrase, the regular resources of previous biographers, are of only marginal use for the purposes of the present study. This necessarily requires a large book, such as this one. That in itself is no advantage. The relevant advantage, and it is no small one, is that much of the best of Burke, at present not readily accessible, or readily comprehensible out of context, is within these covers and situated, in every case, in its immediate context.

The 'commented anthology' aspect makes this book unusual, in that it contains what it is about, and is about what it contains.

In a word, the basis and essentials of a Burke revival are here, especially in those pages where Burke himself is heard to speak. There are already signs of such a revival, especially in France, hitherto partes infidelium where Burke is concerned. France has a way of setting fashions, and I hope this good fashion will come round in time for the bicentenary of Burke's death, in 1997.

Religion and Reticence

Paul Cardinal Cullen and the
Problem of Religious Biography in Ireland

Desmond Bowen

Philip Magnus began his able biography of W.E. Gladstone by re-marking: 'the vast majority of mankind have believed, however imperfectly, throughout the ages, that the whole of human life is in the service of God'.[1] Gladstone certainly was convinced that God would call him personally to account for his every thought, word and deed, and by his mid-twenties he had obtained over himself a work-ing self-mastery through his use of will and prayer. In this struggle he was an exemplar of so many of the Victorians, strong-minded and religion-obsessed individuals, who were intent upon making their civilization a reflection of God's order in time and space. We know much about Gladstone and his spiritual life, as the many bio-graphical studies of the man testify, for, like a seventeenth-century Puritan, he kept a close record of how he could justify his thoughts and actions. Such a perpetual confrontation with the deity was a terrible ordeal for this God-obsessed political figure with his great abilities, passions and energy. The tensions within him between creativity and destruction were strong, as was his human capacity for self-delusion, but to a remarkable degree he controlled himself in the service of what he believed to be a transcendental purpose.

A struggle to serve the deity through perpetual self-oblation was, as might be expected, also the concern of the great ecclesias-tics of the time, and not least the four Roman Catholic cardinals who had much influence in shaping affairs in Ireland, Wiseman, Newman, Manning and Cullen. Each of them was born in the first decade of the nineteenth century, when the old regime in Europe was passing out of existence and, except for Wiseman, who died in 1865, they lived through a time of social evolution and imperial expansion which greatly altered the lives of people in both Britain and Ireland. What was interesting about these four great ecclesi-astics was that, to differing degrees, they were never at home in the earthly Protestant Zion of nineteenth-century Britain, for they served an alternative imperial power, that of the Roman pontiff, who proclaimed himself the Vicar of Christ upon earth. Romantics

and idealists, they believed themselves to be harbingers of a new
spiritual and temporal order for the disillusioned European society that had found wanting the rationalism of the Enlightenment
and the revolutionary designs of the Napoleonic world. Each of
them was highly intelligent, able and dedicated, and we know a
considerable amount of the life-processes of each of them—with
the exception of Paul Cullen. The mystery of why we know so much
about Newman and Manning, less about Wiseman, and so little
about Cullen as a person, is worth exploring for its own sake. It begs
also the wider question of why some religious figures are expansive
about their personal and spiritual lives, and others are exceedingly
reticent.

Assuming that Alexander Pope was right when he believed that
'the proper study of mankind is man',[2] that history is essentially
'about chaps', it is incumbent upon biographer and historian alike
to consider the thought-processes of the creative individuals of an
age. To know something of their hopes, ideals, anxieties and fears is
to know something of the potentials and values of the age that nurtured them: 'highest justice is found in the deepest sympathy with
erring and straying men'.[3] In the soul-searching of a John Henry
Newman one can see the great concern of the Victorian middle-
classes: 'a passionate and sustained earnestness after a high moral
rule, seriously realized in conduct'.[4] We are told so much when Cardinal Manning could ask the labour leader, Ben Tillett, whether
the workers in the London Dock strike of 1889 were 'in a state of
Grace'.[5] What an insight into the intrigue within the court of Rome
is provided when Manning, in a rare moment of candour, wrote to
his fellow convert, the aristocratic papal chamberlain, George Talbot, about Newman:

> What you write about Dr. Newman is true. Whether he knows
> it or not, he has become the centre of those who hold low views
> about the Holy See, are anti-Roman, cold and silent, to say no
> more, about the Temporal Power, national, English, critical of
> Catholic devotions, and . . . I see much danger in an English
> Catholicism of which Newman is the highest type. It is the old
> Anglican, patristic, literary, Oxford tone transplanted into the
> Church. It takes the line of deprecating exaggerations, foreign de-
> votions, Ultramontanism, anti-national sympathies. In one word
> it is worldly Catholicism, and it will have the worldly on its side,
> and will deceive many.[6]

In truth, however, Manning was always as 'English' in his own
way as Newman, and his correspondence indicates how much his
imagination was captivated by England's imperial expansion and

civilizing mission. He could rejoice that 'as the Greeks and Latins of old, so the Saxon blood and speech are now spread throughout the earth, prelude now as then, of some profound design of God.'[7] It is interesting to consider that the two great Oxford converts, Newman and Manning, seemed always to be torn in some respects between their allegiance to the competing imperialist powers of Westminster and Rome. This was never the case with the Spanish-born Irish cradle Catholic, Nicholas Wiseman, nor his almost exact contemporary in age, Paul Cullen. Such ideological tension may account for the ready exposure of thought on the part of the two English prelates, whereas lack of it may have encouraged the relative reserve of Wiseman, and the laconic reticence of Paul Cullen. Much has been written about Manning and Newman, who were, comparatively speaking, writing constantly about themselves, but little about Wiseman, in spite of his flamboyant personality, and nothing of a biographical nature has appeared regarding the taciturn Paul Cullen.

Peadar MacSuibhne has spoken of 'the warm, lifelong friendship' between Wiseman and Cullen, but there is no real indication that their relationship was anything more than the cautious, guarded respect to be found among curial figures. Wiseman came from an Irish family that traded in wine between Waterford and Seville, and he had been born in Spain. After schooldays in England he was sent to the English College in Rome at the age of sixteen, just two years before Paul Cullen began his studies at Propaganda. He was ordained priest about three and a half years before Cullen, and moved with him in the group of young intellectuals who were being groomed for curial service. Wiseman was to act as agent of the English bishops in Rome, just as Cullen was to serve zealots who found their identity in the ultramontane court which emerged during the pontificates of Leo XII and Gregory XVI. Wiseman was a rather effusive personality and he made much more of a public impression than the retiring Cullen. It was Wiseman who welcomed to Rome visiting members of the English ruling class, or prominent converts like the ardent and ascetic Hon. George Spencer, the architect Augustus Pugin, the wealthy Ambrose de Lisle, and many others. Away from Rome, however, Wiseman was uncomfortable with the English Catholics generally, as he found during his time at Oscott between 1840 and 1845. When he returned to England in 1850, armed with what a Catholic peer called 'an edict of the Court of Rome'[8] to re-establish the hierarchy in England, he never had an easy time with the English Catholics who resented his triumphalism. His feeling of isolation contributed to his dependency upon Manning during his latter years, when he was very ill, and looking for someone like himself who cared, apparently, for nothing but the Church.[9]

Manning has been ill-served by both his 'official' biographer, E.S. Purcell, and by Lytton Strachey, who suggest at times that Wiseman's faith in the ambitious and illustrious convert may have been misplaced. Coming from the same evangelical background as Newman, who confessed that he was past forty before he could rid himself of his conviction that the Pope was the Antichrist,[10] Manning's movement towards Rome was a tortuous one, as his journals revealed. When Newman told Manning of his intention to move into the 'one true fold' of Christ, Manning's emotional response revealed the depth of his own torment over the prevailing Erastianism of the Church of England.[11] At the time that members of his extended family went over to Rome he confessed his deepening unease over his own ecclesiastical allegiance:

> There seems to be about the Church of England a want of antiquity, system, fullness, intelligibleness, order, strength, unity; we have dogmas on paper; a ritual almost universally abandoned; no discipline; a divided episcopate, priesthood and laity.[12]

Manning's leaving the Church of England was not easy. He agonized about religion with Gladstone and others, particularly during a time of serious illness in the spring of 1847; visited Rome, where Pio Nono saw the English archdeacon on his knees as the papal carriage went by; returned to a church filled with controversy; and by the end of 1850 the 'parting of friends' had begun.[13] At the time of Manning's final questioning Wiseman had just issued in Rome his flamboyant and hugely tactless pastoral 'From out the Flaminian Gate,' its imperialistic assertions so grating that they annoyed Queen Victoria. The response of the Protestant public to the 'papal aggression' was such that the newly converted Manning had no time for further introversion. Wiseman showed that he had every intention of using Manning's intellectual and administrative talents as he patronized the new convert who was to succeed him at Westminster in a mere fourteen years' time.

However much Purcell's biography of Manning and Lytton Strachey's essay in *Eminent Victorians* are dismissed because of their portrayal of Manning as a 'designing prelate' his career after his conversion did give evidence of an inordinate ambition. Wiseman invited him to address the English bishops in synod within a year of his conversion, and his rise to favour in the English Catholic church was matched by his success in Roman circles when he visited the Holy See in 1852. Whereas Newman had offended even the Pope by his criticism of Rome's fawning on worldly-minded fashionable

English visitors, Manning made use of his fluent Italian to charm the ultramontanes in particular, and to establish a reputation as an orator. Pio Nono was impressed enough that he wanted to keep Manning in Rome.

Wiseman managed to get his protégé back, however, and he became invaluable to the cardinal, acting as an intermediary both with the Irish hierarchy and with the government. There was never any doubt who would succeed Wiseman, whose health was rapidly deteriorating in the months before his death in 1865:

> Cardinal Wiseman was slowly dying; the tiller of the Church was slipping from his feeble hand; and Manning was beside him, the one man with the energy, the ability, the courage and the conviction to steer the ship upon her course.[14]

Once he was in power as Archbishop of Westminster Manning used all his formidable energy and intelligence to promote the same ultramontane domination of the church in England that Cullen was establishing in Ireland. Along the way he began to lose the friendship of Gladstone, however, as he courted those like the Irish M.P.s who might be of use to his mission: 'the man is gone out . . . and has left nothing but the priest'.[15] He was also too extreme in his opinions at the Vatican Council, where he acted as chief whip of the English bishops, and the *troppo fanatico* convert made enough enemies among the cardinals that the red hat did not come his way until 1875.[16]

Though Manning never again went through the religious soul-wrestling that had preceded his conversion, he was always at war ideologically as his ultramontane convictions deepened. A real breach with Gladstone developed from the time he sent him his pamphlet, 'Ultramontanism and Christianity'.[17] The work arrived when Gladstone was losing the election of 1874, and it produced from him his 'venomous' reply, *The Vatican Decrees in Their Bearing Upon Civil Allegiance*, which questioned the loyalty of those who served the papal power. Manning, of course, replied quickly to Gladstone's assault,[18] but what caught public attention was Newman's *Letter to the Duke of Norfolk*, a brilliant riposte which managed not only to chasten Gladstone but also to question the 'maximizing tendencies' of the 'partisans of Rome'.[19] This was considered 'irreverent' by some in Rome who were never sure what their response should be to Newman, whom they could never place ideologically in the way they could Manning.[20]

Manning's estrangement from English contemporaries like Gladstone and Newman was not easy to bear; he had put the world from him, but what he wrote about himself indicates that he found little peace following his conversion. He was in later years obsessed with Newman whom, he believed, had never been able to identify himself fully with the Roman ultramontane cause:

> Newman was not in accord with the Holy See. I am nobody, but I spoke as the Holy See spoke. But almost every newspaper in England abused and ridiculed me. My name was never mentioned, but his was brought in to condemn me; his name was never mentioned, but mine was brought in to despite me. If only we had stood side by side and spoken the same thing, the dissension, division and ill-will which we have would never have been, and the unity of Catholic truth would have been irresistible. But it was not to be so.[21]

Neither Newman nor his contemporaries doubted the sincerity of his submission to papal authority when, after a long agonizing, in October 1845 he made his commitment. At the end of the month he went to Oscott College near Birmingham where the president, Nicholas Wiseman, confirmed him. Wiseman told Charles Russell of Maynooth: 'he opened his mind completely to me; and I assure you the Church has not received at any time a convert who has joined her in more docility and simplicity of faith than Newman'.[22] Newman wanted to maintain a 'simplicity of faith', without doubt, and when he wrote his Augustine-like *Apologia* he began the last section, 'Position of My Mind Since 1845', with the statement: 'From the time I became a Catholic, of course, I had no further history of my religious opinions to narrate'.[23] He told Wiseman he wanted to be strictly under obedience and discipline for a period of time, and it was decided he would go to Propaganda College in Rome. When he got there he was shocked by 'the poor state of both philosophy and theology':

> There was no study of Aristotle, nor of St. Thomas Aquinas. A few searching questions from his distinguished student completely confused the startled lecturer at Propaganda. The Roman theologians, Newman realized with dismay, simply had no 'view'.[24]

He was impolitic enough, when he left the college, to send a criticism to the rector on matters like the ban on reading books, which might have stimulated the students who were generally dissatisfied with their circumstances. Clearly Newman was going to find it difficult to avoid narrating his religious opinions.

On his return, he devoted himself to establishing the English Congregation of the Oratory, gave himself to writing and preaching, and avoided any controversy during the 'papal aggression' hysteria.

Then Paul Cullen, Archbishop of Armagh, and papal delegate for Ireland, wrote to ask him in the spring of 1851 if he would help in the establishment of a Catholic University, to be modelled on the one in Louvain in Belgium. Newman responded positively to the offer of what he hoped would become a 'Catholic university of the English tongue for the whole world'. He was to be the first rector, dividing his time between Dublin and the Birmingham Oratory, and soon he began to prepare his first lectures:

> It is a most daring attempt but first it is a religious one, next it has the Pope's blessing upon it. Curious it will be if Oxford is imported into Ireland, not in its members only, but in its principles, methods, ways and arguments.[25]

After he began his work in Dublin, however, his lectures — published in 1853 as *Discourses on the Scope and Nature of University Education: Addressed to the Catholics of Dublin* — displayed a 'new ambiance', which was a first indication of Newman's difficulties in Ireland: 'I am out on the ocean with them, out of sight of land, with nothing but the stars'. In the *Discourses* is 'a more or less covert attack' upon 'the narrow dogmatism of a defensive clerical Catholicism.'[26] Newman's tensions with the rigidly orthodox Paul Cullen had begun.

Newman's idea that the Catholic University should be one for the English-speaking world was not the concept which Cullen envisioned, as both men found out when the question of appointments came up.[27] Newman wanted Wiseman as chancellor, and Manning as vice-rector, and the best qualified men for professorial posts whether they were priests or laymen, political activists or not.[28] For his part, Cullen had in his mind a Roman seminary-type model for the university, with restrictions on the laity in its teaching staff, and no room within it for the liberal nationalists of Ireland whom he loathed as brethren of Mazzini. Cullen insisted upon appointing as vice-rector a Vincentian priest, James Taylor, who was his secretary. He also foisted on Newman, as Professor of Canon Law another of his staff, Laurence Forde, whom Newman found 'intolerable'.[29] Cullen's reservations about Newman had increased since Newman had suggested what the ideal of education should be in a university, a formation which: 'makes not the Christian, not the Catholic, but the gentleman'.[30] Not only was Newman to feel that he was under surveillance by the papal delegate, but Cullen was to ignore his requests for consultation about the university to the point of rudeness. Newman found it very difficult to deal with the suspicious Cullen, who operated, he presumed, as he had in Rome: 'to act, not to speak — to be peremptory in act, but to keep his counsel; not to commit himself on paper; to treat me, not as an equal, but as one of his subjects'.[31]

Newman had a respite in this tension when Cullen was absent in Rome for almost a year in 1854–55, attending the ceremonies associated with the promulgation of the dogma of the Immaculate Conception, while he persuaded Propaganda and the pope to stand firm against his pro-nationalist critics, such as the Quaker convert, Edward Lucas, editor of the *Tablet*. Newman heard of Cullen's conduct in Rome and he confessed in a letter to his confidant, Ambrose St. John, about Lucas: 'Dr. Cullen's treatment of him at Rome is too painful for me to talk of'.[32] He told St. John that Cullen had warned him off Lucas: 'and I, of course, would not be warned'. By this time, however, he was aware of the 'narrowness and party-spirit' of Cullen and had reconciled himself to the inevitability of leaving the university project:

> Poor Dr. Cullen. . . . The great fault I find with him is that he makes no one his friend, because he will confide in nobody and will be considerate to nobody. Everyone feels that he is emphatically close, and while this conduct repels would be friends, it fills enemies with vague suspicions of horrible conspiracies on his part against Bishops, Priests and the rights of St. Patrick.[33]

In April 1857 Newman sent Cullen notice that he was leaving the university, because of the fatigue occasioned by journeying between Dublin and Birmingham. Cullen did not reply to this formal letter, but by this time Newman knew there was to be no meeting of minds between himself and the enigmatic papal delegate. Earlier there had been a suggestion by Wiseman that Newman become a bishop, to enhance his authority in Ireland, but because of political manoeuvring in Rome this did not take place. Newman knew by the manner in which he had been informed that the appointment was not to be made and that Cullen had a hand in this embarrassment, as did Cardinal Wiseman: 'the Cardinal never wrote to me a single word, or sent any sort of message to me in explanation of the change of intention about me till the day of his death.'[34] Newman was learning something of the Roman way of handling ecclesiastical affairs, which ignored even 'the received rules of courtesy'. He felt Wiseman was 'unjust' in his treatment of him, and at the time of Wiseman's death he noted in his private journal: 'every year I feel less and less anxiety to please Propaganda, from a feeling they cannot understand England'.[35] When in later years he had an uncomfortable conversation with Bishop Ullathorne, recently returned from Rome, he commented wryly: 'I think Bishops fancy that, as justice does not exist between the Creator and his creatures, between man and the brute creation, so there is none between themselves and their subjects.'[36]

Newman was not happy about proceedings at the Vatican Council, where the ultramontanes made use of the ideas in his *Essays on Development*, and he mused about the corruption which had arisen so often in papal history; at the same time he affirmed his appreciation of Rome's central authority which alone safeguarded the local church from political domination. He paraphrased Lord Acton's dictum:

> Where you have power, you will have the abuse of power — and the more absolute, the stronger, the more sacred the power, the greater and more certain will be its abuse.

As for the scandalous politicking at the Council that finally allowed Cardinal Cullen and the other ultramontanes to produce their dogma of papal infallibility, he cautioned: 'Let us be patient, let us have faith, and a new Pope and reassembled council may trim the boat'.[37] His *Letter to the Duke of Norfolk* enabled him to argue for the faithful that there was little to be feared from the new declaration of papal power, for whatever was deemed to be an infallible judgment would still need interpretation by the 'general Catholic intelligence'. He also stressed the sovereignty of conscience, 'the aboriginal Vicar of Christ'.[38] The subtlety of Newman's mind was inevitably resented by the ultramontanes, and Manning showed, after the death of Pio Nono, little enthusiasm for Newman being made a cardinal.[39] The impression left by his life experience, within the Roman Catholic Church as he knew it, was that of a man who could prove to himself that in it he had found his spiritual home — but only with extreme reservations:

> If it strains credulity to accept the claims of the Catholic Church, it tests the intellect still more to make such a commitment, and then hedge it about with reservations. Newman's mind, it may be reckoned, was equal to the task, but then Newman's mind had been able to see the Thirty Nine Articles as a repository of Catholic doctrine. The man leaves the impression that he could have proved whatsoever he wished, which leaves the sceptic all the more wary of being convinced.[40]

If Newman had the greatest number of reservations about the imperial power he served, the prelate we have mentioned in passing, Paul Cullen, had the fewest, if any. He was born just eight months after Wiseman, in April 1803, and just three months before

Robert Emmet's rising. His extended family had suffered much during the '98 rising, but his father had been spared through intercession by local Quakers and the Protestant Archbishop of Cashel from the ravages of the largely Catholic militia and yeomanry, although the family farmland was laid waste. The Cullens had prospered, even during the penal days, and continued to do so after the rising. John Devoy claimed in later years that the Cullen clan had the reputation of being the 'chief land grabbers' in counties Carlow, Kildare and Queens. Paul Cullen's brothers Michael and Thomas were sent to Liverpool to establish an extremely profitable cattle importing business. The family also did well through the church, with a great number of them taking orders or becoming religious. They formed a 'truly Levitical family',with three of the priests, including Cullen, becoming bishops.[41] It is likely that most members of this family, who were representative of the strong Catholic farmer class, in competition with their Protestant neighbours, were as 'close' about their affairs as was Cullen.

This was certainly the characteristic applied to him by many of his contemporaries, and it alone has probably precluded a biography of the man appearing. He was the most important personage in Ireland's history between O'Connell and Parnell, but when a man considers it a virtue to reveal as little as possible about himself, matters like his motives at any juncture of his life can only be inferred. This does not make it easy to produce a biography, particularly of someone like Paul Cullen, nurtured in the Roman school of diplomacy, who was by nature secretive and devious. Wiseman, of course, went through the same formation as Cullen in Rome, but we know he had a 'dark night of the soul' during his time at the English College, which apparently Cullen never had, and his natural flamboyancy has enabled some scholars to conjecture much about him in their biographies of the first Archbishop of Westminster, the cardinal who restored the hierarchy in England.[42]

Paul Cullen was sent to Propaganda College in Rome while Wiseman was still a seminarian in the English College. He arrived in 1821 when Pius VII was still alive, the pontiff who had caught the imagination of Europe's conservatives and romantics by the heroic opposition he had shown during the Napoleonic period. Cullen witnessed the triumphal coronation of Leo XII in 1823, and even then seemed to identify himself with the *zelanti*, the conservatives in the curia who encouraged the new pontiff to reinforce the Index, strengthen the Holy Office, condemn Freemasonry, and put the Jews back into the ghetto. Cullen had no criticisms to make of these reactionary measures; indeed he expressed shock when Carbonari revolutionaries who were about to be publicly executed attempted to preach their cause from the scaffold. What he thought of Roman politics can only be inferred, however, for nowhere does he make comment on the intense political struggle that was in progress in the curia and resulted in the eclipse of the great Cardinal Consalvi, the long-serving Secretary of State.

It was soon clear to Paul Cullen that so long as he was diplomatically circumspect he had a brilliant career ahead of him. His intellectual gifts were such that he was called 'the eagle of the schools', and when he defended his doctoral thesis the occasion attracted not only the Pope, but two of his successors, and nine cardinals. Immediately after his defence the Pope surprised everyone by drawing the young Cullen aside for a conversation about Irish affairs. He was appointed professor of oriental languages at Propaganda, a position he held when Leo died in 1829 to be succeeded by one of Cullen's patrons, Gregory XVI, who had been prefect of Propaganda. The new Pope was a rigorous conservative, a Camaldolese monk devoted to building up the authority of the Holy See. He thought highly of Cullen, appointed him rector of the Irish College, and allowed him to delegate many of his duties to his vice-rector while Cullen devoted himself to acting as agent for the Irish bishops in curial affairs.

Cullen's letters home were by this time becoming less frequent, but there is little doubt that he took his duties and himself very seriously. Even his brothers addressed him formally as 'My dear Doctor'. He had few friends, apparently none of the spiritual questionings that plagued Nicholas Wiseman, and his whole identity was subsumed in his vocation as a trusted servant of the very ultramontane Gregory XVI and a champion of the universal mission of the Holy See. The friends he had were men like the vice-rector, a devotee of Ignatius Loyola, Tobias Kirby, who wrote his thesis on *The Right of Appeal to the Holy See*, and was renowned among the students for his rigorist rules—such as having them walk in a 'crocodile' when proceeding between the Irish College and their lectures in the Roman College. When Cullen was in Ireland in 1840, one class wrote him to give assurance that they were 'becoming each day more obedient, docile and punctual to all the rules'.[43] The formation that Cullen and Kirby wanted for the Irish seminarians was the total oblation of themselves in service to the Vicar of Christ upon earth, so that they might extend papal authority in the Irish Catholic Church, or wherever Rome directed them to serve.

Cullen probably had no real confidants but he was close to successive prefects of Propaganda, such as Cardinal James Philip Fransoni, and his successor Cardinal Alessandro Barnabo. He was trusted in Propaganda, and it was this authority that persuaded the Irish bishops to make use of him as they pressed their various causes in what seemed, in Roman eyes, to be their never-ending divisions. Their two main factions were the 'old Gallican' bishops led by the saintly Archbishop of Dublin, Daniel Murray, who tried to work with the British government, and the 'new Gallicans', who identified themselves with the O'Connellite nationalist movement. The latter had as their champion the irascible Archbishop of Tuam, John MacHale. Cullen listened to all their complaints, often against each other, and long before he went to Ireland as papal delegate and primate he had in dossier form a very intimate knowledge of each Irish bishop, including his moral and other failings. He was sophisticated enough in his position that he kept his balance between the warring factions, but once, in 1844, he overly identified with the MacHale faction, who were agitating over the Charitable Bequests Act, a government regulation of church gifts. This caused Cullen to flounder, however temporarily, when, for a while, it looked as if he would lose the trust of the curia, and be accused of being a nationalist partisan. Such was his terror at that time that he was on the verge of a breakdown. From that time forward he vowed he would never allow himself to become, in his words, 'vassal of a popular party'.

Cullen's attitude to the perennial violence in Ireland was shaped by his curial identity. Ideally Rome wanted a union of throne and altar in its religious and cultural mission, and it was always unsure how to handle the anomalous situations in Belgium prior to 1830, in Poland, and Ireland, where the rulers were schismatics or heretics. It was uncertain how to control the spirit of nationalism which swept so many parts of Europe in the post-Napoleonic years, particularly that of the Carbonari, and of the followers of Mazzini and Garibaldi, who threatened the temporal rule of the popes in the Papal States. The natural tendency of Propaganda was to interpret the agitation in Ireland in the O'Connell years as an extension of Mazziniism, an agitation fomented by atheistic Freemasonry and militant Protestantism. Cullen completely accepted these presuppositions, which were nurtured during his twenty-nine years in Rome, and there is no indication that he ever modified them.

'Outrage' was particularly prevalent in Ireland in the years following Catholic Emancipation in 1829. This was the era of the 'tithe war', with which Cullen probably had some sympathy; for the anti-tithe agitators were supported by the strong farmer class who wanted to get rid of paying tithe to the parsons, and Cullen came from that class. On the other hand, his reaction was thoroughly Roman when he was told by his correspondents about such scandals as a mob in Waterford jostling and spitting on Bishop Abraham in

1833; about two curates leading the mass of the people in Birr into secession from the church in 1835; or the Bishop of Clogher apologizing about never holding a chapter-meeting on the grounds that a clerical gathering of this nature would result in violence.[44] By the time that O'Connell was holding his monster Repeal meetings in 1843, Rome could not decide how to assert its authority over the Irish bishops and clergy who were so totally involved in the political *agitazione* that William Higgins of Ardagh had threatened to close all chapels and to use them only for Repeal meetings. The British government was making sure that the Propaganda knew of the press reports of denunciations from the altar that often resulted in assassinations. Crisis followed crisis with the coming of the Famine, the death of O'Connell, and the new agitation of Young Ireland.

Cullen's antipathy towards revolutionary nationalism was hardened by the experiences of 1848 in Rome, when the new Pope, Pius IX, was forced to flee to Gaeta, leaving Roman affairs in the hands of Cullen, who believed himself safe from the mob because he was a British citizen. He saw the revolution at first hand when the papal Prime Minister Rossi was murdered, and from this time onwards he was convinced that the greatest enemy of the Roman Catholic church in his age was the agitazione of the nationalists who were at heart secular and anti-clerical, no matter how much they might try to make use of the church. It was at this time that news came to Rome of the death of William Crolly, Archbishop of Armagh, who had long been dismissed in Ireland as a Gallican, a tool of the British government.

When Pius IX returned to Rome he was a thoroughgoing reactionary conservative, at war with all the revolutionary movements of the age which he was to denounce in the future in his Syllabus of Errors, attached to the encyclical *Quanta Cura* of 1864. With the encouragement of the *zelanti*, the conservative cardinals at the heart of the ultramontane movement, he initiated a massive counterattack against the principalities and powers of his world by the church militant. In England the campaign was to be directed by Nicholas Wiseman in the 'papal aggression' of 1850; in Ireland the restoring of Roman discipline in the church, and the reinforcing of Roman authority in society, was delegated to Paul Cullen, who was appointed to succeed William Crolly. The situation in Ireland was a desperate one, for in the years following the famine Evangelical proselytizers from England had begun a massive campaign which was successful enough to alarm the authorities in Propaganda, as well as Cullen when he visited the west of Ireland. There he found Archbishop MacHale bitterly resentful of any Roman intrusion into his province, where scandals abounded, such as the abandonment of parishes by priests during the time of famine and pestilence. MacHale had even returned financial aid to Cardinal Fransoni of Propaganda, saying there was no need for such charity in Connaught.[45]

From the time that Cullen arrived in Ireland to exercise his legatine powers there were murmurings about the Roman functionary who had been appointed directly by the Pope.[46] The nationalist prelates, led by Archbishop John MacHale of Tuam, were not an immediate problem for Cullen, for they considered he might be on their side in their struggle with the Gallicans, led by Archbishop Daniel Murray of Dublin. Cullen's clash with the latter took place at the Council of Thurles which he called, using his legatine authority, and there he managed to win by one vote a condemnation of the state-supported Queen's Colleges, which Murray strongly favoured. Using tight procedural methods he ably controlled the fractious prelates, and had them agree to a series of decrees which emphasized the ultimate authority of the Holy See in religious and ecclesiastical affairs.[47] At the same time he began to plan the replacement of the Gallican bishops, many of whom were aged, with strong ultramontanes when they died. He also indicated to the government that his intention was to impose law and order upon the Irish church, and when Daniel Murray died in 1852, Cullen was translated to Dublin where he could more easily carry through his mission to place the church under Roman control.

Before his move Cullen was made perpetual apostolic delegate, and as soon as he had settled in Dublin he began his campaign with a reshaping of the church in the archdiocese. He wrote to Cardinal Fransoni in Propaganda to recount his introduction of Roman devotions which, he said, the people attended in great numbers, their public devotions being 'most edifying'.[48] Then he set about attacking the Protestant establishment in every way possible, displaying an amazing streak of bigotry while he did so, telling Kirby in Rome about scandals like Lord Palmerston being tried for adultery, and Sir Robert Peel for assault. He encouraged a kind of social apartheid on the part of Catholics, boasted to Kirby that he had never dined with a Protestant, and he quipped about how he had slept in a bed in a Protestant hotel.[49] The American evangelists, Moodie and Sankey, were dismissed by him as 'irreverent ranters', and no mercy was shown in his attacks on the proselytizing missions in Dublin. Most serious was his attack on Richard Whately, the Protestant Archbishop of Dublin, which resulted in Whately's works being withdrawn from the curriculum of the National System of Education, and his retirement from the board.

When Cullen was made a cardinal in 1866 his triumphalism was grating on the Protestants, who realized that even on social occasions the new prince of the Roman church was the dominant presence. His triumphs were recounted for Kirby, with the note that they were to be drawn to the attention of the very worldly Cardinal Secretary of State, Antonelli. He relished telling of one *conversazione* where he met the Prince and Princess of Wales:

> About 3000 people were present. . . . There were two or three hundred dignitaries of the Protestant Church who looked at my red cloak with horror and amazement. They must have been terribly mortified when they saw me called up to the dais on which the Prince and Princess were placed whilst all the Protestant clergymen were left in the crowd.[50]

When the Catholic university was formally opened in 1864, there was a dinner in the Mansion House at which 'The lord mayor gave the pope's health in the first place, and the queen in the second place . . . you can imagine what annoyance such a proceeding has given to Protestants'.[51] Holy Cross seminary at Clonliffe, which was first opened in 1859 and was added to year by year, became notable as a symbol of ultramontane power in Dublin. In 1876 Clonliffe church was dedicated to the Sacred Heart in front of a huge assembly including the entire Irish hierarchy and Cardinal Alessandro Franchi. In terms of triumphalism, however, the greatest accomplishment of Cullen was his direction of the Irish campaign which resulted in the disestablishment of the Church of Ireland in 1871.[52] During this struggle he kept in constant contact with Cardinal Antonelli in Rome who, he admitted, was the real strategist of the enterprise.

Cullen's most important work was not on the level of diplomacy but the steadfast pursuit of his goal of crushing all opposition to papal direction of the Irish church. The old Gallican party had broken up with the death of Murray, but a new, strongly Gallican movement, allied with Irish political nationalists, had emerged, led by Archbishop John MacHale. Nothing could be done with this fierce old ecclesiastical warrior who outlived Cullen, but the papal delegate made sure that whenever an episcopal appointment was made the new prelate was a sound ultramontane who would oppose MacHale and his followers. For example, he had Propaganda appoint to the diocese of Galway, which was besieged by Protestant proselytizers, John MacEvilly, who was strongly Roman in his allegiance. MacEvilly kept a close watching brief on MacHale, whom he succeeded as Archbishop of Tuam in 1881. Other important appointments were made by Rome, and by the time of the Fenian crisis the great enemy of Irish nationalism was clearly the increasingly disciplined church led by Cullen.

One of the ways in which Cullen tried to redirect the nationalist spirit in Ireland was to have it serve the cause of Rome in Italy. The Holy See was trying to maintain its temporal authority in the states of the church against the attacks of Garibaldi and the other Italian nationalists, and to defend them Cullen organized an army of Papal Zouaves in Ireland. When they were raised the Irish detachments were told of the support Britain was giving to the Italian insurgents, and large sums were raised from the Irish poor to pay for the papal defence, a fact which the Irish Protestants did not fail to notice.[53] When the Irish contingent arrived it fought for only a few weeks, suffering considerable casualties, and the criticism of Cullen mounted. Even loyal bishops complained about Cullen trying to get money for the papal cause out of the pockets of people on the verge of starvation.[54] No further attempt was made to enlist directly for the papal army, although in the last campaign before the fall of Rome some Irish did serve in Franco-Belgian Zouave regiments.

Cullen by the early seventies was one of the most important cardinals in Rome, and it was widely believed that if Pio Nono had died at that time Cullen would have been the choice of the conservative cardinals for Pope. In the event that did not happen but, when Vatican Council I met, Cullen was already a dominant figure among the assembled bishops, most of whom were ultramontaners appointed by Pius IX during his long reign. During the council he made several brilliant and learned speeches and with Cardinal Bilio was the author of the formula which defined the dogma of papal infallibility.[55] Cullen was needed as a front-line ultramontane general, however, and as soon as the Council was over he hurried back to Ireland to continue the battle. Almost immediately he was confronted with Gladstone's strictures on the Vatican Council, which Cullen was never to forgive, as well as Newman's *Letter to the Duke of Norfolk*, which he viewed as a defence of Gladstone's ideas. Then he devoted himself to holding a plenary council at Maynooth which ensured that the hierarchy would continue to promote the initiatives of ultramontane reform first introduced at Thurles twenty-five years earlier.

During this period he encountered the greatest of challenges to ultramontane authority in the person of a stubborn old priest, Robert O'Keeffe, of Callan in the Ossory diocese. He was a strong supporter of the National System of education, and when he fell out with his bishop he appealed to Cardinal Barnabo of Propaganda, demanding that the bishop be tried for various offenses in a Roman court. Cullen then suspended O'Keeffe, who had the temerity to begin a civil lawsuit against the cardinal. Cullen appointed his nephew, Patrick Francis Moran, the future Cardinal Archbishop of Sydney, as co-adjutor of the diocese of Ossory, a disastrous move as Moran's home at Leighlinbridge was not far from Callan. Quickly the feud became one between two rival ecclesiastical farming families, the O'Keeffes and the Morans, there were contending altars in Callan, and the press began to focus on the scandal which was to Cullen a great embarrassment. Cullen, of course, saw behind the whole imbroglio the sinister hand of Freemasonry. By the time of the trial what had been raised was the old issue of *praemunire*: which authority ruled in Ireland, that of the crown or that of the papacy? The trial lasted sixteen days, with the judge ordering Cullen in the end to pay all legal costs. This caused a new trial on appeal and finally O'Keeffe, rendered penniless by legal costs, was forced to drop all charges against the Cardinal. Cullen had been badly frightened by this encounter, and did not like the press's interpretation of himself as the papal legate who would make the Irish priests 'slaves of the prelates, and without even the slave's privilege of complaining against injustice'. In a real sense O'Keeffe had at least checked the ambitions of 'the gloomy ascetic who now rules the Roman Catholic church in Ireland' as he sought 'to rivet on Irish priests the chains of ultramontanism'.[56]

The other check on the 'Cullenization of Ireland' that the cardinal legate pressed so successfully was provided by the Irish nationalist movement. Its leaders were Young Ireland zealots, like Charles Gavan Duffy, whom Cullen drove out of Ireland, Frederick Lucas, the convert editor of the *Tablet*, and Archbishop John MacHale. The latter brought their complaints about Cullen's opposition to their movement to the curia, during the Immaculate Conception ceremonies in Rome in 1854. This brought Cullen to a state of fury, for he was being attacked in the very centre of his power, and he treated Lucas very harshly. He also succeeded in making an open enemy of John MacHale, who from that time did all in his power to oppose Cullen's work.[57] The battle of the MacHaleites was fought not only in Irish parishes, but in places like the Irish College in Paris, where nationalist students used weapons and violence in their religious infighting and succeeded in driving successive rectors into breakdown.[58] One of the most prominent of the Paris agitators was Rev. Patrick Lavelle, who was nominally a priest in MacHale's archdiocese during the Fenian years, although he spent much of his time agitating in Dublin. Cullen tried at this time to organize a National Association to counter the Fenian hysteria by directing public passion into support for Roman concerns, like educational reform, and for the disestablishment of the Church of Ireland. This body was an abject failure, however, and was dismissed as 'a fresh attempt to Ultramontanize the Irish people'.[59] Nobody was happier than Cullen when the government came to his rescue by crushing the Fenians, who were always to the papal legate 'the disciples of Mazzini' and a threat to the Roman Catholic church.

In the 1868 period Cullen lived on Eccles Street in Dublin, next door to Isaac Butt, the one-time Orangeman and politician.[60] Cullen was only ten years older than Butt, who had defended Fenians in their state trials, and without doubt he must have met his neighbour who was notoriously a womanizer and a bankrupt. Such propinquity may account for Cullen's intense personal dislike of Butt, as well as the Home Rule movement he began. So far as Cullen was concerned the new organization was suspect, if only because some Protestants supported it. In his report to Rome he played down the importance of the Home Rulers' success in the election of 1874, but he recognized that a new political battle was coming: he would need to devote his energies to keeping the bishops, clergy and laity united in the storm that was coming.[61] He knew he would have no peace with a political movement in Ireland that welcomed ex-Tories, Protestants, and even active Orangemen. They were not the men who would support what mattered to Cullen: denominational education, the closing down of the Queen's Colleges, a charter for the Catholic University, and support for Pio Nono's *Kulturkampf* in Germany. Fortunately for Paul Cullen he died in 1878, just a few months after Pius IX, and was spared the challenge of dealing with the rise to power of the 'uncrowned king of Ireland', the Protestant Charles Stewart Parnell.

It was typical of Cullen, who was always defensive and intensely reserved about anything he said about himself, or the campaign he had in hand, that at the end of his life he was 'close' even in reporting to Kirby or Cardinal Barnabo in Rome. Particularly when he felt himself vulnerable, as he did in his last four years of life when Home Rule was gathering momentum, his reaction was to say nothing. It is very difficult to write a biography of a man who was neither expansive nor introspective, but was cautious, prudent, suspicious by nature, by training and because he was always at war. What he sought was invulnerability for the sake of his legatine mission, and he was fully open only to suggestions that came to him from the Pope himself. Even in his dealings with Antonelli, the papal Secretary of State, or the authorities at Propaganda, he was cautious and guarded. Of his actual communication with Pio Nono, at a time like that of the struggle with Lucas and MacHale in Rome, we would, as a matter of principle, know nothing. Nor do we have any insight, apart from passing comments in letters to Kirby or P.F. Moran, about his strategic considerations as he sought to impose his militant and divisive ultramontane culture upon the Irish people. One of his final exhortations to Tobias Kirby was to carry on the battle against the Protestant ascendancy:

> There is no chance of getting anything from them through love of justice, so speak stoutly . . . yield nothing and threaten that you and all Catholics must join the enemies of the government if they refuse us justice.[62]

Yet what Cullen accomplished in Ireland, as a dedicated individual working eighteen hours a day, seven days a week, for twenty-eight years, was considerable; it was never for self-glorification or national assertion. It is difficult to disagree with the leading editorial in the *Times* which appeared the day after his death on 24 October 1878:

> To him Rome was everything and he looked askance even at social pleasures which threatened to blur the line between her fold and that of heresy. To him obedience to . . . word of command was the first condition of order, and order the first necessity of a church. He was an ecclesiastical imperialist and he governed in a perpetual state of siege. Such a man could not have the play of mind or the broad sympathies which bring mental or moral influence, but the very narrowness of his view tended to give him fixity of aim, and to show him the shortest way to victory . . . He will be chiefly remembered as the prelate who made Ireland an essentially Ultramontane country.

A modern American scholar has said: 'by 1878 Paul Cardinal Cullen had indeed come to symbolize all that was real about Roman power in Ireland'.[63] Such a total oblation of personalty, of course, had ensured that Cullen would not prove to be an attractive subject for biographers, for in so many ways he became a living symbol of obedient ultramontane virtue, which is all he ever wanted to be.

He was apparently a lonely man, particularly in his later years, when he became of some concern to his secretary Laurence Forde, who told Kirby of Cullen's 'eremitical life' once his nephew P.F. Moran left Dublin. Yet this was an existence he chose, a reflection of his early formation in Rome. Like Wiseman, he found it difficult to delegate responsibility, which would have brought him fellowship.[64] He never chose familiarity, even with the chosen students whom he favoured in their ecclesiastical careers. James Quinn, who had been one of the most brilliant students at the Irish College in Rome, and had a distant family connection with Cullen, made a great mistake when, shortly before he was consecrated as

Bishop of Brisbane, Australia, he approached Cullen as an acquaintance rather than an ecclesiastical superior. Cullen's reaction was such that Quinn wrote to him 'on my knees and before God' to ask pardon for his presumption.[65]

Cullen was, so far as we know, a simple man when it came to religious belief. He never, apparently, had the terrible time of spiritual doubting that almost destroyed Wiseman in his time in the English College in Rome, nor did he have any journey in faith like that of Manning or Newman, which has given to biographers so much material. He was like the later ultramontane, John Cardinal Heenan, who once told an astonished Malcolm Muggeridge that he had 'never had a serious doubt in his life'.[66] Vatican Council II was to unleash the great anti-ultramontane rebellion that nearly broke Heenan before he died, but Cullen was throughout his life never denied reinforcement for his views from the triumphal Roman court of his generation. His friend and patron, Cardinal Barnabo of Propaganda predeceased him by only four years; Cardinal Antonelli, the Papal Secretary of State, by two years; and Pio Nono by a mere eight months. It is unlikely that in his latter years Cullen had any serious doubts about the ultimate victory of the ultramontane papacy. Just six months before his death he wrote to one of the Irish bishops from the Irish College in Rome a comment on what the new pontificate of Leo XIII promised — a continuation of the good fight:

> The new pope is gaining the hearts and good wishes of everyone. He will be another Pius IX. He is exceedingly kind to all the Irish who approach him and he is most friendly with me. The good man will have a great deal to suffer as his enemies are numerous and most rabid. They were hoping in the beginning that he would abandon Pius IX's line of action, but being disappointed they are now furious.[67]

It is an interesting question why, when thousands of Cullen's letters are available to scholars, the usual marmoreal two-volume exercise in pseudobiography did not appear in the Victorian years after his death, or indeed since. Perhaps it was felt that any biography would emerge as an exercise in ecclesiastical hagiography where 'the church and its works were the important matters; man was only an instrument'.[68] When you know little about the inner workings of a cleric like Cullen, even in the midst of the many struggles of a man who was always at war, no portrayal of him will be three-dimensional. The easy answer to the question as to why he has had no biographer is that in his thinking and actions he was always so constrained: never revealing his moments of human despair, or times of intellectual questioning in his lonely Irish mission — not even to an intimate friend, for he had none. If what is interesting in religious personalities is ultimately their 'struggle between the sacred old and the prophetic new',[69] then the staunchly 'Syllabist' (referring to the Syllabus of Errors) Cullen has not been a personality worthy of biographical study. He was simply an ultramontane exemplar, a nineteenth-century Roman 'apparatchik' who served the papal court so well that it is next to impossible to disassociate the man from his legatine rôle.

This may account, in large measure, for the absence of a biographer, but another reason may lie in the complexities of Irish history. Leopold von Ranke argued that 'in power itself a spiritual essence manifests itself'.[70] In Cullen's legatine authority was summed up the 'spiritual essence' of ultramontane Rome, one of the great imperial powers of the age, and any Irish scholar who attempts a biography of Paul Cullen needs to acknowledge how successful he was in bringing the Catholic church in Ireland under papal direction, and in imposing an ultramontane culture upon its people. For generations Irish nationalists have been reluctant to do this and, especially in our own day, Irish Catholic churchmen have felt uncomfortable when they consider what the 'Cullenization' of Ireland has meant. When Gladstone wrote on the Vatican decrees in 1874, he saw clearly what Paul Cullen and other papal delegates were persuading Catholic people everywhere to accept:

> Absolute obedience, it is boldly declared, is due to the Pope, at the peril of salvation, not alone in faith, in morals, but in all things which concern the discipline and government of the church. Thus are swept into the papal net whole multitudes of facts, whole systems of government, prevailing though in different degrees, in every country of the world.[71]

In Ireland the 'prevailing' has been to a remarkable degree highly successful as, since Cullen's day, the Roman central office has maintained its authority over the Irish Catholic church, and relentlessly imposed its ultramontane culture among the people. In the present day this imperialistic power is increasingly resented in Ireland, not only by the Protestant minority, but by an ever increasing number of Irish Catholic people. Yet to criticize Roman authority in Ireland is still a venture most scholars would wish to avoid. One suspects this is the real reason why scholars are reluctant to consider a biography of the papal delegate, Paul Cullen, who so successfully brought not only the Irish Catholic church but the Irish Catholic people under Roman obedience.

Notes

1. Philip Magnus, *Gladstone: a Biography* (London: Murray, 1963), p. xi.
2 David Knowles, *Historian and Character* (Cambridge: Cambridge University Press, 1955), p. 3.
3 William Stubbs, *Constitutional History* (Oxford: Clarendon, 1873–78), III, p. 639.
4 R.W. Church, *Oxford Movement* (London: Macmillan, 1891(, p. 19.
5 Llewellyn Smith and V. Nash, *Story of the Dockers' Strike* (London: Unwin, 1889), pp. 186–87.
6 E.S. Purcell, *Life of Cardinal Manning* (London: Macmillan, 1896), II, pp. 322–23.
7 Shane Leslie, *Henry Edward Manning, his Life and Labours* (London: Burns, Oates and Washbourne, 1921), p. 114, letter to Lady Herbert, December 1864.
8 David Mathew, *Catholicism in England* (London: Longmans, 1937), p. 198. Cf. G. Albion in G.A. Beck (ed.), *English Catholics, 1850–1950* (London: Burns and Oates, 1950), pp. 88–97.
9 Wilfrid Ward, *Life and Letters of Cardinal Wiseman* (London: Longmans, 1897), II, p. 510: cf. S.W. Jackman, *Nicholas Cardinal Wiseman* (Dublin: Five Lamps, 1977), pp. 130ff.
10 J.H. Newman, *Apologia Pro Vita Sua* (London: Collins, 1959), p. 100.
11 Robert Gray, *Cardinal Manning: a Biography* (London: St. Martin's, 1985), p. 106.
12 E.S. Purcell, *Life of Cardinal Manning* (London: Macmillan, 1896), I, p. 484.
13 David Newsome, *Parting of Friends* (London: Murray, 1966), pp. 368–69.
14 Lytton Strachey, *Eminent Victorians* (London: Penguin, 1948), p. 75.
15 Gray, *Manning*, p. 221.
16 Derek Holmes, *More Roman than Rome: English Catholicism in the Nineteenth Century* (London: Burns and Oates, 1978), p. 142.
17 H.E. Manning, 'Ultramontanism and Christianity,' *Miscellanies* (London: Burns and Oates, 1877), II, pp. 165–99.
18 *Times*, 7 November, 1874.
19 J.H. Newman, 'Letter to the Duke of Norfolk,' in *Certain Difficulties Felt by Anglicans in Catholic Teaching* (London: Longmans, Green, 1891), II, pp. 297, 300.
20 C. Butler, *Life and Times of Bishop Ullathorne* (London: Burns and Oates, 1926), II, p. 104; cf. Manning to Ullathorne, in *Dublin Review*, April 1920, p. 216.
21 Purcell, *Manning*, II, p. 351.
22 Wilfrid Ward, *Life of John Henry Cardinal Newman* (London: Longmans, Green, 1912), 1, p. 99.
23 J.H. Newman, *Apologia Pro Vita Sua*, ed. David DeLaura (New York: Norton Oxford University Press, 1968), p. 184.

24 Ian Ker, *John Henry Newman: a Biography* (Oxford: Oxford University Press, 1988), p. 327.

25 Newman to Ambrose St. John, November, 1950, *ibid.*, pp. 376–77.

26 *Ibid.*, pp. 382–83.

27 Fergal McGrath, *Newman's University: Idea and Reality* (Dublin: Browne and Nolan, 1951), pp. 180ff.

28 John Henry Newman, *Autobiographical Writings*, ed. H. Tristram (London: Sheed and Ward, 1956), p. 328.

29 Peadar MacSuibhne, *Paul Cullen and his Contemporaries* (Naas: Leinster, Leader, 1962), II, pp. 376, 295.

30 J.H. Newman, *Idea of a University* (Oxford: Longmans, 1912), p. 120.

31 Ker, *Newman*, p. 401.

32 Ward, *Newman*, I, pp. 381–84.

33 *Ibid.*, p. 370.

34 *Ibid.*, p. 357.

35 Ker, *Newman*, p. 570.

36 *Ibid.*, p. 595.

37 *Ibid.*, p. 660.

38 Alvan Ryan, *Newman and Gladstone: the Vatican Decrees* (Notre Dame: University of Notre Dame, 1962), p. 129.

39 Butler, *Ullathorne*, II. pp. 121, 158–60.

40 Gray, *Manning*, p. 282. Cf. Walter E. Houghton, *The Victorian Frame of Mind* (New Haven: Yale University, 1963,) pp. 94, 145, on the tension many felt between private judgement and external authority.

41 MacSuibhne, *Cullen*, I, p. 339: Cullen, cardinal, Archbishop of Armagh; P.F. Moran, cardinal, Archbishop of Sydney; Michael Verdon, Bishop of Dunedin, New Zealand. James Quinn, Bishop of Brisbane, Australia, and Matthew Quinn, Bishop of Bathurst, Australia, were brothers and distantly related.

42 Brian Fothergill, *Nicholas Wiseman* (London: Faber and Faber, 1963), p. 36; R.J. Schiefen, *Nicholas Wiseman and the Transformation of English Catholicism* (Shepherdstown: Patmos, 1984), p. 17.

43 Desmond Bowen, *Paul Cardinal Cullen and the Shaping of Modern Irish Catholicism* (Dublin: Gill and Macmillan, 1983), p. 25.

44 *Ibid.*, pp. 87–89.

45 *Ibid.*, p. 94.

46 *Freeman's Journal*, 21 January 1950.

47 Emmet Larkin, *The Making of the Roman Catholic Church in Ireland, 1850–1960* (Chapel Hill: University of North Carolina, 1980), pp. 27–58.

48 MacSuibhne, *Cullen*, III, p. 139.

49 Cf. the guest register, Hunter's Hotel, Rathnew, Co. Wicklow, 8 September 1858.

50 Bowen, *Cullen*, p. 143.

51 *Ibid.*, p. 146.

52 *Times*, 16 November 1868.

53 *Belfast Newsletter*, 7 February 1860.

54 Bowen, *Cullen*, p. 202.

55 Katherine Walsh, 'The First Vatican Council, the Papal State and the Irish Hierarchy', *Studies*, Spring 1982, pp. 58, 65–66.

56 *Daily Express*, 14 December 1872, editorial. For details of the trial cf. Court of Queen's Bench (Ireland), *Report of the Action for Libel brought by the Rev. Robert O'Keeffe, P.P. against His Eminence Cardinal Cullen* (London, 1874), pp. i–xxxviii, 1–594.

57 *Nation*, 28 January 1854.

58 Bowen, *Cullen*, pp. 259–62.

59 *Dublin Evening Mail*, 10 January 1865.

60 A.B.R. Young, *Reminiscences of an Irish Priest, 1845–1920* (Dundalk: Dundalgan, n.d.), p. 101.

61 Emmet Larkin, *The Roman Catholic Church and the Home Rule Movement in Ireland, 1870–1874* (Chapel Hill: University of North Carolina, 1990), p. 261.

62 Bowen, *Cullen*, p. 295.

63 Emmet Larkin, *The Roman Catholic Church and the Creation of the Modern Irish State, 1878–1886* (Philadelphia: American Philosophical Society, 1975), p. 391.

64 E.E. Reynolds, *Three Cardinals, Newman–Weisman–Manning* (London: Burns and Oates, 1959), p. 261; cf. W.J. Fitzpatrick, *Life of Father Thomas N. Burke, O.P.* (London: Duffy, 1885), II, p. 188ff. for Burke acting as a kind of 'court jester' for Cullen when the cardinal entertained.

65 Charles Hayes, 'Cullen, Newman and the Irish University', *Recusant History*, 1980, XV, p. 206.

66 Adrian Hastings, *History of English Christianity, 1920–1985* (London: Collins, 1987), p. 480.

67 MacSuibhne, *Cullen*, V, pp. 254–55.

68 J.A. Garraty, *Nature of Biography* (New York: Knopf, 1957), p. 55.

69 Paul Tillich, *Systematic Theology* (Chicago: University of Chicago, 1967), III, p. 367.

70 G.C. Iggers, *New Directions in European Historiography* (Middletown: Wesleyan University, 1975), p. 22.

71 Ryan, *Newman and Gladstone: the Vatican Decrees*, p. 41.

Writing Women
into Irish History
The Biography of Fanny and Anna Parnell

Jane McLaughlin Côté

My interest in the Ladies' Irish National Land League and in the lives of its founders, Fanny and Anna Parnell, was first awakened by references to them in Michael Davitt's The Fall of Feudalism in Ireland, or the Story of the Land League, published in London and New York in 1904. Wishing to know more about these remarkable sisters who had led a political organization of women dedicated to Irish land reform and Home Rule, I went confidently to my local library only to discover that no book on the Ladies' Land League had ever been published. Lengthy modern studies of the Irish land agitation of the 1880s contained only the briefest references to the Ladies' Land League, invariably of a dismissive nature; thumbnail portraits of Anna Parnell describe her as 'Parnell's fanatical sister'[1] or as possessing 'a tincture of revolutionary fanaticism'.[2]

Paradoxically — or so it seemed to me at first — some of the contemporary accounts of the land agitation written by men active in the movement describe the activities of the Ladies' Land League and of its leaders, whom they knew personally, with a measure of sympathy. Not with full-hearted approval, it is true; the idea of Victorian women taking to the public sphere in the interests of Irish nationalist politics was too startling an innovation to be taken easily in stride. Nevertheless they wrote of the Parnell sisters and their League with respect and an admittedly grudging admiration. By 1910 the tone had turned to ridicule; by the 1920s it was 'Anna Parnell and her female fanatics.'[3] Although I was familiar with the concept of 'writing women out of history,' this was my first experience of seeing the phenomenon at work.

Fortunately, a new generation of Irish historians has rejected the dubious moral judgments of their predecessors and is attempting to deal fairly — if briefly — with the Ladies' Land League and to appraise its contribution to the land agitation and to Irish history in general. Nevertheless, a full-scale study of the organization from its beginnings in New York, where it was founded by Fanny Parnell in October 1880, until its demise two years later in Ireland, where it had been headed by Fanny's younger sister Anna, remained to be written. Since no one else seemed disposed to undertake the project I decided to take it on myself.

From preliminary research in secondary sources and in Irish, Irish-Canadian and Irish-American newspapers of 1879–82 it became evident that the story of the Ladies' Land League in Ireland is first and foremost the story of Anna Parnell, just as that of the League in the United States and Canada belongs to her sister Fanny; without their unique blend of talents and personal qualities, such an organization would have been unthinkable in the late Victorian era, particularly in conservative, Catholic Ireland. What began, then, as a study of the Ladies' Land League soon evolved into a biography of its founders and principal organizers, with just over one half of the final book devoted exclusively to their involvement with the Ladies' Land League. By tracing the family background, the early lives and adolescence of Fanny and Anna Parnell, I hoped to discover why these two gently bred daughters of a Protestant Anglo-Irish landlord and his American wife rejected the beliefs and attitudes of their caste to become ardent Irish patriots dedicated to the cause of the mainly Catholic, landless Irish peasants. At the same time it would be necessary to explore the prevailing economic and social conditions that made it possible for them to emerge as the leaders of an important political organization in an era when women had no vote and little access to education, were barred from the professions and were relegated to the private sphere.

During the three years devoted, more or less full time, to researching the book, a number of problems and considerations presented themselves; some are common to all biographers, and many are unique to biographers of exceptional women engaged in such unconventional activities as political agitation.

First among the considerations that are common to all biographers to-day is whether the approach to the subject's life, character and achievements should be thematic or whether the more traditional chronological treatment is more appropriate. My own choice of a chronological biography was based on a personal preference for that approach, since it captures best the dynamism of a life as it is lived from day to day, revealing (ideally) the development of character as the subject progresses from childhood through adolescence, maturity, old age and death. While the thematic approach can offer new insights into the character and achievements of a well-known historical personality who has been the subject of previous (well researched) studies, this was not the case for Fanny and Anna Parnell.

Another problem common to all biographers (although not all biographers are willing to admit it) is the realization that their ideal goal of objective truth is impossible to achieve; that the beliefs, interests and experience of the biographer inevitably intrude upon her writing. Even the selection of sources, and the manner in which the facts gleaned are presented, depend on the writer's own view of what is important both in the subject's life and in the long run of history. Clearly the historians who wrote the Parnell sisters and the Ladies' Land League out of Irish history either neglected the sources I found so fruitful or regarded the facts revealed by those sources as inconsequential and not worth inclusion. Indeed, the very choice of subject reflects the writer's preoccupations. In my own case, a long-standing interest in nineteenth-century women involved in social and/or political reform made the accidental 'discovery' of the Parnell sisters a logical subject for a biography. Even the decision to write a biography tells much about the writer: her belief in the importance of individual action and in the possibility of free will; a rejection of the undiluted positivist/scientific/marxist/Annales School approach to history which tends to discount the importance of the individual in favour of the inanimate forces of geography, history, demography and so on. Ironically, Anna Parnell herself believed very firmly that the individual personality or character is unimportant in the long run of history, a view evidently derived from Henry Thomas Buckle's influential History of Civilization in England (published in two volumes, 1857–61). In keeping with this conviction, Anna Parnell attempted to purge her later writings of any personal content, even referring (in her written account of the land agitation[4]) to her then famous brother, Charles Stewart Parnell, as simply the 'President of the Land League'. Fortunately for her biographer, Anna Parnell's published and unpublished writings inevitably reveal much of their author and of her most deeply held convictions. More of this later.

Having then realized that they themselves stand in the way of that elusive goal of objective truth, conscientious biographers will attempt to recognize and take into account their own biases. Even this laudable aim is difficult to achieve. A case in point is George Orwell, who warned his readers that unless they followed his own example and faced the unpleasant possibility that they might, unknown to themselves, harbour anti-semitic sentiments, the canker of racial and religious bigotry would never be eliminated. At the same time Orwell could cheerfully mock a colleague who believed that 'if a woman was brought up exactly like a man she would be able to throw a stone, construct a syllogism, keep a secret, etc.'[5] Clearly he saw his belief in the natural inferiority of women as irrefutable fact and thus could not recognize his own anti-feminist bias.

The inability to recognize clearly our own biases is no reason to despair; it at least serves the purpose of making the biographer alert to possible bias in others. In my own study of secondary sources I discovered that the authors who needed particular scrutiny were not those overtly hostile to the Parnell sisters and the Ladies' 'Land League but those who, on the surface, were sympathetic to them. It was not until well along in my research that I realized that Michael Davitt's description of the Ladies' Land League and of the aims and objectives of the Parnell sisters, seemingly so laudatory, in fact completely distorted their views, words and actions. For reasons of his own[6] Davitt chose to portray the Ladies' Land League as a group of women bent on making Ireland ungovernable during the imprisonment of Parnell by inciting the Irish peasants to commit acts of violence such as arson and intimidation. In this way, Davitt concluded, they succeeded in forcing Gladstone to release Parnell and to bring into law a Land Act which achieved the aims of the land agitation. In fact, Anna Parnell abhorred the futile violence of the Secret Societies as did her sister Fanny. She had attempted to encourage the Irish farmers to use novel but peaceful strategies that Davitt and indeed most Irishmen were unable to understand. She also scorned the imaginary victory attributed to the Ladies' Land League since she believed that the land agitation had failed, that the Land Act of 1881 was nothing but a pathetic 'mouse that had raised a whole island'. Although Anna Parnell wrote *The Tale of a Great Sham*[7] in order to counter Davitt's glorification of the Land League (the 'great sham' of the title) and his vicious lies about her own and her sister's aims and objectives, she could never find a publisher for her manuscript. Thus Davitt's *The Fall of Feudalism in Ireland* became the 'authoritative' contemporary account of the land agitation of 1879–82, on which later writers relied in order to ridicule and discredit Anna Parnell and the Ladies' Land League.

Among the problems faced primarily by biographers of women engaged in political or social reform is the scarcity of original papers. Because historians traditionally assigned little space to the participation of women in the major political movements of past centuries, the task of modern scholars attempting to recover women's lives and achievements has been made needlessly arduous. Documents that escaped destruction were not made the subject of careful study; considered of minor importance, perhaps the subject of a footnote or two, they were consigned to the back shelves, got mislaid and all too often disappeared completely. Biographers consumed a lot of time in tracking down elusive clues contained in those cryptic footnotes only to discover once more that the original papers cannot be found or are so well hidden in scattered collections around the globe that they are as good as lost.

This discouraging state of affairs was brought home to me on many occasions throughout my research. One will suffice to illustrate. Having reason to believe that Fanny and Anna were in correspondence at a particularly crucial stage in their adult lives with their great-aunt by marriage, Mrs. Fenno Tudor of Boston, I traced the papers of their aunt's branch of the Tudor clan to the Baker Library at Harvard. The voluminous papers of her husband Frederic, the 'Ice King' of Boston, were carefully indexed and stored in the appropriate acid-free folders and boxes. A note dated 1941 and appended to the index informed me that 'Mrs. Tudor's papers were returned to the family.' Since the papers had been deemed by the Baker archivist to be of no historic value, they were destroyed by the family. Although Mrs. Fenno Tudor was a wealthy business woman in her own right, a member of the executive of the American Women's Suffrage Association working in close contact with Mary Eastman and Julia Ward Howe, a founder and generous benefactor to many still existing institutions in Boston, her papers were not deemed worthy of shelf room—not even worth sending, it seems, to the nearby Schlesinger Library of Radcliffe College. Thus a promising lead came to nothing.

Despite several notices in journals and newspapers and a lengthy combing of likely archives in Canada, the United States, Ireland and England, nothing in the way of private journals, memoirs, or family correspondence from or to Fanny or Anna, came to light, although an interesting selection of letters to Anna on Land League business, including one from as far away as New Zealand, did turn up. Biographers of Fanny and Anna's brother, Charles Stewart Parnell, are less dismayed by the lack of his private papers since Parnell is known never to have put pen to paper if he could possibly help it, relying throughout his adult lifetime on the telegraph to keep in touch with friends and family alike. His love letters to Katharine O'Shea, published in her memoir in 1914, owe their existence to Parnell's imprisonment in Kilmainham in 1881–82 and his inability for obvious reasons to get to the telegraph office. This was not the case with his sisters; Fanny, and to a lesser extent Anna, were assiduous letter writers.

The disappearance of Fanny's private papers is particularly difficult to understand. From 1880 until her sudden death two years later at the age of 33, Fanny was effective head of the Ladies' Land League in the United States and consequently maintained contact with hundreds of correspondents including her sister Anna, then in Ireland. Only a handful of these letters could be traced, none unfortunately of a personal nature. During these three years Fanny was living with her mother Delia Parnell at 'Ironsides', the Stewart estate in Bordentown, N.J., which Delia inherited in 1869 from her father Commodore Charles Stewart. It is logical to assume therefore that Fanny's papers disappeared when 'Ironsides' was sold at auction and its contents were dispersed, in the early years of this century. Yet the voluminous papers of four generations of Delia Parnell's maternal ancestors, the Tudor family of Boston, which were in Delia's possession at 'Ironsides' in the early 1890s, found their way safely into the Houghton library of Harvard and the Massachusetts Historical Society. Why then did only Fanny and Delia's papers disappear? More than likely they suffered the same fate as those of Mrs. Fenno Tudor, and the 'scholars' who rescued the family papers of the Tudors did not see fit to do the same for two (then) obscure women.

How then is one to understand the character and motivations of women active in the public sphere whose private voices are never heard?. The biographer can only turn to the public voice which, with careful study, can throw much light on the private person. Unlike their unbookish brother Charles, who left on record only his public speeches, Fanny and Anna Parnell published newspaper and journal articles, political pamphlets and collections of poems — mainly political — amounting to many thousands of words. In addition, Anna left her 70,000 word unpublished manuscript, *The Tale of a Great Sham*, and upwards of 30 public speeches fully reported in the Irish provincial press. Although none of these is biographical in character or intent, they do in fact reveal a great deal about their authors: their extensive reading in economics, political science and history, and in French, American and English literature; their precocious interest in Irish nationalist politics, beginning in adolescence; the evolution of their political thought from pro-Fenian poems (written by Fanny) in 1865, when she was 16, to their espousal of passive resistance as the only effective means of obtaining land reform and ultimately Home Rule; their personal philosophy, rooted in the writings of de Tocqueville, John Stuart Mill and Thoreau, and based on a belief in individual liberty and the rights of the minority.

Even their style of writing gives valuable clues to the characters of the two sisters, which were borne out by their actions. Fanny's discursive and at times prolix style pointed to her willingness to employ the acceptably feminine means of making a point by being charmingly persuasive. Anna's crisp, spare prose and dismaying ability to cut opponents down to size with a telling phrase or two are indicative of her direct and single-minded approach which, in the person of a Victorian lady, was seen as aggressive and provocative.

Certainly this knowledge of the political and philosophical views of Fanny and Anna Parnell was helpful in understanding and analyzing the intentions, actions and achievements of their public lives, which, unlike their early years, are well documented. But it did not explain how two young Anglo-Irish Protestant ladies came to hold views so contrary to the received opinion of their caste. Nor did it point to the source of their belief in their own right, as Victorian women, to enter the public arena of Irish nationalist politics. It seemed to me that an explanation might be found in their family background and early life. Unfortunately, in the absence of early diaries or letters, the only sources of information on Fanny and Anna Parnell's childhood are the published memoirs of an older sister, Emily Monroe Dickinson, and an older brother, John Howard Parnell. Both memoirs were written late in life when their authors were hard up and needed the money that a book dealing mainly with the life of their famous brother would bring in. Consequently they are highly personal, mainly anecdotal, short on dates, confused as to chronology and have little to offer in the way of solid information concerning their two much younger sisters. They do, however, provide valuable insight into the complex relationships within the large Parnell family (10 surviving children) — the hidden tensions, resentments, rivalries and alliances among the children and between the parents.

It is also clear from both memoirs that the early death, at age 48, of their father, John Henry Parnell, when Anna was 7 and Fanny 11, profoundly disrupted the lives of all the family. Debts contracted by John Parnell in the year before his death forced the family to rent out the beloved home 'Avondale' and begin the peripatetic existence which would be the pattern for the later lives of Fanny, Anna and their mother. Further, John Parnell's will caused lasting resentment in those of his children who believed with good reason that they had been unfairly treated; Delia Parnell and her six daughters were left an annual allowance of £100 while the three surviving sons inherited a landed estate each. Although Anna Parnell would later write with great bitterness of this custom of the Anglo-Irish gentry, who would give 'all or nearly all to the sons and nothing or hardly anything to the daughters',[8] she would in another context refer to her father as a friend.

In view of all this, there was a strong temptation to indulge in a spot of psychobiography based on the concepts of ambivalence and compensation. The temptation however was easily resisted. Despite Peter Gay's persuasive case (*Freud for Historians*) for employing Freudian psychoanalytic theories to help in understanding the motivation and actions of an individual, they do not seem to be very helpful in the case of women engaged in unconventional activities such as movements for social or political reform; the desire to engage in such movements is seen as abnormal and an indication of a dysfunctional personality. The question asked is not, 'What forces and inspirations enabled this woman to perform remarkable feats?' but rather, 'What unresolved conflicts led her to reject marriage and domesticity in order to seek satisfaction in "masculine" pursuits?' I chose to see the death of John Parnell, a conventional and unimaginative man who was firmly embedded in the beliefs and attitudes of his caste, as a door to freedom from constraint and contradiction for his two young daughters. Under the tutelage of their easy-going American mother from an early age, Fanny and Anna Parnell enjoyed a physical and intellectual freedom that their older sisters, who were brought up during the lifetime of their father and who lived conventional and unhappy lives, were denied.

A technique now much favoured by family therapists, the use of the genogram,[9] offers an alternative to the Freudian psychoanalytic approach for exploring unconscious motivations and can be usefully adapted to the needs of biography. The use of the genogram is based on the realization that we all acquire from our families not only a genetic inheritance but an inheritance of models of behaviour which are transmitted through the collective family memory, that is, the stories told about family members and which are passed down from one generation to another. Thus a long-dead grandmother or great-aunt — even a distant cousin — who lives on in family stories as an admirable character of strong will and independent mind or, more likely, as a model of selfless maternal devotion, can cast a long shadow over the women and the men of succeeding generations. By constructing a genogram — a family tree on both sides of the family in both diagrammatic and narrative form and going back at least three generations — the individual can often reach an informed understanding of the family past and of the ways in which it has influenced her choices in life. There is nothing very new in the notion that families influence their members in all manner of subtle and unrecognized ways. Traditionally, however, it has been thought sufficient by therapists to look at the direct influence of the immediate family — a practice followed by historians and biographers. The genogram goes beyond this and considers the possible influence of every member of the extended family, living and dead, of whom the individual has 'inherited' any knowledge.

It seemed to me then that if I could locate extensive archives from Fanny and Anna Parnell's family background — particularly on the maternal side (since they were raised mainly by their voluble American mother) — I might find a plausible explanation for the unlikely turn their adult lives would take. Although biographers of Charles Stewart Parnell have almost invariably attributed his Irish nationalism to anti-English sentiments acquired from his American mother and her family (who in fact were all ardent anglophiles), they have never supplied any reference to Tudor or Stewart family papers which would substantiate their claim of anti-Englishness (which is simply taken as a given). This seemed to indicate that no such papers existed. However, in order to leave no stone unturned I addressed a letter of enquiry to the Boston Public Research Library and was rewarded with the information that three large collections of Tudor papers were held in Boston at the Houghton and Baker libraries of Harvard and at the Massachusetts Historical Society. All are readily available to researchers. A subsequent trawling expedition in Gardiner, Maine (inspired by a hunch), turned up a fourth large cache of family correspondence, still in the possession of the descendants of Emma Tudor Gardiner, the great-aunt of Fanny and Anna Parnell. This last collection was particularly valuable for the new and detailed information it contained concerning the unhappy childhood, the adolescence, courtship and early married life in Ireland of Delia Tudor Stewart Parnell.

These extensive Tudor archives, many of which date from before the American Revolution, include private journals, business diaries and records, and many hundreds of intimate family letters. They enable one to follow year by year, at times day by day, the agitated lives of that remarkable family. The Tudors of Boston included men of letters, visionary and successful business entrepreneurs, holders of high office in peace and war, and highly literate and self-confident women in an age when little more than ornamental graces were required of them. Throughout the Tudor archives the stuff of family myths and legends abounds. The independent, pro-British great-grandmother who carried out cold drinks to the weary British soldiers filing past her Boston home after the Battle of Bunker Hill, the gallant great-grandfather who swam across the channel to East Boston to visit his young fiancée under cover of darkness during the siege of Boston, were only two of the more colourful family stories. Others concern their great-uncle, Frederic Tudor, the 'Ice King' of Boston, and his heroic struggles against great odds to make a large fortune by shipping ice to the tropics. The brilliant social success in aristocratic London society of their grandmother, whom Fanny and Anna knew well as children, and the tragic failure of her marriage to the naval hero of the War of 1812, Captain Charles Stewart, all loom large in the correspondence, as well as in the reminiscences of the Parnells' mother Delia Tudor Stewart Parnell.[10] In short, this rich treasure trove compensated in large measure for the absence of Fanny and Anna's private papers, and enabled their biographer to uncover a trail that led from Revolutionary Boston to *The Tale of a Great Sham*.

In conclusion, it is worthwhile to draw attention to yet one more problem faced by biographers of women engaged in unconventional political activity. That is, the danger of slipping into hagiography. The Parnell sisters, like so many politically active women of the past, have been unfairly treated by historians who have distorted their motives and misrepresented their characters and personalities. Writing their biography became not just a question of recovery but of rehabilitation. It was tempting to right the balance by over-looking Fanny and Anna Parnell's faults and failures and concentrating instead on their virtues and achievements. This, however, would have simply compounded the original error by distorting their lives and characters in another direction. By presenting them for the first time in all their rich complexity, neglecting neither their failures nor their achievements, I hope I have established for them the important place they deserve in nineteenth-century Irish history.

Notes

1 T.N. Brown, *Irish-American Nationalism, 1870–1890* (Philadelphia and New York: Lippincott, 1966), p. 115.

2 F.S.L. Lyons, *Charles Stewart Parnell* (London: Collins, 1977), p. 178.

3 St. J. Ervine, *Parnell* (London: Ernest Benn, 1925), p. 235.

4 A. Parnell, *The Tale of a Great Sham*, ed. D. Hearne (Dublin: Arlen House, 1986).

5 G. Orwell, *The Collected Essays, Journalism and Letters of George Orwell*, Vol. I, eds. S. Orwell and I. Angus (London: Secker, 1968), p. 136.

6 J. Côté, *Fanny and Anna Parnell: Ireland's Patriot Sisters* (London, Dublin and New York: Macmillan, 1991), pp. 242–45.

7 See A. Parnell, *The Tale of a Great Sham*, ed. D. Hearne (Dublin: Arlen House, 1986).

8 *Ibid.*, pp. 85–6.

9 See M. McGoldrick and R. Gerson, *Genograms in Family Assessment* (New York: Norton, 1985).

10 See Delia Tudor Stewart Parnell to T.D. Sullivan, 21 January 1880. Sullivan papers (MS 8237(6)), National Library of Ireland.

Excavating Nora

Brenda Maddox

Beginning

'I suppose,' people say, 'you feel you know her better than any-one you've ever known in your life.' Then: 'you must see a lot of yourself in her.' The answer to both is *No*.

The myths of biography run deep. Biography is very popular these days; some would say too popular. Why it should be so is one of the questions I will try to answer. Along with the popularity of the genre has come a surge of theory of biography. It has inspired a lot of nonsense. Let me say at the start that I wrote the life of Nora Joyce, not because I felt I knew her — or wanted to learn more about myself — another question people ask — but because I didn't know her. She was a mystery to be solved, a story waiting to be told. Why we read it is part of a larger question I'll try to answer later. But first, and not unrelated to the larger questions, I'd like to talk about what many have asked me — a problem I had to solve: how do you go about writing a biography of a woman who left no diaries and next to no letters. Written records are the stuff of biography.

The way to start, certainly the way *I* started, was not to think of it as a biography at all. The late Richard Ellmann had warned me at the start that there was 'nothing to say.' Nora was an uninteresting woman, he said. And from his point of view — that of one of the century's great literary biographers — he was correct. Nora, seen from one point of view, did nothing but shop. Ellmann told me that there was not enough material to warrant a book — not even, he ventured, a feminist treatise. She wrote no letters, he said, as they had never been separated. And all the Joyces' old friends were dead.

When I persisted, however, he kindly invited me to lunch at New College, Oxford. As we sat in his study — it was in March, 1984, before his cruel illness overtook him — I told him that I did not think of it as a biography, but rather as a 'book about' Nora. I simply wanted to know more about Joyce's wife.

That there was more to know I had no doubt. I have been a journalist for 30 years and an author for nearly 20. My experience has shown me that real people leave real traces. I could write a book about my grandmother, or yours.

How could anyone doubt, considering the mountains of Joyce material in libraries around the world, that there was bound to be somewhere, in the boxes and folders, unused information about his wife? I also went equipped, although lacking a Ph.D. in English or comparative literature, with basic journalistic principles. And even if the Joyces' friends were dead, their friends' children were not. I mused to my daughter that it was as if someone came along 50 years from now and wanted to write a book about the wife of a famous scientist friend whom she has seen only several times. 'I could tell them a lot,' she said.

In other words, in working for four years on *Nora*, I went about it the way I would go about reporting for a newspaper. I was gratified to learn how very well some fundamental truths of journalism applied. If you want a good story, send somebody who knows nothing about it. The truth — or an approximation of it — is available to anybody willing to dig. There is no last word on anything. There is always room for a fresh eye, which adds up the evidence differently. And the first sign that you are on to a good story is someone telling you to go away — there *is* no story.

But 'lives' are not 'stories' — public events. There is a hostility to any biography except autobiography. The British writer Auberon Waugh said that no outsider can possibly describe the life of anyone else. I don't share that view. We are all many selves. We are the children of our parents, the parents of our children. We are writers to our publishers but self-employed businesspeople to the taxman. Biographies are subjective — they are the author's view of the subject, one of an infinite possibility of portraits. Good biographies may be rare, but good autobiographies are rarer. Most subjects give themselves a very soft ride.

However, I never imagined that, in examining the private lives of James and Nora Joyce, I was anything but an outsider. But a friendly curious one. Nora in the past has been described as an unlettered chambermaid from Galway, an unworthy consort to whose company Joyce was mysteriously addicted. It was clear, certainly, from Joyce's letters and from Ellmann's biography, that Nora had more to her than that. Everything she said made me laugh. I never believe that stupid people can be funny. Ellmann himself reminded me of her remark to Joyce, overheard by Mary Colum, that a possible new flat she had gone to inspect 'was not fit to wash a rat in.'

Nora made me laugh even when she was bad-tempered and scolding. One of her sharpest retorts was relegated to an Ellmann footnote. In 1931, for example, Nora had made yet another attempt to break free from James Joyce. With his friend Stuart Gilbert as a witness, Joyce sat disconsolate in their hotel room and watched Nora pack up. He begged her to change her mind. 'We could take a trip,' he volunteered — as if their whole life together had not been one long trip. Nora did not just say no. 'I wish,' she said, 'you would go drown yourself.' No one else talked to the great modernist master like that, just as no one else told him what Nora told all his literary friends: 'Jim should have stuck to singing.'

Nora Joyce, née Barnacle, did not interest me as a mere 'wife of' but as a personality in her own right. Who was this tall bold red-haired girl from Galway who dared to run away from Ireland — unmarried — in the harsh moral climate of 1904 — with a young writer with nothing in his pocket but two tickets to Zurich? How could she have been, as her reputation had it, an almost illiterate while mastering three languages and dining out in Paris and London with Samuel Beckett, Ezra Pound and the Yeatses? What did she see in James Joyce?

And then there were unanswered questions in the Joyce story as it had been told. Why *had* the Joyces bothered to marry in 1931 after 27 years loyal cohabitation? Why, after Joyce died in Zurich in 1941, did Nora remain there until her own death, in 1951? And what happened to all the money his books eventually earned? There clearly was no shortage of things to write about.

When I began, of course, I had to trust my intuitions about Nora's character — or to make leaps of imagination when there simply was no evidence. But I did not make these leaps without checking that what evidence there was would support them — and I made a cardinal rule *not* to take any biographical information from Joyce's fiction. Just because Molly Bloom commits adultery in *Ulysses* does not mean that Nora did, although Joyce lived for many years in terror of such a betrayal. Nor did I put any words into her mouth or, without evidence — in the form of a letter, a memoir or an interview — thoughts into her head.

When I say, as I do in Chapter One, 'As Joyce entered the hotel, in dirty canvas shoes and a straw hat, seeing the shabby way he was dressed, Nora wondered if she should entrust herself to him', that is because I had a good find. In the cellar of his house in Dublin, Roderick Power, son of Arthur Power, dragged out his father's notes for *Conversations with James Joyce*. They confirmed that Nora told that to Power. I trusted him, and footnoted the fact.

I used Joyce's own portrait — 'O Nora Nora Nora — I am speaking now to the girl I loved, who had red-brown hair and sauntered

over to me and took me so easily in her arms.' I did a book outline based on Stanislaus Joyce's descriptions, e.g. 'Miss Barnacle
has magnificent hair but a common expression on her face,' — and
glimpses in literature. The way Gretta Conroy, the red-haired West
of Ireland wife in Joyce's short story, 'The Dead', leaves her clothes
after she undresses for bed, for example, makes her cautious husband mistrust her:

Perhaps she had not told him all the story. His eyes moved
to the chair over which she had thrown some of her clothes. A
petticoat string dangled to the floor. One boot stood upright, its
limp upper fallen down: the fellow of it lay upon its side.

A psychoanalyst friend of mine, Norman Zinberg, who, sadly,
died last month, read my outline. He asked me over for a drink.
'Shall I tell you what I think Nora was like based on what you've
said?' A person with very little conflict, someone who does what
she does with no regrets. Running away with Joyce, writing erotic
letters: she'd go along with it. That kind of person, he said, is very
attractive to a person racked with guilt — as Joyce was.

Sources

So I felt I was on the right track. I was convinced that a real
woman was there. Not so much a biography, more an excavation. I
set out to find the pieces, and like an archaeologist, to number them
so that people would not think that I had made them up. Unlike an
archaeologist, I set out in every direction at once: friends, books,
libraries, public documents, academia, Joyce's work — fiction and
letters. First, to find the old friends who were still alive: Maria
Jolas, Moune Gilbert (Stuart Gilbert's widow) and Arthur Power,
all in their nineties. Their memories, of doubtful value, or the factual details. But their sense of the person. 'I'm glad you're doing
Nora,' they all said. 'She has not been fairly treated.' Second, to
comb published memoirs and library archives. Hard as it may be
to believe, new material is still coming to light — such as the letters
of Joyce's daughter, Lucia, who died in 1982. Her letters, of which
hundreds exist, are mainly at Buffalo and University College London. Many collections contain unique newspaper cuttings. It was
from one of these, from the *Figaro Littéraire* of 1976, that I learned
that Carola Giedion Welcker, who had been present at Joyce's funeral, heard Nora say, as the coffin was lowered into the grave,
'Jim! How beautiful you are!'

(I checked this quote — pure gold for a biographer — with Ellmann. He had a high opinion of Mrs. Giedion Welcker. 'If she said
it, I'd believe it,' he said.)

And then there were the Joyce relatives. I began with Stephen Joyce, Joyce's only grandson and direct descendant. He lives in Paris with his wife. They were very kind to me and gave me many addresses. Stephen Joyce was the only person — then — who believed with me that his grandmother was as important as his grandfather. Then there was Joyce's niece, Bertha, who lived with the Joyces in Trieste; there was the son of Joyce's brightest sister, May, Ken Monahan, outside Dublin. There were quite a lot around in fact — people now in their seventies — who made me feel as if Nora and Jim were real people who had just walked out the door. In Washington the daughter of Joyce's best Irish friend, Constantin Curran, gave me the details of what was blindingly obvious from photographs but had never before been commented upon — that Nora was a fashion plate. Nora loved couture, Curran's daughter told me, and Joyce indulged her in it; she patronized the house of Lucien Lelong.

And then there was the search through public records. As a journalist I was gratified to find how much that was new could be learned by a patient searching out of birth, marriage, death, divorce and probate documents, some going back to the last century.

After about a year — and my first Joyce conference, the Ninth International James Joyce Symposium, at Frankfurt — I began to get the sense of fun of being 'on' to something. Several scholars had pointed me to the learned papers that claimed that Nora was an unworthy consort of James Joyce, that she could not cook or keep the house in order. But already, reading as I had been for references to Nora, I could think of half a dozen mentions of her roast chicken, her shining household, page after page of references to her cooking. Why had no one collected them? The result was a paper, 'Could Nora Cook?', which I presented to the Joyce Conference the following year, at Philadelphia. Complete with recipes furnished me in Paris by another lucky find, the niece of Nora's best friend, Kathleen Bailly, I was able to lay to rest, forever, one small corner of the case against Nora the incompetent.

Let it be clear — the primary source was Joyce's letters. Not only the erotic ones, all of them. If you have an author for a husband, you have no need of a biographer. Joyce knew Nora, and he explained her to his brother. He wrote his own biography by keeping such an extensive correspondence — and he wrote hers. We know — from him — what she looked like: 'O Nora! Nora! Nora! I am speaking now to the girl I loved, who had red-brown hair and sauntered over to me and took me so easily into her arms and made me a man.'

In a letter to Stanislaus on December 3, 1904, from Pola, Joyce wrote:

> Uncle Michael supports Mrs and the children, while Papa bakes and drinks in a distant part of Connacht. Uncle M is very rich. Papa is treated very contemptuously by the family. Nora says her mother would not lie with him. Nora has not lived at home but with her grandmother who has left her some money.
>
> She has told me something of her youth, and admits the gentle art of self-satisfaction. She has had many love-affairs, one when quite young, with a boy who died. She was laid up with news of his death.

Let's take a closer look at this boy who died. Ellmann's biography identifies him as Michael Bodkin, a University College Galway student who left university to work in the gasworks and who died in February 1900 and is buried at Rahoon Cemetery. He is, according to the accepted view, the prototype of Michael Furey in 'The Dead', who caught his death by singing 'The Lass of Aughrim' in the rain outside Gretta's window.

In Dublin, in October 1948, I had an interview with Patrick Henchy, former Keeper of Books at the National Library of Ireland. It was a grey Dublin January afternoon, a coal fire, a drink. Henchy is from Galway, and he said, 'Nora had lots of boyfriends, you know. Ellmann was all wrong about that Michael Bodkin.'

Henchy had gone along, as a kind of native guide, when Ellmann a quarter of a century ago had traversed Galway researching his biography of Joyce. Nora's sister, Kathleen, talked about a much earlier boyfriend, Michael Feeney, who had died. Ellmann was not interested, said Henchy; he was hung up on Bodkin. But Henchy noticed, as the talk in Galway was (and still is) that Nora was one for the boys. She had boyfriends much earlier than Bodkin, the boy from the gasworks, who, as a matter of historical fact, died in 1900 when Nora was 16.

'Look for Michael Feeney in Rahoon Churchyard,' said Henchy. 'I'm sure you'll find him.'

Looking through a west of Ireland cemetery is best done by letters from London, and you had best not be in a hurry. Many requests for records from Ireland are returned with the laconic reminder that many records were destroyed in the burning of the Customs House in the civil war of 1922. But Galway's were not, and with time the Cathedral sent back the record of grave number 1, that of a Michael Feeney, who died in 1896.

More letters, to the County Health Board this time, revealed the death certificates, and not only the relevant one, for Michael

Feeney — a common name, and he might have been 80 years old, but this one was 16 years old. A pupil teacher. Died in February in the workhouse, after typhoid pneumonia.

I asked for another death certificate, that of Nora's grandmother. It was even more interesting. We know that she was fostered with her grandmother at the time when her grandmother died. It had appeared from Joyce's letters — maybe even he had believed it — that Nora's grandmother had died when she was a young adult, not long before she ran away from home to Dublin at the age of 19.

But the death certificate said — could it be right? — that Nora's grandmother, Catherine Mortimer Healey, had died in 1896 — New Year's Day. Three months before Nora turned 13. And just six weeks before Michael Feeney's death. No wonder she was 'laid up with news of his death.'

The pieces began to fit. Joyce's letter saying, 'She has had many lovers, one who died, when she was quite young. She was laid up with news of his death,' took on new meaning. Nora had lost her boyfriend just when she lost her grandmother, and therefore had lost her home too, in the early months of 1896, just as she began work as a portress at the Presentation Convent. She was young indeed to have had a boyfriend at 12. No wonder Joyce wanted to think she was older when she suffered this heartbreak.

With this news background, we can read again the closing passage from 'The Dead', when Gabriel Conroy reaches out to embrace his wife, only to have her burst into tears because the song, 'The Lass of Aughrim', she has just heard, makes her think of a boy she knew long ago. Who was this boy? her husband wants to know.

'It was a person I used to know in Galway when I was living with my grandmother, she said.'

Gabriel asks coldly if she intends to look up this old lover when next she visits Galway.

'He is dead, she said at length. He died when he was only seventeen. Isn't it a terrible thing to die so young as that?'

And what did he die of?, Gabriel asks.

'I think he died for me,' she answered.

'It was in the winter, she said, about the beginning of the winter when I was going to leave my grandmother's and come up here to the convent. And he was ill at the time in his lodgings in Galway and wouldn't be let out, and his people in Oughterard were written to.'

The proximity of Michael Feeney's death in February to that of Nora's grandmother on New Year's Day, as well as, the occasion of her leaving her grandmother's home make Feeney a closer model for the fictional Michael Furey — his name even sounds the same —

than Nora's later admirer, Michael Bodkin. Feeney was five months short of 17 (and Joyce needed to make his teenage lovers plausible: a Nora of 12 and a Feeney of 16 would lack dramatic credibility) and Bodkin was 20 when he died.

Fair to take it as biographical? From an author who said, 'Imagination is memory'? I took it: Nora Barnacle: a pretty redhead, street-smart, bereft by the loss of her grandmother, worried about her power over men — and added to it Joyce's note to *Exiles*:

> 'Bodkin died. Kearns died. Mankiller they called her at the convent.'

If we are only interested in Joyce's literary work, it hardly matters where he got the facts for 'The Dead'. He arranged his material to suit his art and ear. But to understand Nora — and to understand the nature of the Joyce's marriage, what manner of man and what manner of woman they were — it helps a lot to know that as early as 12, she lost her substitute mother, a boy she loved, and for the boy's death she felt responsible.

Copyright

I have talked about excavating Nora. Many of the pieces of the puzzle I found were in libraries. Here I ran into a problem I had not foreseen, one which perhaps does not hamper the archaeologist. The pieces belong to someone, the copyright owner. Just to have discovered them does not entitle you to display them — that is, to quote them in your own work.

Many — such as the unpublished letters of James Joyce to Harriet Shaw Weaver in the British Library or the unpublished letters of Nora to Jim in Cornell — cannot be quoted without permission of the trustees of the James Joyce Estate, which is administered by the Society of Authors in London. For others, such as the letters of J.F. Byrne in the Humanities Research Centre, the copyright owner cannot be traced.

Byrne suggested that Joyce's friend, Vincent Cosgrave, may have been a lover of Nora's before Joyce — an accusation, you will know, if you know Joyce's life, that deeply upset him and was part of the genesis of *Ulysses*, the story of a cuckold. In 1909 Joyce, leaving Nora behind in Trieste with their two small children, revisited him. On that visit Cosgrave told him that he had been seeing Nora during the same summer that Joyce had been courting her.

It has been widely believed — although no evidence has existed either way — that Cosgrave was lying. Byrne's letter suggested otherwise — that Joyce simply could not accept what was common knowledge in Dublin — that he was not the only man in Nora's life. But if I wished to I would quote the letter I had to write, vainly as it turned out, in search of the widow or descendants of Byrne. None appeared. But if they do, I will be happy to ask their permission.

I have no objection to copyright. Indeed I, as an author, live by it and have not hesitated to ring the lawyer when I find large chunks of a book of mine in somebody else's. I do accept people's right to be arbitrary and selfish, just as we all have had neighbours who would not let you walk across their grass, or who share in some way that would cost them nothing.

I do object when owners of rights use them as a means of censorship. If you may not quote, that is one thing. If you may not quote, when others are permitted to do so, or unless I have an advance look at what you say, that is another. If people wish to bequeath papers and put a timelock on them that is universally applicable, that is their business. But to pick and choose, with no known guiding principle, is not the business of serious scholarly trustees.

And I would hope that libraries — when accepting letters, memoirs, notes for the collections — would do all they can to see that the material is given free of restrictions. If time-limits are to be imposed — no quotations until all immediate descendants have died — or not until the year 2020 A.D., that might be fair. But not arbitrary — pick and choose — permissions.

You may have read that a chapter had to be deleted from my biography because of objections from Nora's grandson, Stephen Joyce. That is true: the next-to-last chapter, in fact. Let me make it clear that Mr. Joyce did not object to what I had written, because he had not read it and said he had no wish to read it. It was the subject matter, pure and simple — the life of Lucia Joyce after her mother's death in 1951 — that he had decided should not be written about. Although he had not told me so in advance.

As many know — those who have read the chapter in the American proof copy that was circulated before this ban was imposed — there was nothing sensational or alarming in it. It contained a poignant, and I thought, touching portrait of the quite reasonable life Lucia had made for herself at the very pleasant St. Andrew's Hospital, Northampton. Lucia retained very warm memories of her mother. In her own autobiography Lucia wrote:

Nora was the prettiest girl in the county Galway. She was a very well-dressed woman who liked to entertain friends and go to the opera alone.

But the chapter had to go; this was part of the delicate negotiations for copyright permission to use much other Joyce material, including passages from unpublished letters, especially Nora's. I am grateful for those permissions. They help us to understand Nora. They help her to speak in her own voice. One in particular shows how she not only spoke — but wrote — with the earthy forthrightness of Molly Bloom.

In August 1917 she and the children, Giorgio and Lucia, had left Joyce in Zurich while they went to Locarno. 'I hope you are writing Ulisses,' she said, 'without us to bother you.'

The children, at 12 and 10, were with her. 'I havent any trouble with them,' she wrote, without punctuation or pause, 'except in the morning before they get up its a regular game with them they have a boxing match in the bed and of course I have to pull the two of them out on the floor Georgie is very shy he is afraid of my life I might see his prick so that he rolls himself up in the quilt now I must wash my hair its the only trouble it continues to fall out very much hope this will find you well best love from children Nora.'

Libraries

'Surely,' people say, 'all the Joyce materials are in one place.' Ireland is the place that usually springs to mind. They are not. There is no Great Curator up in the sky to make sure that all the Leonardos are in Florence, all the Wyndham Lewis in the British Library, and that the Getty Museum in Malibu does not get a disproportionate share of anything.

One of the new experiences in writing the book was the discovery of libraries. They can be forbidding. I have learned to allow for 20 minutes of tension — worse than checking in with an airline — when you first approach the desk and ask to see the Special Collection. There is a barrage of Who are You, What are Your Credentials? Some demand a photograph (British Library), a letter of accreditation. Then they relax — the collections are there, after all, to be used. In the end they all were extremely kind and helpful. But not at the start.

I would like to make a plea for Special Collections to be made user-friendly. And more welcoming to travellers. Few have any accommodation, and why should they? But they might do more to supply information to the scholar or writer who has come, at their own expense, from out of town to consult the collection.

"Where can I stay?" I asked one library in the mid-American hinterland. I was given the name of a Holiday Inn more than a mile from the campus. 'You *could* walk there,' they said, 'but we would not advise it as you have to pass through a not very nice part of town.' Another gave me the address of a motel across the street. But it turned out to be across the street from the *old* campus — and the street was an eight-lane highway. The new campus, where the collection was, was a 15-minute taxi ride away.

No one can complain that Special Collections need special handling. They are, I accept, colder than other parts of the library because of climate-control of manuscripts. But there cannot be any universal imperative about the petty restrictions they impose, for they differ from place to place. Some will not let you use your own pencils. Others forbid your own pencil sharpener. At Texas you must write on yellow paper only and wear white gloves to look at photographs. Most blanch at the sound of the word photocopy while others provide not only a handy machine but a bill-changer as well.

Lap-top computers have added a new twist to the game. Some ban them. Others permit them. The Berg Collection at the New York Library allows them as long as they do not beep. In my Good Library Guide the toughest is the Beinecke at Yale. It is like Alcatraz with a sculpture garden; closed-circuit cameras pan the room as you read, and the compulsory divestiture of belongings is most strict — a ritual hard on women without pockets, who need to get through with the odd dime, kleenex, and telephone numbers.

Security is necessary but the average scholar, having gone through the labyrinth to get permission to enter, is less likely to write in red lipstick on Gutenberg Bibles than the ordinary library or museum visitor — and is, in any case, under constant surveillance by librarians in near empty rooms.

But the worst and most unnecessary restriction — the only one I can really complain about — is the limit on hours. Most university libraries are open until 11 pm or midnight. And they are used by students who live nearby. But Special Collections — almost by definition — are used by people with special interest — 'Oh, does Cornell have a Joyce collection?' someone high in the Cornell English Department asked me — from out of town.

But Special Collections close at 5 o'clock, which means the books start banging and the staff looking impatient at half past four. Some are open Saturdays. Buffalo's is not. I worked very hard to get through those boxes, including 100 letters from Lucia Joyce.

I think libraries with unique collections, especially those away from metropolitan centres which people travel from the ends of the earth to see, have a duty to make the collections as accessible as possible to those who come to visit them and to make travellers feel like welcome visitors to the campus.

The best in my Good Library Guide would be the Library of Congress: photocopying machines, assistants more interested even than you are in tracking the documents, easy catalogue, super assistance, cardboard folders to hold your clobber, lockers right on the spot which actually return your quarter. The least bureaucratic, the most user-friendly. 'We don't have enough money to be bureaucratic.'

I rescued Nora from Special Collections. Gradually, a real woman began to emerge from the pieces scattered over the Joyce trail from Trieste to Palo Alton. Nora's letters to her sister-in-law Eileen and the letters from her mother at Cornell. At Southern Illinois the notes from Claud Sykes to Herbert Gorman saying, ' I believe that Mr. Weiss was in love with Mrs. Joyce.' Needless to say, that did not make Gorman's biography of Joyce, nor Ellmann's. And at Texas — in a memoir of Lucia Joyce — 'Mr. Weiss was in love with my mother.' Also at SUI the questionnaire that Gorman sent round to James Joyce. Joyce's own hand: 'Nothing special happened on June 16, 1904.' Joyce covering his own traces.

Personal Interviews

It was useful to learn that in Galway people still gossip about Nora as a fast piece of goods who made herself an easy mark picking up a man on the street like that. And there were the neighbours in Bowling Green. Always I had to be on guard against what Hugh Kenner has called 'the Irish fact'. I sought out, on many people's urging, the butcher across the road. Peter Feeney. I had to track him down in the local hospital, where he was recovering from a heart attack. But that did not stop him from sitting up and telling me graphically how upset his neighbour, Nora's aunt (?), Mrs. Annie Barnacle, had been at the news of James and Nora's marriage in London in 1931. When they came to Galway, he said, she tore a strip off the two of them. You could hear her voice from one end of Bowling Green Close to the other. A wonderful story — except that Nora had not visited Galway after 1922 and James Joyce not since 1912.

But when Mr. Feeney told me that Mrs. Barnacle was a very tall woman who used to sit on a hard-back chair outside her house, wearing a long black cardigan and taking snuff — I chose to believe him.

And Arthur Power's notes. As I say in the introduction to my book, what Power wrote was: 'After leaving the theatre, the Joyces often call in at the Café Francis before going home.' The editor changed it to: 'After leaving the theatre Joyce often calls in at the Cafe France before going home,' which deftly obscured the fact that Joyce went nowhere without Nora and that she was an experienced theatre-goer, and suggested rather a shrew of a wife waiting at home.

Another truism is that all the memoirs have been published. I would advise anyone using published memoirs for a biography to try to find the original drafts. People censor themselves furiously in the long process between notes and publication. Sylvia Beach progressively lost her nerve at each stage of *Shakespeare and Company*. In Princeton, you can find what she really thought — far darker, bitterer, more appropriate to a real woman who was near-paralyzed by migraine headaches than the brisk cheery Girl Scout leader of the final version.

In her notes at Princeton I found the missing piece in what to me was the most revealing discovery I made in my book: that the break with Sylvia Beach was part of the deal, the intricate closely linked chain of events between Joyce's own surprising marriage in 1931 and his son's a year earlier. It was a chain that began with Giorgio Joyce wanting to marry the New York divorcee, Helen Kastor Fleischman, and ended with Random House fighting the court case that resulted in *Ulysses* being legally published in the United States — and Joyce being presented with the grandchild he longed for.

An unforeseen consequence of Joyce and Nora's wedding — which Helen insisted on before she would have a child — was that the Joyce marriage hit the papers, revealed their long cohabitation and their children's illegitimacy, and helped drive Lucia Joyce over the edge into insanity.

'I did it for the best but I only succeeded in breaking up my home and bringing trouble after trouble.'

Why Biography?

So then why do we read biography? Just as I began my book I attended a debate of the Folio Society in London in 1986. The assembled literati were there to discuss a declaration of George Eliot's that 'Biography is generally a disease of English literature.'

The proposition was resoundingly defeated. Biography is to England what psychoanalysis is to America. The English disease is terror of being discovered. Literary biography offers release to the eloquent race that fears the unconscious and psychoanalysis, confession and open government. It seems to be the one form in which secrets — or the inner truth — can get out.

The most eloquent of English biographers, Victoria Glendinning, won the day. Biographer of Edith Sitwell, Elizabeth Bowe, Rebecca West and, her greatest, Vita Sackville-West, she said the biographical impulse was the same that produces all literature. Far from prurient, 'it brings before the reader the great psychological constants and the irrational, emotional inner life of significant individuals.'

To the English, she said, biography is particularly important because they are a people both reticent and not deeply religious. 'We have to make sense of life on earth,' she said. 'Human beings just do not have enough information about the conditions of their existence.'

Amen. I would apply that even to an insignificant individual: Nora Barnacle Joyce. I disagree totally with Robert Adam, who said, 'Joyce's work is the only reason we are interested in her — or in either of this pair of scruffy Celts.'

I think we are all interested in how people play the cards they're dealt. Fate dealt Nora a most unusual hand. She played it well, with nothing but charm and self-assurance. Joyce knew that the ordinary was extraordinary. Nora, to be sure, looked at one way, was a woman who did nothing but shop. I hope I have done her justice.

Oh yes. And what did I learn about myself? Quite a bit, as it turned out. I found I had much to draw on — my father's family's Irish roots, a wonderful neighbour in my hometown, Susan Kiernan Balboni, who had come to America as an Irish servant — also a beauty and a wit — who wept every St. Patrick's Day that she was not back in Ireland. I drew on my husband's Welsh family — and know well how Nora faced the likes of Ernest Hemingway and Samuel Beckett: the Celts have absolutely no sense of awe. They are sure of themselves — oversure — not great forward planners.

I used what I know about women, about children, about families, about marriage. About the kind of girl who is fostered out — and who is pretty enough to make heads turn — in a small town. About marriage. I never made the mistake of wondering how Joyce could be interested in Nora when she wasn't interested in his work.

Nora is the prototype of all of us wives who do not take our husbands' work seriously. She is Everywoman. And no one knew that better than James Joyce.

Writing is not easy for any writer I know, certainly not for me. It is always a silent choice among alternatives, with the certain knowledge that once you have fixed certain choices in words, you have forever blocked out other possible paths. It is even more so when writing a 'life of'. There have been complaints about invading privacy. A real question when the person, or their children are alive, as Sylvia Plath's children certainly are. But after a writer and his nearest are long dead or very old, and they have become myths of their time, privacy—to my mind—cannot be invaded. Those who argue, but he was my husband, brother and so forth, I would remind that we are all many selves. We are the children of our parents, parents of our children. To our publishers we are producers of product. To the taxman we are small business people. All these selves co-exist and overlap. A biographer may focus on any one of them—the spouse, the artist, the disastrous friend. And whatever perspective is taken, biography is an act of selecting from the chaos of the material the details that fit the biographer's sense of the subject. It is here that biography parts company with reporting. There is no externally imposed event around which to organize the selected details. The biographer is as subjective as the portrait painter. As the examination I remember most clearly from my undergraduate years said: Auden's poem on the death of W.B. Yeats tells us much about Yeats, but more about Auden.

That is the fascination of Nora. Make no mistake. She was ordinary. She did nothing but shop. We would not be interested except for her relation to James Joyce—or these scruffy Celts, said Robert Adam in the *New York Review of Books*.

Maybe he wouldn't. But I would. I would also like to write the life story of my grandmother, an Italian immigrant, who ran away unmarried with her lover when she was 16 and did not marry until ten years later when they wanted to make a return visit to Italy. I would happily write the life story of my childhood neighbour in Bridgewater, Mass., Susan Kiernam Balboni, an Irish beauty, who married an Italian mechanic after serving as maid to the only rich family in our town. She had five children, said her rosary, told earthy stories about her married life I cannot repeat here, and wept real tears every St. Patrick's Day. But I doubt whether Houghton Mifflin or Hamish Hamilton would have backed me.

So Nora then, for two reasons. Because she was Joyce's muse, and because she was untouched.

The interesting life of a woman who, with nothing but courage and charm, could make her life a cosmopolitan life — and never lose her sense of self — and inspire the greatest female literary creation in English literature since Chaucer invented the Wife of Bath.

Looked at one way, she did nothing but shop. I am grateful to all the other biographers who saw her that way and left her for me. She was a wonderful, fabulous character to write about.

Bio As It Auto Be

From the Letters of George Bernard Shaw

S.F. Gallagher

'The truth is I have a horror of biographers': words taken, my dear siblings — I'm no sexist — from the umpteenth epistle of Saint Bernard Shaw to the infidel Frank Harris. For the noble art of auto-biography Shaw had even harsher words. During his early career of book-reviewer, he suggested that an autobiography is 'usually be-gun with interest by reader and writer alike, and seldom finished by either' (*S:A*, I, vii). Later, in various contexts, he describes the au-tobiographer as 'the dog returning to its vomit'; asserts that '[a]ll autobiographies are lies . . . not unconscious, unintentional lies . . . deliberate lies' (*S:A*, I, i); and declares, 'All autobiographies prove . . . that no man has an accurate knowledge of his own life, and that when an autobiography does not agree with a biography, the biography is probably right and the autobiography wrong' (*CL*, 3, 51).

From the Preface to his first novel *Immaturity* (1879, but pub-lished 1930) to his *Sixteen Self-Sketches* (1949, the year before he died), Shaw wrote autobiographical fragments — primarily, he claim-ed, to correct the errors of his biographers — but he modestly re-fused to attempt a formal autobiography: 'Were I to tell the truth about myself I must needs seem vainglorious: were I to tell less than the truth I should do myself an injustice and deceive my read-ers' (*S:A*, II, vii). However, Shaw's form of collaboration with his biographers, or would-be biographers, might justly be described as the imposition of autobiography upon biography; hence the ti-tle I've given this paper. None of Shaw's biographers escaped his sometimes cantankerous but usually good-natured interventions. He corrected their errors, insulted their intelligence, and sometimes suppressed what he thought irrelevant, damaging to his contempo-raries still living, or simply improper. Reprimanding Frank Harris for his 'obsession with the sexual cuckoo', Shaw tells him: 'I have always been impatient of the continual attempt to make the read-ing of books a substitute for sexual experience. Such books are not records of experience: they are mostly the delusion of impo-tence described for the consolation of inexperience' (*P & P*, 90). In

this instance, Shaw had been provoked by Harris's prurient curiosity about what Shaw himself repeatedly describes as the 'innocent'
ménage à trois of his father, his mother and her instructor in voice
(that's *voice*, not *vice!*) Vandaleur Lee, at Torca cottage during his
boyhood. Several of Shaw's biographers had already, or have since,
probed this matter; indeed, it has become a pernicious obsession
of Michael Holroyd's current biography: a work that, like *Playboy*,
I tend to consult mainly for its illustrations. But I digress; or do I?

Since it would be impossible, in the time to allotted me, to deal
with Shaw's letters to his several biographers, I must focus on just
one selection: those to Shaw's first, and indeed only authorized,
biographer, Archibald Henderson; and, even then, only on their
early correspondence (1904–12)—from Henderson's first, tentative
approaches to Shaw and the playwright's ambivalent acceptance
of them; through the painful gestation and birth of Henderson's
first biography; to the post-publication *contretemps*, triggered by
Shaw's published comments on the work, and its amiable resolution.

Archibald Henderson, destined to write, over fifty years (1904–
56), eight books on Shaw—including three major biographies—
was, initially, hardly the most obvious candidate for this monumental undertaking. A twenty-five-year-old instructor in Mathematics
at the University of North Carolina, he had been absorbed by his
research on 'the Twenty-seven Lines on the Cubic Surface', until he
was dragged by a friend to an amateur performance in Chicago of
Shaw's *You Never Can Tell*, protesting the 'pretty frothy title' of
the play by an author he had never heard of. Years later, he would
recall the interdisciplinary rapture he experienced:

> I sat through that performance . . . feeling as if I were being sub-
> jected to some sort of mental electrification; and, although this
> anticipated the researches of Millikan, Compton and Kohlhörster,
> I had the sensation, in fancy, of being immersed in a shower bath
> of cosmic rays . . . I emerged from the theatre a changed man. I
> had discovered a genius. (*MC*, xiv–xv)

Within a year, Henderson's metamorphosis had progressed far
enough for him to send Shaw his earnest but inchoate proposal for
'a small book, biographical and interpretative' (*MC*, xvi). Shaw,
having added Henderson's name to his card-list of 'Disciples', responded within the month (June, 1904). His letter supplied some of
the information requested, discouraged the disciple from producing
'a panegyric by an untutored idealist' (*MC*, xvi–xvii), and implicitly
commended one of Henderson's assumptions: 'It is quite true that
the best authority on Shaw is Shaw. My activities have lain in so

many watertight compartments that nobody yet has given anything but a sectional and inaccurate account of me except when they have tried to piece me out of my own confessions' (*CL*, 2, 427). This encouraged Henderson to issue 'a long list of inquiries', to indicate at least that he had studied Shaw's career and 'knew what pieces were missing to fill out the puzzle' (*MC*, xxvii). It was December before Shaw could find time to reply, by postcard, apologizing for the delay and telling Henderson not to bother about some sources he had mentioned: 'I can tell you all that is necessary . . . ' (*CL*, 2, 471–72). The following month, another postcard was sent: 'I had hoped to send you a letter by this post; but it is not yet finished; I have only arrived at the 41st(!) page so when it comes it will keep you busy for some time. If this business is to come off, *we* may as well do it thoroughly' (*MC*, xix; emphasis added). The postcard concludes, 'Have you a spare photograph of yourself? I should very much like to see you. Failing that, your picture would be a help'. Henderson, who had in fact asked Shaw for *his* photo, was unnerved by this counter-request. Eventually, and with much misgiving, he sent Shaw the best photo he could find — one that his wife had pronounced the 'least forbidding' of an 'unspeakable' set — and was immeasurably relieved when Shaw replied, 'Thanks for your own portrait. You seem to be the man for the job' (*MC*, xx).

The lengthy letter alluded to in Shaw's second postcard was begun January 3, 1905, and completed January 17; it ran to fifty-four holograph pages. It addresses ten of the numbered questions posed by Henderson. Some of the answers are brief, referring Henderson to appropriate sources of information; others provide details of Shaw's evolution as an orator, of his Fabian experiences, of his family, and of his early days as 'a genteel sort of office boy' in Dublin. In explaining that when he was fifteen there was no money for a university education, Shaw parenthetically comments: '. . . which, by the way, I despised, half ignorantly, half penetratingly, because it seemed to me to turn out men who all thought alike, and were snobs' (an interesting anticipation, don't you think, of Yeats's sentiments in 'The Scholars': 'All think what other people think'?) This epic epistle concludes with an invitation to Henderson 'to devise fresh questions', that is, if he seriously intends 'to go ahead with this job':

> When you began it, I knew quite well that you had no idea of what you were attempting — that a complete life of me in my public capacity would be a history of all the 'movements' of the last quarter of the XIX century in London, with very little about me personally in it. . . . I do not think what you propose is important as my biography; but a thorough biography of any man who is up

to his chin in the life of his own time as I have been is worth writing as a historical document; and therefore if you still care to face it I am willing to give you what help I can. Indeed you can force my hand to some extent; for any story that you start will pursue me to all eternity; and if there is to be a biography it is worth my while to make it as accurate as possible. (*CL*, 2, 506)

A month later (10 February 1905), Shaw is advising Henderson to go slowly with 'the book' until it has grown on his hands to its full size, and accusing him of not taking himself seriously enough as a university professor: Henderson must avoid anything resembling a mere 'theatrical biography', which would be immediately dismissed as 'a mere puff', and 'keep on the lines of Boswell's Johnson, Lockhart's Scott, not to mention Plutarch':

> . . . I cannot impress this too strongly on you—a merely theatrical biography of me would be a most unworthy waste of your time, and an unspeakable annoyance to me. My plays speak for themselves. . . . I want you to do something that will be useful to yourself and to the world; and that is, to make me a mere peg on which to hang a study of the last quarter of the XIX century. . . . If you shew me as a ghastly little celebrity posing in a vacuum, you will make both of us ridiculous. Unless you can shew me in the context of my time, as a member of an interesting crowd, you will fail to produce the only thing that makes biography tolerable. (CL, 2, 510–11)

And if Henderson should discover that he has something much bigger on hand than a biography of Shaw, and discard Shaw altogether, so much the better.

Not long afterwards, Henderson receives from Shaw another 'weighty counsel of perfection, by which any biographer might profit' (*MC*, xxii). Shaw asks Henderson if he is going to write 'a natural history', like a true Shavian, or 'a romance', like an incorrigible anti-Shavian. He suggests that Henderson might begin with a vivid romantic picture of 'the miraculous Shaw, the wonderful personality, the brilliant, the witty, the paradoxical, the accomplished' critic of a thousand arts and master of half a dozen: 'Having got this off your afflated chest, then get to business' (*CL*, 2, 515). For Shaw, getting to business means emphasizing the common humanity of the *real* Shaw. Then Henderson must attempt to explain 'how this prosaic reality produces this romantic effect, and does actually get a certain quality into his work, creative and critical, which distinguishes it from the work of men with much more remarkable qualifications'. In this way, Henderson will lay down the lines of a 'scientific biography' without drily ignoring the glamour: 'Of course you will have to snuff out what you call my "astounding personality" and smash your idol; but you cannot possibly do yourself a greater service. Until you know me from behind the scenes, you may be my dupe, but not my biographer'. The letter concludes:

> Be as accurate as you can; but as to being just, who are you that you should be just? That is mere American childishness. Write boldly accordingly to your bent; say what you WANT to say and not what you think you ought to say or what is right or just or any such arid nonsense. You are not God Almighty; and nobody will expect justice from you, or any other superhuman attribute. This affected, manufactured, artificial conscience of morality and justice is of no use for the making of works of art: for that you must have the real conscience that gives a man courage to fulfil his will by saying what he likes. Accuracy only means discovering the relation of your will to facts instead of cooking the facts to save trouble. (*CL*, 2, 516)

Shaw's letters for the remainder of 1905 address themselves to more of Henderson's consecutively numbered questions: they cover such topics as Shaw's championing of Wagner in England; his art criticism; the putative influence on Shaw of Nietzsche, Strindberg, William Morris and Marx; and Shaw's reaction against Darwinian materialism (See *CL*, 2, 536–58, *passim*). In a postscript to one of these letters Shaw hopes that the sheets 'are not too difficult to read' and explains that he has had to spoil his handwriting 'in order to make a carbon duplicate to keep in case of miscarriage' (*CL*, 2, 558).

By mid-1906, Henderson had sent Shaw the manuscript of a portion of the biography, the receipt of which Shaw acknowledges by postcard:

> I received the MS just as I was starting for Paris to sit to Rodin. So I sent it to the typists to be copied, and have since kept the two copies in different houses to reduce risk of loss by fire etc. I shall presently send you back the original; but I shall work on the typed copy & correct it. It is a remarkable work; but there is no use in being in a hurry about it, as it will improve in value every day. I have a bibliography, genealogy, & deuce knows what not for it. And you must come over and see me some time or other: the vision is still wildly romantic. (*CL*, 2, 628)

A couple of months later, August 1906, in response to Henderson's prodding, Shaw writes: 'I am taking what is called a holiday by the sea: that is, I am getting my work concentrated on me with an intensity impossible in London. I am not at all insensible to the importance to you of getting the biography afloat; and I am not indifferent to it on my own account either, as its publication will save me a great deal of trouble and misrepresentation. But this is a terrible year for me' (*CL*, 2, 639–40). It was, indeed, even for Shaw, an unusually demanding period. To avoid the lapse of their European copyright, he was trying to arrange performances on the continent of all seven of his *Plays: Pleasant and Unpleasant*; *John Bull's Other Island* and *Major Barbara* had to be provided with Prefaces and seen through the press; he had promised his wife, Charlotte, a preface to her English edition of three French plays; he was embroiled in a newspaper controversy about German Social-Democracy; and he had just begun another play, *The Doctor's Dilemma*. 'What I hope to do', he told Henderson, 'is to wait until you send me the rest of your MS, when I will get it copied as before, and then turn myself to it as if it were a book of my own'. He had obviously been through what he had already received, since he chides Henderson, again, for 'signs here and there in your manuscript, that you still regard me as a fantastic figure in a Pantheon rather than as a human being', offers some suggestions for its eventual publication and translation into German, and placates his impatient biographer with the prospect of academic eminence:

> The book should be an important professional one — a *debut* for you into first class literature; . . . you have put your back into it; and you must come in on the top grade, every inch a university professor. You see, if you make yourself an ornament to the University of N.C. you will be able to make them let you spend six months of every year in some civilized place, and finally become wholly independent of teaching differentials to passmen, which ought not to be the final doom of a mathematician. . . . Be patient: there is an end to everything, even to my biography. (*CL*, 2, 640–41)

Shaw also invites Henderson to visit him, 'as it is not desirable that the only American now living who has not called on me should be my biographer' (*CL*, 2, 640).

In late March 1907, Shaw attempts to console Henderson for further delay, on the grounds that much has yet to be done to ensure 'more completeness and more authority' for the book: 'In fact I should not hurry the book at all if it were not that I am anxious to get you well out into the limelight as the only genuine American authority on Shaw'. He upbraids Henderson for not yet having visited him — 'we are still personally strangers' — but cautions him: 'Remember: you must not come in July August or September. All the other Americans come then, and are disgusted to find nobody but themselves in London. Can't you get a research scholarship, and travel for a year or so on that? (*CL*, 2, 675). Henderson did visit London that year, arriving June 17. Shaw met him at St. Pancras railway station and was introduced by Henderson to one of his fellow passengers, Samuel L. Clemens.

During Henderson's visit, Shaw confirmed, orally, that Henderson's book would be the 'authorized' biography of Shaw. Henderson, indeed, had earlier suggested that its title be 'George Bernard Shaw: Biography and Autobiography', and Shaw's own typescript bore that title. Even if the suggestion was hardly intended as ironical acknowledgment of Shaw's constant intervention in, and rewriting of, the book, the epithet 'author-ized' seems singularly apt. Henderson says that 'no document' of their agreement 'was then or later drawn up and signed', but he does give a text of what he calls Shaw's 'views regarding our relative positions'. This, though lengthy, I think you should hear whole:

> I never intended to write an autobiography because I do not think that, psychologically and practically, it is possible to 'tell all' — Cellini, Rousseau and Company to the contrary notwithstanding. I have written, at one time or another, enough biographical reminiscences to serve the purpose of anyone wishing to write about me. In your case, I hold myself in readiness to answer, as far as my knowledge goes, and with due consideration for the feelings of others, any question you may ask me. In designating you my authorized biographer, I am making this position unique. There shall be only one authorized biographer: yourself. Two authorized biographers would be unthinkable: they might not agree with each other. It's bad enough to have one. A man cannot have two father confessors. Imagine having to confess all your sins to both! I authorize you, in the only rational sense of the term: I will supply you with abundant information and materials, essential facts you can learn from no one else; undertake to see you make no errors of fact; and leave you entirely untrammelled regarding opinion and interpretation; and promise to revise your narrative both in manuscript and proof. Thus you become my authorized biographer — the Great Panjandrum; and there shall never be another. (*MC*, xxv)

Several years after Shaw's death, Henderson affirms that this 'gentleman's agreement' was 'faithfully kept'.

Henderson, however, was less than happy with 'Shaw's maddeningly dilatory tactics', and illustrated such by the following extract: 'Your mimeographed twelve chapters have not arrived. When they do, I shall begin to make excuses for delay in sending them back to you. But after all, you have only written the book twice over, and

I fully expect that what will finally get into print will be the sixth, if not the twelfth complete version, and that it will appear the week after my death' (*MC*, xxvi). In fending off Henderson's importunity, Shaw's tone is not always entirely jocular: 'Why are you in such a confounded hurry?' he writes in March 1910, 'You admit that it is only six years since you began the book? I told you it would take twenty-five. All the disappointment you have suffered has arisen from your rooted conviction that I always mean exactly the opposite of what I say. . . . You must remember that if you have to write the life, I have to live it; and whilst time persists in going sixty minutes to the hour, it is not physically possible to hurry me up' (*CL*, 2, 903-04). Almost a year later, February 1911, when he had belatedly browsed Henderson's revised typescript, Shaw wrote:

> . . . before I had turned over two pages at random I gave you up as hopelessly spoiled by mathematics. . . . When you were an innocent boy you believed that a miss is as bad as a mile; that the whole is greater than its part; and that accuracy and strict logic are the foundation of all sound intellectual and ethical superstructure. But the higher mathematics taught you that this is mere intellectual priggery; that a miss is as good as a Bull's eye if the target is only far enough off; and that the part is as great as the whole when the whole is infinite. They proved to you that you could get good working results by proceeding on impossible assumptions and inconceivable data. And when you took to literature, you naturally applied to it the methods of the infinitesimal and differential calculus. (*CL*, 3, 8–9)

When Henderson attempted to defend what he had written, by sending Shaw the notes he had taken of their conversation, Shaw replies, 'Your notes are all right, but you do not understand them.' He completes a detailed explication, and observes, 'My total failure to drive this into the solid ivory of your skull, has led you to write patent nonsense.' Then, having dealt with other blemishes in the publisher's proofs, he becomes curiously concessive:

> However, it does not matter. The providence which guides drunken men along the edges of precipices, and deposits them unhurt on soft places when they fall over, evidently loves you. I like the sample of the book: on the whole, it comes out right, and quite unlike the usual conventional biography. . . . When the book appears, I will send you an annotated copy for your guidance in correcting the second edition if it ever comes to that. God knows what blunders you will make; but you will always save the situation somehow; and your hits reach the bull's eye. (*CL*, 3, 19–21)

But this time Henderson will not be placated by faint praise; with a vehemence worthy of the master, the disciple replies:

> As to your criticisms, I think them worthy neither of you nor me. They are too petty to arouse any feeling in me except of wonder that a man of your critical intelligence could so waste his time and mine in making them. . . . It is not at all a case of my understanding, or misunderstanding of what you said. If you expressed yourself incoherently, so much the worse for you. It is the old, old story of your public character—that you are forced to spend one half of your time explaining the things you say in the other half. . . . The cosmic jest of a man jeering at his biographer may tempt your idiosyncrasy for the comic and the novel. But it is not the great line to take; it is not the line I have taken in writing your life; it is not 'cricket.' (*CL*, 3, 21–22)

Henderson wrote this from Berlin. Later that year (1911) he was in Paris when the biography *George Bernard Shaw: His Life and Works* appeared and a *Morning Post* reviewer, Charles Whibley, suggested that the term 'authorized' on the title-page signalled that Shaw, rather than Henderson, had written the book. Shaw promptly wrote the newspaper, saying it wasn't so, but conceding that the fault was his rather than Henderson's: 'He strove to make me read my own life in manuscript, and strove in vain: I had had enough of it whilst living it.' He disclaimed responsibility for some statements in the book which he said had escaped his eye while the manuscript was in his possession, and advised that readers should bear in mind Henderson's profession:

> Now the higher mathematics are based on the discovery, made simultaneously by Newton and Leibnitz, that by proceeding on inconceivable assumptions, provisional proclamations, and impossible hypotheses, you can arrive at trustworthy working results. Professor Henderson has used this method freely, and the general effect, on the whole, justified him, but I must earnestly protest against being held responsible for his data. (*CL*, 3, 35)

Henderson, tired of this Shavian line, was not amused. In what Dan H. Laurence describes as 'a long, polite but blistering rebuttal', he wrote the *Morning Post* that he had no reason to believe that any portion of the biography had escaped Shaw's scrutiny, and warned his readers that Shaw was

> a dialectician, which means that, if necessary, the same words can mean to him two different things, whereas I am a mathematician, which means that they can mean only one. . . . Quite conceivably he did not mean what he said (as quoted in the biography), or his

casual remarks may have acquired an unexpected significance in print. But he is a man of many words, and he is unaccustomed to being confronted with them. When he is, his invariable and quite natural response is to "repudiate" them. (*MC*, xxvii–xxix)

Though consoled somewhat by one of Shaw's statements in the *Morning Post*—'I think that, as a whole, the book is a most remarkable achievement, and is perhaps as near the facts as it is in the nature of such a book to be' (*MC*, xxix)—Henderson remained unmollified until the publication several months later of Shaw's letter to the American publishers of the autobiography, Stewart and Kidd. This letter began with the statement I quoted earlier—that when they disagree, 'the biography is probably right and the autobiography wrong'—and diplomatically emphasizes the friendship that had developed between Shaw and Henderson:

> Henderson, in an intercourse with me which has been very intimate, . . . has had to put into shape a mass of unceremonious and irresponsible autobiographies received by him *viva voce*, besides making a desperate attempt to recover a biography from a period of which he . . . has had no direct experience. The very friendliness of our relations has been an obstacle to him, for I have been less helpful to him than I would perhaps have been to one whom I should have had to treat with more ceremony. . . . Under these disadvantages, I think he has done extraordinarily well. There are mistakes, of course, but they do not matter. . . . The fact that its publication has left my friendly relations with the author quite unaltered—except in so far as they are enhanced by the service he has done me—speaks for itself, and leaves room for hope that any further edition may be still nearer the mark. . . . (*CL*, 3, 51–52)

The efficacy of this fence-mending may be inferred not only from Henderson's gratified quotation from it forty-five years later—in the Preface to his *George Bernard Shaw: Man of the Century* (1956), where he alludes to their brief estrangement as 'a rather annoying yet not unamusing contretemps'—but also from his immediate response: 'It is', he wrote Shaw early in 1912, 'a thoroughly frank and kind-hearted letter, nor is there a single statement in it to which the most meticulous person could possibly object. . . . [I]t is thoroughly characteristic of the genial, kindly man to whom I was so much drawn when I first met him in 1907' (*CL*, 3, 50).

The reconciliation endured and their collaboration continued. In 1932 Henderson published his two-volume *Bernard Shaw: Playboy and Prophet*, and when, in 1948—recently retired and now in his seventy-second year—he informed Shaw that he proposed to write his biography de novo for the third time, Shaw replied:

> I am now in my 93rd year and statistically and actuarily dead. I will answer any questionnaire from you as long as I am alive and not hopelessly dotty; but my memory is failing so damnably that even in this you must not count too much on my co-operation.
>
> I advise you most urgently to consult no documents. Go on your old reading and your knowledge of human nature, and you will be readable and interesting even it the result be a life of Henderson rather than of Shaw. Go on the documents, and if you live to go through them exhaustively your book will be a monument of unreadable dullness. This is the lesson of my own experience. What I invent turns out to be true. What I copy in paraphrases from 'authorities' is invariably wrong. (*MC*, xxxi–xxxii)

The aged Shaw's final injunction to his ageing disciple was: 'As there is no end to a job of this kind, set yourself a time limit for what it is worth, and when you have reached it STOP' (*MC*, xxxii). The Master has spoken: I must obey.

Works Cited

Henderson, Archibald. *George Bernard Shaw: Man of the Century*. New York: Appleton-Century Crofts, 1956. [*MC*]

Laurence, Dan H., ed. *Bernard Shaw: Collected Letters 1898–1910*. London: Reinhart, 1972. [*CL*, 2]

——, ed. *Bernard Shaw: Collected Letters 1911–1925*. London: Reinhart, 1985. [*CL*, 3]

——, ed. *Bernard Shaw: Collected Letters 1926–1950*. London: Reinhart, 1988. [*CL*, 4]

Weintraub, Stanley. *The Playwright and the Pirate: Bernard Shaw and Frank Harris: A Correspondence*. Gerrards Cross: Colin Smythe, 1982. [*P & P*]

——, ed. *Shaw: An Autobiography 1856–98*. New York: Weybright and Talley; Toronto: Clarke, Irwin, 1969. [*S:A*, I]

——, ed. *Shaw: An Autobiography 1898–1950*. New York: Weybright and Talley; Toronto: Clarke, Irwin, 1970. [*S:A*, II]

John Butler Yeats. *W.B. Yeats, 8 December 1897*.
The National Gallery of Ireland.

Memories into Images in Modern Irish Painting

James White

Many critics of Ireland will put forward the idea that memories have been our downfall. But the tradition of the seventeenth- and eighteenth-century hedge schools, where teaching was by word of mouth and by memory, has brought about a peculiar facility in verbal expression. As a result, the memorized stories become images and part of folk memory. During the past century, a number of Irish painters have woven this store of memories into the fabric of their pictures, and in the area of portraiture in particular they have attempted to portray the characteristics of the subject rather than its outer shell. John Butler Yeats (father of poet W.B. and the painter Jack B.) was perhaps the progenitor of this style, a little over a hundred years ago. More is known about the way John Butler Yeats's mind worked in relation to the problems and nature of art than is known about most painters because of his marvellously illuminating letters to his sons, which have been published. All his life he was engaged in an encounter with the personalities of those he chose to portray. He knew exactly what he wanted to do. It was to capture those moments of illumination that are revealed in a gesture or expression; to recognize those glimpses of human sympathy and understanding which are suggested by a smile or a grimace and to draw together the observations he made as he talked with those friends and companions who contributed to the world of Dublin in the last twenty years of the nineteenth century, a world which had such an influence on our history and the literary and artistic movements which became part of it.

For John Butler Yeats, the artist began to define his stance only after he had made the necessary observation of the details and facts surrounding his subject. It was then that he must bring his imaginative insight into play. 'Art only comes when there is abandon, and a world of dreaming and waiting and passionate meditation,' he wrote in one of his letters. He believed that the artist must search for feelings which are universal in their application.

John Butler Yeats. *John O'Leary.*
The National Gallery of Ireland.

> Love by itself is lust, that is, primitive animalism. And anger,
> what is it but homicide! Art lifts us out of the sphere of mere
> bestiality, art is a musician and touches every chord in the human
> harp — in other words, a single feeling becomes a mood and the
> artist is a man with a natural tendency to thus convert every single
> feeling into a mood — he is a moody man.[1]

All his life he wrote to his sons admonishing them to avoid worldly
success, to think nothing of courting those who are famous and in
the limelight. He wrote:

> I think it is a great matter for Ireland that she is a small island,
> and that she refuses to take any interest in the great affairs of the
> British Empire. She is like a child lost in a great fair, who being
> naughtily intrepid is not at all frightened, and on the contrary
> delighted to be lost. Thus we have escaped the collective mind,
> which for so many years has dulled the lustre of English life and
> tarnished the brightness of its poetry.[2]

When he returned from his sojourn in London, he became very
attracted by John O'Leary because of his independence of mind
and because he, O'Leary, had returned from Paris where he had
shared rooms with Whistler, the great American painter, and with
Swinburne, the poet. O'Leary had been involved with the Fenian
movement and had edited *The Irish People*, the official organ of
the I.R.B., and as a result he was sentenced to twenty years' penal
servitude in 1864. However, he was later released and returned
to Ireland in 1885, where he published his recollections of Fenians
and Fenianism. He kept a literary salon in his house in Terenure
in the Dublin suburbs, which included Douglas Hyde, AE, Stephen
Gwynn, John Butler Yeats and his two sons, amongst many others.
He aimed primarily to encourage the writing of prose and poetry
with a national content. This also fired John B. and his son Jack B.,
and successively their work represented the emerging spirit which
led to the rising and, in the case of Jack B., to a lifetime refusal
to accept any form of conservatism where Irish independence was
concerned.

In his portrayal of the characters of this period, John Butler
Yeats succeeded in showing the most diverse and individual figures
with dignity and calm, and his affection and admiration for their
qualities is apparent. His method was the impressionist manner of
the late nineteenth century, using combinations of light and colour
appropriate to the spiritual environment of his sitter as he inter-
preted it. The movements and flickers of the eye seem to be invoked
by this use of brush strokes of various tones, so that when we examine the picture we feel drawn to contact the personality.

Robert Ballagh. *Joseph Sheridan Le Fanu*, 1976.
The Arts Council of Ireland.

He passed on to his son Jack B. much of this feeling for finding pictorial equivalents of the elements of human weakness and dignity combined in the subjects which were to attract him. Early on in his career, he was commissioned to paint a series of characters in oil to illustrate *Irishmen All*, a book by George A. Birmingham (pseudonym of Canon J.O. Hannay) by the publishers Frederick A. Stokes Company of New York, in 1913. These demonstrate a series of quite different characteristics, associated with contemporary country life, but based on the painter's childhood memories in Sligo. Of them, Canon Hannay wrote to Jack on 15 September 1913, 'Considering that neither of us saw each other's work, the illustrations and the text fit together extraordinarily well.'[3] His father wrote from New York of their 'liveliness and their actuality — and a sort of poetic truthfulness — you satirize but with such a kind heart.'[4]

W.B.'s favourite painting by his brother Jack was called 'Memory Harbour,' and it showed the scene of their childhood at Rosses Point, somewhat compressed to bring many elements into focus, something we all tend to do when we allow our minds to recover past memories — we select those dear to our hearts and forget others. In two other works Jack Yeats uses that process again, relying more on racial memory as passed on to us by the storyteller and the historian. In 'A Race in Hy Brazil,' the scene is the mythical submerged island some hundreds of miles west of the coast of Ireland in the Atlantic. The prow of a vessel hung with rose garlands on the right recalls the 'Departure for Cythera' by Watteau, which caused Sam Beckett to comment, 'Yeats grows Watteauer and Watteauer.'[5] The other, 'In Memory of Boucicault and Bianconi,' records the Italian emigrant Bianconi whose carriages plied around Ireland and carried the travelling players to towns where theatre had never before been seen until Bianconi brought in the Boucicault dramatist and his players to perform. This picture shows the characters of 'The Shaughraun' taking a moment before the Glencar waterfall at Sligo in a pause on their journey.

As in most other countries, present-day contemporary Irish painters employ the varied methods and styles which emerged from Cubism and Expressionism. However, there are those amongst them who rely on the power of memory to transcend time and recollection and give immediacy to the dim and distant past. One excellent example of this is Robert Ballagh's portrait of Joseph Sheridan Le Fanu, commissioned in 1976 by the Irish Arts Council, which happens to occupy the house in Merrion Square where Le Fanu once lived. Le Fanu was one of the first of the psychological novelists, and his horror stories are built up to play on the reader's

. . . J.M. Synge.

. . . James Joyce.

. . . Thomas Kinsella.

. . . John Montague.

Louis Le Brocquy. *Drawing Towards An Image of . . .*

mind. During his last illness, he had a recurring dream about a house falling down. So Ballagh painted Le Fanu standing inside a Georgian window such as can be found in Merrion Square, but he allowed the window panes to be slightly ajar so that through the crack could be perceived the falling house of the writer's dream and of his interior world. The assembly of facts relating to the character of his sitter are his more usual method, as one can see in the images of Hugh Leonard and Myles Na Gopaleen.

Ballagh's concentration on the actual countenances of his sitters is in contrast with Louis LeBrocquy, who has emerged as the portraitist who seeks to encourage the inner compulsion and intellectual force of his subjects to shine through their facial exteriors. When one considers the comparative unimportance of the facial appearance of Shakespeare, as compared to the wonders he created and his contribution to the growth of literature, one can understand LeBrocquy's enterprise in attempting to surmount it with what he calls 'Studies towards an Image of Shakespeare,' an exhibition which was shown in many of the world's capitals in 1982. In some sixty-five paintings, each quite different, he explored many facets of the great playwright's personality as he saw it. He has used this method for his portrait researches over the past twenty-five years and has created a gallery of writers, poets and painters which perhaps reflects his own tastes. They do not replace the exact photographic image, which each of us will be curious to examine in these cases which are of particular interest to us. Nevertheless, they make a remarkable contribution towards our understanding of the varied aspects of humanity and insight within the creative artist. LeBrocquy has himself written:

> To attempt today a portrait, a simple static image of a great artist such as Joyce appears to me to be futile as well as impertinent. Long conditioned by photography, the cinema and psychology, we now perceive the human individual as facetted, kinetic. And so I have tried to draw from the depths of paper or canvas these changing and even contradictory traces of the man.[6]

He adds later:

> But to a Dublin man, peering at Joyce, a particular nostalgia is added to the universal epiphany, and this perhaps enables me to grope for something of my own experience within the everchanging landscape of his face, within the various and contradictory photographs of his head which surround me.[7]

LeBrocquy has, of course, also illustrated a number of literary works, including the translation of 'The Tain' by Thomas Kinsella, an epic poem, the first written record (dating from the twelfth century), and a fine volume of Joyce's *Dubliners*. Altogether, his output makes a superb contribution to the visual records of the literary figures of our time and, strangely enough, is produced on the European continent, not too many miles away from the places where James Joyce's works were created.

Notes

1 J.B. Yeats, *Letters to His Son W.B. Yeats and Others 1869–1922*. ed. J. Hone (London: Faber and Faber, 1944), p. 185.

2 *Ibid.*, p. 239.

3 Hilary Pyle, *Jack B. Yeats: A Biography* (London: Routledge and Kegan Paul, 1970), p. 115.

4 *Ibid.*, p. 115.

5 Thomas McGreevy, *Jack B. Yeats* (Dublin: Victor Waddington Publications, 1945), pp. 14–15.

6 *Studies towards an Image of James Joyce*, Catalogue of the exhibition in Geneva, 1977 (also Zurich, London, Belfast, Dublin, New York, Montreal, and Toronto, 1978), p. 33.

7 *Ibid.*, p. 37.

II

APPROACHES
TO AUTOBIOGRAPHY

On The Nature
of Autobiography

James Olney

As I am sure everyone attending this conference is aware, autobiography has become the darling of literary critics and literary
theorists in the past fifteen or twenty years. The New Critics of
thirty, forty and fifty years ago, for reasons I need not go into here,
had nothing to say of autobiography: it was simply not a literary form that drew their critical scrutiny, and as critical scrutiny
or close reading was their principal strength there is little or nothing to be said of thought about autobiography as a literary mode
during the heyday of New Criticism. Nor were literary historians of that time much interested in the subject. How different
things are now, however, in our post-modernist, post-structuralist
age: Every self-respecting literary theorist of our day (and I use
the term 'self-respecting' in full ironic awareness of the fact that
many post-modernist thinkers would deny any reality, other than
perhaps a linguistic one, to that strange entity 'the self'), whether
that theorist be feminist or Marxist or African-Americanist or de-
constructionist or any combination of these and other possibilities,
has something to say about autobiography; and thus autobiography, in spite of — or more likely because of — its literary impurity
and instability, has in recent years become, paradoxically, something like the paradigmatic literary form. Given this state of affairs,
what I would like to do is to meditate a bit on the nature of autobiography, not as I have done in the past, in a kind of old-fashioned
mix of philosophy, psychology, and literary criticism, but rather in
the terms, which are somewhat but not altogether alien to me, of
post-structuralist and post-modernist thinkers. Beyond this — beyond investigating what such thinkers as Jacques Derrida, Paul de
Man, Maurice Blanchot, Emile Benveniste, Philippe Lejeune, and,
especially, Roland Barthes have said about and done with autobiography — I want to suggest how strikingly and perhaps astonishingly
certain Anglo-Irish figures — notably George Moore, W.B. Yeats,
Oliver St. John Gogarty, Sean O'Casey, and Samuel Beckett — in
their writing of autobiography, anticipated, in some instances by

many years, what theoreticians (most of them French) have latterly been saying on the subject.

In 1975 Roland Barthes published a little book, *Roland Barthes par Roland Barthes*, that quickly became a kind of classic of post-modernist autobiography (if the term is not hopelessly paradoxical, for the very idea of a classic is inimical to post-modernist thinking) and at the same time was taken by many of its readers to represent the most advanced thinking about the subject of autobiography and the possibilities for it in our time. In other words, the book was thought to be at one and the same time, in the best modernist/post-modernist way, both an autobiography and, in Shirley Neuman's phrase, a meta-autobiography. One of the most striking formulations in the book at a meta-autobiographical level—so striking that Barthes pulls it out of the text and puts it to redoubled use as a scribbled epigraph standing before the text—is this sentence: 'All this should be taken as if spoken by a character in a novel' (French ed., inside front cover and p. 123; American ed., pp. 1 and 119). Given that the U.S. publisher at least described the book as an autobiography, this Barthesian formulation caused a little flutter of delight in the hearts of genre critics, who saw him as calling for a new kind of autobiography and a reordering of genres appropriate to a post-modern age. Indeed, Philippe Lejeune, writing within a year or two of the appearance of Barthes's book said, 'Barthes's self-portrait will probably remain a classic example for studying these problems [i.e., problems of person and subjectivity in autobiography]' (40). It's a pity that those who were so excited by Barthes's bold gesture, as they understood it to be, were not familiar with the note in the front of Gogarty's *As I Was Going Down Sackville Street*, published in 1937, i.e., thirty-eight years before *Roland Barthes par Roland Barthes*: 'The names in this book are real,' Gogarty declares in his note, 'the characters fictitious' (vi). Gogarty's note would seem almost designed to add insult to injury, as it not only anticipates Barthes' epigraph by quite a number of years—by a good generation as those things are measured—but it is also a good deal wittier as well. It only makes matters worse for Barthes' originality when Gogarty adopts as a subtitle—if that is the proper word: the phrase comes before rather than after the main title—the words 'a phantasy in fact.' And Gogarty, like Barthes, carries the generic anomaly a step further by including in his text photographs bearing the real names—W.B. Yeats, Talbot Clifton, Augustus John, and so on—of these fictitious characters, these characters in a novel.

Gogarty was not the only Anglo-Irish autobiographer, however, who was years ahead of Roland Barthes in asserting the essential fictionality of autobiography. Writing in 1975, Barthes declares, 'The substance of this book, ultimately, is . . . totally fictive. The intrusion, into the discourse of the essay, of a third person who nonetheless refers to no fictive creature, marks the necessity of re-modelling the genres: let the essay avow itself *almost* a novel: a novel without proper names' (French ed., p. 124; American ed., p. 120). It was this kind of thing that caused reviewers to en-thuse about Barthes' book. 'Barthes is an extraordinary virtuoso,' Frank Kermode wrote. 'Highly original, extremely fertile and in-ventive, he really does represent . . . a new kind of writing.' And Susan Sontag, in a similar vein, refers to Barthes's 'brilliance,' his 'naked originality and generosity of speculation' (both quotations from the book flap). To Barthes' cautious injunction, '[L]et the es-say avow itself *almost* ["almost" in italics] a novel: a novel without proper names,' the Anglo-Irish autobiographer seems to respond, but years in advance of Barthes, 'Let the essay avow itself *alto-gether* a novel: a novel *with* proper names.' Here, for example, is George Moore in a prefatory note to the first volume of the U.S. edi-tion of *Hail and Farewell*, chiding reviewers of the English edition of the volume for referring to it as simply a book of reminiscences (though the note is signed 'The Publisher,' it sounds to me very like George Moore writing in the third person): 'Mr. Moore has in no way attempted to include herein his reminiscences. In fact he has rather tried to produce something quite different. His intentions were to take a certain amount of material and to model it just as he would do in a novel. The people in his book are not personalities; they are types of human characters. . . . Yeats [for instance] is not only the man who has gone to America to explain the Abbey The-ater to the American people; he is the typical literary fop' (*Ave*, v). And I might point out that if these are in fact Moore's words rather than the publisher's, as I assume is the case, then Moore, writing in 1911, has once again stolen a march on Barthes and anticipated him by sixty-four years in adopting the voice of, in Barthes's words, 'a third person who nonetheless refers to no fictive creature.' Like-wise, Sean O'Casey maintains a third-person, non-fictive persona for six volumes of autobiography that read at least as much like a novel as *Hail and Farewell* and much more like one than *Roland Barthes by Roland Barthes*.

When O'Casey or Barthes — or Henry Adams, for that matter — produces third-person autobiography it is grounded in the sure sense that the 'I,' the first-person, personal pronoun, is the most fictive element in autobiography and that the subject, or subjectivity, is always an effect of language. 'It is in and through language that man constitutes himself as a *subject*,' Emile Benveniste writes in

Problems in General Linguistics, and he goes on: '[W]e hold that
. . . "subjectivity," whether it is placed in phenomenology or in
psychology, as one may wish, is only the emergence in the being of
a fundamental property of language' (224). Barthes was, of course,
well aware of what Benveniste had to say about subjectivity and
the subject, and he is only paraphrasing the linguist, though in this
instance without attribution, when, in *Roland Barthes by Roland
Barthes*, he writes, referring to himself in the fictive/non-fictive
third-person, 'He wants to side with any writing whose principle is
that *the subject is merely an effect of language*' (French ed., p. 82;
American ed., p. 79). This is to say that the 'I' of autobiography is
the ultimate shifter, without lexical definition and without reference
except in the instance of discourse that contains it. As Benveniste
puts it: 'What then is the reality to which *I* . . . refers? It is solely a
"reality of discourse," and this is a very strange thing. *I* cannot be
defined except in terms of "locution," not in terms of objects as a
nominal sign is. *I* signifies "the person who is uttering the present
instance of the discourse containing *I*" ' (218). Carry this but a step
further, which Barthes gladly does, and autobiography, like any literary performance, becomes sheer language play, an endless play
of signifiers that never reach so far as to join to a signified. 'Writing begins with style,' Barthes declares in the heading to one of his
fragments. He himself began writing, he says, by imitating the style
of writers who were very much concerned with substance and signifieds: 'Yet this style serves to praise a new value, *writing*, which is
excess, overflow of style toward other regions of language and subject. . . . But above all, style is somehow the beginning of writing:
however timidly, by committing itself to great risks of recuperation,
it sketches the reign of the signifier' (French ed., p. 80; American
ed., p. 76). Simply put, for Barthes style took over from substance
and the signifier from the signified, but in what writer are style and
the signifier more everything than in Moore, in Gogarty, in Samuel
Beckett?

Here is Roland Barthes contrasting the pleasure of writing—
pure pleasure or *jouissance* as he terms it elsewhere (the verb he
uses in the present passage is *jouir*[1])—with the necessity, enforced
by a mercantile society, to produce an *oeuvre*, a body of saleable
work:

> The contradiction is one between writing and the work. . . . I
> delight ['Je jouis'] continuously, endlessly, in writing as in a per-
> petual production, in an unconditional dispersion, in an energy
> of seduction which no legal defense of the subject I fling upon
> the page can any longer halt. But in our mercantile society, one
> must end up with a work, an '*oeuvre*': one must construct, i.e.,

> *complete*, a piece of merchandise. While I write, the writing is
> thereby at every moment flattened out, banalized, made guilty by
> the work to which it must eventually contribute. How to write,
> given all the snares set by the collective image of the work? —
> Why, *blindly*. At every moment of the effort, lost, bewildered,
> and driven, I can only repeat to myself the words which end
> Sartre's *No Exit*: Let's go on. (French ed., p. 140; American ed.,
> p. 136)

I expect many of you will already know what I want to quote by way
of Franco-Anglo-Irish anticipatory response to this passage. Rather
than the end of Sartre's *No Exit* Barthes might well have referred
to the end of Beckett's *The Unnamable*. Now, I am not claiming
that *The Unnamable* is an autobiography in the traditional sense,
but rather that it is precisely what Barthes calls his text: 'Le livre du
Moi,' the book of the self (French ed., p. 123; American ed., p. 119).
And this is exactly what current theory is saying of autobiography:
that it is a categorical error to imagine that an autobiography is
the biography of the author. In spite of the common etymology
of the words, biography and autobiography, as writing practices,
are just about as different as they could well be. Hence, in writing
about Beckett, Porter Abbott suggests, and wisely I believe, that
we should speak of autography — self writing — rather than of autobiography, leaving out, as it were, the historical life, the *bios*. We
might adduce Yeats at this point, writing, à la Barthes, on the frag-
mentary notes — the *writing* rather than the *oeuvre* — that compose
one of his volumes of autobiography, *Estrangement*: 'To keep these
notes natural and useful to me I must keep one note from leading
on to another, that I may not surrender myself to literature. Every
note must come as a casual thought, then it will be my life. Neither Christ nor Buddha nor Socrates wrote a book, for to do that is
to exchange life for a logical process' (461). Were the effect not so
entirely bathetic, we might add to that list of grand forerunners the
name of Roland Barthes — 'neither Christ nor Buddha nor Socrates
nor Roland Barthes wrote a book' — but of course Barthes was not
a forerunner at all but very much an after-runner. Here, at any
rate, to get back to my original anticipatory response to Barthes,
is Beckett on the nature of writing, on signifiers and signifieds, on
words and on going on:

> I don't know, that's all words, never wake, all words, there's
> nothing else, you must go on, that's all I know, they're going to
> stop, I know that well, I can feel it, they're going to abandon me,
> it will be the silence, for a moment, a good few moments, or it will
> be mine, the lasting one, that didn't last, that still lasts, it will

be I, you must go on, I can't go on, you must go on, I'll go on, you must say words, as long as there are any, until they find me, until they say me, strange pain, strange sin, you must go on, perhaps it's done already, perhaps they have said me already, perhaps they have carried me to the threshold of my story, before the door that opens on my story, that would surprise me, if it opens, it will be I, it will be the silence, where I am, I don't know, I'll never know, in the silence you don't know, you must go on, I can't go on, I'll go on. (414)

And of course Beckett did go on, seeking the words that will 'find me,' that will 'say me'; fearing conclusion and closure, he continually renewed the autobiographical or autographical act. Just so, Yeats wrote multiple *Autobiographies* (not, as the U.S. title has it, *The Autobiography of W.B. Yeats*); Moore wrote volume after volume and revised endlessly *Confessions of a Young Man*, with a new preface each time to show that he was still alive, still going on; and Gogarty produced a string of volumes, each of which could bear the subtitle of *It Isn't This Time of Year at All*: 'an unpremeditated autobiography.' Likewise, the modernist autobiographer par excellence of French letters, Michel Leiris, went on through volume after volume pursuing 'the written formulation of that immense monologue that in a sense is given me, since all its substance is drawn from that which I have lived, but which in another sense obliges me to a constant effort of invention, since I must introduce an order in that indefinitely renewed substance, churn up its elements, adjust them, refine them until I manage in some measure to grasp their significance' (cited by Brée 198). Leiris, like Beckett, committed himself to the incessant writing of the book of the self, continually beginning and rebeginning, never ending, circling around and drawn to a centre which is silence, fearing and fascinated by what Barthes terms 'the last word': 'Liking to find, to write *beginnings*, he [i.e., Barthes] tends to multiply this pleasure: that is why he writes fragments: so many fragments, so many beginnings, so many pleasures (but he doesn't like the ends: the risk of the rhetorical clausule is too great: the fear of not being able to resist the *last word*)' (French ed., p. 98; American ed., p. 94). Maurice Blanchot points to this same fearful seductiveness at the heart of the act of autobiography that draws the autobiographer on to an end that is as fascinating as it is frightful and is also known all the while to be impossible. 'The proof that a book of autobiography respects the centre of truth around which it is composed may be that such a centre draws it toward silence. Whoever sees his book through to the end has not come to the end of himself. If he had, his speech would have been "cut short." Yet, the drama—as well as the power—in all "true" confessions is that one begins to speak only with a view to that moment when one will not be able to continue. There is something to be said which one cannot say . . . ' (151–52; quoted in Derrida 72–73).

This post-modernist will to non-conclusion and non-closure, this open-ended continuity and circularity in the writing of the book of the self can be seen not only in individual autobiographers of the Anglo-Irish tradition but in the whole conglomerate of them taken together. One might say, in a term that is very current in the literature of and on autobiography, that these volumes of Anglo-Irish autobiography are intensely *intertextual*, and they are so in several different senses: first, any single autobiography from among them exhibits intertextuality with autobiographies by other writers in the group; second, an autobiography may display intertextuality with other works by this same writer; and third, an autobiography may be said to show intertextuality with the text of the writer's life. To take the last of these first: No one, I think, would argue with the notion that what we might call the text of a life, imagining a life to display something of the design or pattern that we expect in a literary work, is related in the most intimate, determinative way to the autobiographical text produced, as we say, out of that life. But the very notion of intertextuality implies not a one-way relationship but a reciprocal and inter-determinative relationship between texts. Thus we can expect and in fact do find that the text of an autobiography turns back to shape the text of the life as much as the life shapes the autobiographical text. Paul de Man, in a piece published in 1979, put it this way:

> But are we so certain that autobiography depends on reference, as a photograph depends on its subject or a (realistic) picture on its model? We assume that life produces the autobiography as an act produces its consequences, but can we not suggest, with equal justice, that the autobiographical project may itself produce and determine the life and that whatever the writer does is in fact governed by the technical demands of self-portraiture and thus determined, in all its aspects, by the resources of his medium? (920)

In order, however, not to give Paul de Man all the credit for this idea about the reciprocal circularity that the act of autobiography involves, I should remark that Montaigne, almost four centuries before de Man, said much the same thing about the activity he was engaged in, and an autobiographer like Yeats, four decades and more before de Man, exhibits the same awareness of his portrait forming him as much as he forms his portrait. 'In modelling this figure upon myself,' Montaigne writes, 'I have had to fashion and compose myself so often to bring myself out, that the model itself has to some extent grown firm and taken shape. Painting myself for others, I have painted my inward self with colours clearer than my original ones. I have no more made my book than my book has made me—a book consubstantial with its author, concerned with my own self, an integral part of my life' (504). Yeats could have said as much of his vast effort in autobiography—indeed did say as much several times, as in the following little poem—

> The friends that have it I do wrong
> When ever I remake a song,
> Should know what issue is at stake:
> It is myself that I remake

—or in this passage from *Estrangement*: 'I often wonder if my talent will ever recover from the heterogeneous labour of these last few years. . . . Has it left me any lyrical faculty? Whatever happens I must go on that there may be a man behind the lines already written; I cast the die long ago and must be true to the cast' (484–85). Georges Gusdorf, who has written as brilliantly on autobiography as anyone I know, put the matter very nicely in a letter to me a few years ago: 'Some German poet,' he wrote, 'said of Mallarmé [and we might say it of Yeats] that he lived his life with a view to the bust that would be made of him after his death. In this sense,' Gusdorf continued, 'autobiography comes before the life, not after it.'

Yeats is also an excellent example of the autobiographer who maintains a continual, reciprocal intertextuality not only between his life and his autobiography but also between his autobiography and his other writings. It seems natural, his head being so filled with verse as he tells us it was, that Yeats should quote lines from Henley or Pater or whichever other poet; but the truth is that Yeats quotes from himself at least as often as from all other poets put together, and his *Autobiographies* are thus like *Roland Barthes by Roland Barthes*, a taking up into themselves of all the earlier writings, the work of his work or the writing of his writings, as it were.

As to the final kind of intertextuality, that between one autobiography and another or others, I should think that there is no group of autobiographies as intertextual in this sense as those by Moore, Yeats, Gogarty, O'Casey, and their cohorts. Yeats began writing his *Autobiographies* in response to Moore's mockery in *Hail and Farewell* and though he went far beyond that initial impetus to the autobiographical act we can nevertheless hear a continual call and response between Moore's volumes and Yeats's—and not in one direction alone but constantly back and forth, back and forth. Yeats's life becomes the great reference for the lives of the other autobiographers, and his voice, as heard by each of the others, echoes through their books in an endless string of anecdotes. 'I have met them at close of day,' as Yeats himself puts it,

> I have passed with a nod of the head
> Or polite meaningless words,
> Or have lingered awhile and said
> Polite meaningless words,
> And thought before I had done
> Of a mocking tale or a gibe
> To please a companion
> Around the fire at the club

— and also, we might add, to please the readers of his *Autobiographies*, for it was in the ears of his readers that Yeats, being in this no different from Moore, Gogarty, and O'Casey, thought to confirm and validate his literary quarrels and literary allegiances. The first chapter of Jacques Derrida's *The Ear of the Other* bears the title 'Otobiography,' replacing 'auto — of the self' with 'oto — pertaining to the ear,' and in that chapter he maintains that the autobiographer signs himself/herself only in the ear of the other. In a sense this is no more than a characteristically punning Derridean version of reader response criticism according to which an author's being is ratified and the meaning of a text is not only completed but half-created by its reader. But *The Ear of the Other* has a peculiarly apt sense when one thinks of our Anglo-Irish autobiographers acting in relation to their audience as the ghost of Hamlet's father tells Hamlet Claudius acted toward him:

> Upon my secure hour thy uncle stole,
> With juice of cursed hebona in a vial,
> And in the porches of my ears did pour
> The leperous distilment

Just so our autobiographers do steal upon their audience, especially their Dublin audience, and in the porches of their ears do pour the leperous distilment of their wondrous and often very funny anecdotes, signing themselves in the ears of others and completing the intertextual circle of their written lives in the now textualized lives of their readers.

Now at this point, as I approach my conclusion, I can imagine an objection to the procedure I have been following — an objection that might be raised by any in the audience who are very familiar with the texts I have been referring to and who would find it at least peculiar, and perhaps illegitimate, for me to quote more often from prefaces and forewords and notes to autobiographies than from the autobiographies proper. This, however, brings me to my final post-structuralist point and once more it is one that can most effectively be made by reference on the one hand to latter-day French criticism and on the other hand to Anglo-Irish autobiography of some fifty, sixty, and seventy-five years ago. Consider what the nature of a preface is: It is first of all one of those varieties of writing practice, existing, *like autobiography itself,* at the margins of literature, which theorists of a Derridean and generally post-structuralist bent are particularly drawn to because what goes on in a preface or a note or an absent-minded aside or in the writing on a postcard — or in an autobiography — often destabilizes and thus provides a point of deconstructive entry into the more staid, longer, formal text to which it has reference and a marginal relationship. Gerard Genette has a full book about such writing, a book that he calls *Seuils,* i.e., thresholds — limina, as it were — the Latin word that gives us English 'liminal,' the term so popular in the most advanced criticism of a few years back (and perhaps still today, I'm not sure).

More interesting, perhaps, is to consider what happens in and to a text when it is preceded by a preface (or, which is textually, logically the same thing, when it is followed by a postface). There is the oddity that a preface, though it appears before a work and is normally the first thing we read, is almost always composed *after* the work has been finished. This gives it a special relationship to the rest of the work — a part of the entire work, certainly, yet separate from it also, a reflection on the entire work and a kind of subsuming of the whole thing at the same time. And this is what autobiography is as well, for an autobiography is a part of a life, a view taken from within a life, that yet claims to account for or give the story of the entire life. Autobiography thus bears a synecdochic relationship to the whole life — a part taken for the whole — and this is the same relationship that obtains between a preface and the text it precedes. Moreover, when a preface appears before a novel or an autobiography or a narrative of any kind then we take it that the author is saying, in effect, 'I am now speaking to you straight, not telling stories, not concocting fictions that may indeed carry a higher truth but are nevertheless fictions all the same.' In the prefaces that Henry James wrote for the New York edition of his novels, do we not take it that he is speaking to us directly as Henry James to his readers, saying, '*The Portrait of a Lady* is a fiction but this that I say now is nonfiction, is "the truth"'? But consider the case when the preface is to an autobiography: Is not the mere act of attaching a preface to an autobiography hyper-modernist? Is it not like prefacing an autobiography with an autobiography? Do we not assume that every autobiographer who really is an autobiographer is speaking to us straight all the time, not telling stories, not concocting fictions? Why should he or she have to come out from behind the author-autobiographer role to speak to us as a living man or woman, no longer compromised as to truth by the assumption that he/she is 'speaking in character'? Does not the mere existence of a preface suggest that the rest of the work is something for which an apologia is necessary? A preface thus casts the rest of the work into the fictional mode; and when, as George Moore did in the case of *Confessions of a Young Man*, an author provides us with a series of prefaces written over a period of many years, each succeeding preface throws the earlier preface(s) into the mode of fiction along with the rest of the work, saying, 'I was not quite straight with you last time, I was still fictionalizing, but this time I am giving you the plain truth.' And if you believe that, you have just been gulled once again by the post-modernist, post-structuralist strategies of pre-modernist Anglo-Irish autobiography.

Note

1. I cannot quite refrain from quoting here a passage from Gogarty's *As I Was Going Down Sackville Street*, a passage in which he describes how he persuaded a very reluctant Yeats to accompany him to the opening of the Spring Show where they were to sit in the box of the then Governor-General, Tim Healy. Gogarty's first persuasive ploy is to say that they will wear silk top hats and thus show their contempt for the opinion of the democratic middle class that would deplore this proper aristocratic dress because it shows respect for the representative of the hated English monarch. The idea of wearing a tall hat to show his disdain for the masses appeals to Yeats but it is Gogarty's description of the dairy maids churning butter and singing butter-making songs that carries the day. 'Only one song of butter-making remains,' Gogarty claims, and yet there was a long and great tradition of butter-making songs. 'Have you got it?' Yeats asks.

> 'Father Claude overheard it in Tipperary, when a buxom maid was churning as she thought all alone. She had buttocks like a pair of beautiful melons. Her sleeves were rolled up. She had churned from early morning. Her neck was pink with exercise. Her bosom laboured, but she could not desist, for the milk was at the turn. Up and down, desperately she drove the long handle: up and down, up and down and up and up for a greater drive. The resistance grew against the plunger. Her hips and bosom seemed to increase in size while her waist grew thin. In front of her ears the sweat broke into drops of dew. She prayed in the crisis to

old forgotten gods of the homestead! Twenty strokes for ten!
Gasping, she sang:

> ' "Come, butter!
> Come, butter!
> Come, butter,
> Come!
> Every lump
> As big as
> My bum!" '

'You are missing not one, but many milk-maids' songs. And
when we are dead, they too shall be; and the folk-lore lost forever
of the dairy and the byre.'
'How does it go?' — He beat time to recall the rhythm.

> ' "Every lump As big as My bum!" '

'Yes. You are correct. But my proposal is that we get these
chants at first-hand and be not depending on Father Claude for
such songs.'
'When does Tim expect us?'
'Any time from four to six.'
' "Come, butter, come, butter," ' he murmured. 'I think I will
join you. Let me know when you can send a car. And there's my
hat to be brushed.' (pp. 113–14)

That there is something approaching Barthesian jouissance in the writing of this passage, as well as in the activity described in it, can hardly
be denied.

Works Cited

Abbott, H. Porter. 'Autobiography, Autography, Fiction: Groundwork for
a Taxonomy of Textual Categories.' *New Literary History* 19 (1987–
88): 597–615.

———. 'Narratricide: Samuel Beckett as Autographer.' *Romance Studies*
11 (1987): 35–46.

Barthes, Roland. *Roland Barthes by Roland Barthes*, trans. Richard
Howard. New York: Farrar, Straus and Giroux, 1977.

———. *Roland Barthes par Roland Barthes*. Paris: Éditions du Seuil, 1975.

Beckett, Samuel. *Molloy, Malone Dies, The Unnamable*. New York:
Grove Press, 1965.

Benveniste, Emile. *Problems in General Linguistics*, trans. Mary Elizabeth Meek. Miami Linguistics Series No. 8. Coral Gables, Florida:
University of Miami Press, 1971.

Blanchot, Maurice. *L'Amitié*. Paris: Gallimard, 1971.

Brée, Germaine. 'Michel Leiris: Mazemaker.' *Autobiography: Essays Theoretical and Critical*, ed. James Olney. Princeton: Princeton University Press, 1980.

de Man, Paul. 'Autobiography as De-facement.' *Modern Language Notes* 94 (1979): 919–30.

Derrida, Jacques. *The Ear of the Other: Otobiography, Transference, Translation*, trans. Peggy Kamuf, ed. Christie McDonald. Lincoln, Nebraska: University of Nebraska Press, 1985.

Genette, Gerard. *Seuils*. Paris: Éditions du Seuil, 1986.

Gogarty, Oliver St. John. *As I Was Going Down Sackville Street: A Phantasy in Fact*. New York: Reynal and Hitchcock, 1937.

——. *It Isn't This Time of Year at All: An Unpremediated Autobiography*. Garden City, NY: Doubleday, 1954.

Lejeune, Philippe. 'Autobiography in the Third Person.' *New Literary History* 9 (1977): 27–50.

Montaigne, Michel de. *The Complete Essays of Montaigne*, trans. Donald M. Frame. Stanford: Stanford University Press, 1958.

Moore, George. *Ave*. Vol. 1 of *Hail and Farewell*. New York: D. Appleton and Company, 1911.

——. *Confessions of a Young Man*, ed. Susan Dick. Montreal: McGill-Queen's University Press, 1972.

Yeats, William Butler. *Autobiographies*. Dublin: Gill and Macmillan, 1955.

Writing
an Autobiography

Garret FitzGerald

I am, I suppose, a compulsive writer. In a way this is not surprising for my father, having started life as a minor poet in pre-First World War London, subsequently interwove with his main career as a revolutionary, a member of the first Irish Government and later an Opposition front-bench politician, the roles of editor of a daily underground newspaper, playwright, free-lance journalist, and Visiting Professor and author of a book on scholastic philosophy. My mother, for her part, having graduated from university had been for brief periods secretary to George Bernard Shaw and George Moore, and an indefatigable correspondent with a host of relatives.

The result was that our house was infested with typewriters; by the time I could read and write there were six of them, which were handed down to my three elder brothers and myself in order of seniority. Urged by my next brother, who at the age of thirteen had gained access to the National Library to copy out the grammar and syntax of the Quichua language of the Incas of Peru, to type out a fair copy of his notes, at seven I started to hammer away with two fingers and a thumb on a model of the late 1880s. Later I graduated to a 1902 portable.

With this dubious skill I turned my hand early in life to writing articles for newspapers; by the time I was 22 I had already published on such varied subjects as domestic air services in Ireland, dietetics, the Aztecs, Azerbaijan and a Russian adventurer in post-Great War Latvia. Subsequently, throughout my twenties and early thirties, in parallel with my careers as an Aer Lingus manager and an economic consultant/university lecturer, I wrote extensively on air transport economics and international affairs and became for a period Irish correspondent of papers in provincial Britain, New Zealand, Australia, Hong Kong, India, Kenya, South Africa and Canada.

From this I graduated to representing the *Financial Times*, the *Economist* and the BBC in Ireland and to writing a weekly economic column for the *Irish Times*. During this period I also wrote books on Irish State enterprises, on economic planning in Ireland, on the Third World, and on the Northern Ireland problem. So by the time

I became a member of the Irish government, eight years after my entry into politics in 1965, I must have "clocked up" at least 4 million words.

Clearly, with such a prolific record behind me, I was more likely than most politicians to write an autobiography when I finally retired from the leadership of my party after a term as Foreign Minister and two terms as *Taoiseach*, or Prime Minister. (In fact, since the foundation of the Irish State seventy years ago, only two politicians have published works of autobiography, neither of which drew on documentary material in relation to their period in government.)

Another important factor that induced me to contemplate an autobiography, however, was my interest in history (my principal degree subject at university), and the fact that from childhood onwards I had always been particularly conscious of the importance of the written record. I kept carefully many letters and papers from childhood and I can vividly recall how upset I was as a teenager on hearing a wartime report that during their withdrawal from Southern Italy the Germans had destroyed the records of the Kingdom of Naples.

While I was never sufficiently disciplined to keep a regular diary, except for one summer as a university student, I did make a contemporary record of certain events that seemed at the time to be of particular interest — for example, what I did on the day the War in Europe ended, my involvement with events during a student revolution in 1969 when I was a university lecturer, and an initiative of mine with regard to Northern Ireland after internment was introduced in 1971.

Moreover, although I was the youngest of four brothers, it was I who took charge of my father's papers after my mother's death — he had pre-deceased her by more than a decade — and edited an autobiographical account he had left of the three years immediately prior to the Rising of 1916. I later lodged these papers in the Archive of my *alma mater*, University College, Dublin of the National University of Ireland, which contains the papers of many other leaders of the Irish independence movement.

During my own period in office I was careful to retain the papers from my Private Office, as my father had done a half century earlier, and at each change of government from 1977 to 1987 I placed these boxes of papers in the same Archive. (In Ireland, unlike Britain, the practice has been for ministers, should they wish to do so, to retain their own papers; moreover there is no Irish tradition of former ministers being required to submit autobiographical works to the Cabinet Secretary for approval.)

I should, perhaps, add that, as Minister for Foreign Affairs I had been careful, in line with the tradition of officials in that Department, to make full notes of meetings with colleagues of other countries that were not attended by civil servants — notes which in most cases I subsequently dictated, giving a dialogue account of these discussions which in some cases were as long as 25,000 words. These reports of meetings with ministers of other countries were naturally very useful to me when I came to write this book.

Finally, as evidence of my concern for the preservation of records, I ought to say that as *Taoiseach* I personally initiated and shepherded through Parliament a Bill to establish an Irish National Archive.

Having this kind of personal history it is scarcely surprising that some months after leaving office in March 1987 I should have embarked on an autobiography. I was in fact approached by four publishers and eventually accepted a proposal by Lord Stockton, of Macmillan, to sign a contract with them for a book to be published jointly by them and their Irish associate company, Gill and Macmillan. The actual publication would be undertaken by Gill and Macmillan under the personal supervision of its Managing Director, Michael Gill. Ambitiously I proposed to complete the work within eighteen months; the publishers suggested cautiously that I might need two years. In fact the task took three-and-a-half years.

Two factors were largely responsible for this longer time-frame. First, I had not allowed for the time it would take — a full year — for my papers to be organized and indexed in a preliminary way by a qualified archivist, Mary Mackey, whom I employed for this purpose so that they would be readily accessible to me during the process of writing about the political part of my career. The extent of the archivist's task may be judged from the fact that when it had been completed there was an index covering 460 boxes of papers. Some of these contain routine material such as copies of all letters written by me as *Taoiseach* or replies to invitations I had received when in office, but they also include records of bilateral meetings with ministers from other governments and of EC Council meetings, accounts of discussions or conversations with politicians in Northern Ireland or Britain, and dialogue accounts of the official-level and ministerial-level negotiations for the 1985 Anglo-Irish Agreement.

A second factor slowing the process of writing this book was the fact that during these years my other activities as a back-bench member of the Dail, lecturer, free-lance journalist and company director absorbed much more of my time than I had expected. In fact it was only during the summer months of the years 1988–90, and in the January of these years, when the Dail did not meet, that I could devote the necessary long and continuous periods of time required for the more demanding parts of the task such as that of describing my work as a member of the Council of Ministers of the European Community or the negotiation of the Anglo-Irish Agreement of 1985. Other less taxing sections of the work could, however, be fitted in during such free periods as I had in the remainder of the year. Slow though the process was, with over forty years of writing behind me, I was never tempted to seek any assistance with the writing of the book.

And another retarding factor was that, as I shall explain in a moment, the book turned out to be very much longer than I had anticipated.

I had envisaged writing the book on a word-processor—which I started to learn to use after leaving office in March 1987. However, at that stage I found it difficult to come to terms with this new technology, and I also found that in undertaking a task that involved drawing on a mass of documents—sometimes I would be drawing on half-a-dozen or more files simultaneously—the presence of a machine in the middle of all this material would have been an impossible complication.

Another factor influencing my choice of method of writing was a recognition that, for the purpose of an autobiography, I should have to adopt a style somewhat different from that which I normally employed. I usually tend to write in long periods, deploying subordinate clauses to qualify within a single sentence the point I want to make. This may be partly because my training as a lawyer—although I never practised law—taught me the importance of such a technique as a means of avoiding ambiguity. But this style is clearly unsuited to an autobiographical work, which above all else must be readable, and I think this stylistic consideration may also have led me to revert to a method I had not employed since my earliest journalistic period in the latter part of the 1940s, viz., handwriting.

I was enabled to employ this somewhat primitive method by virtue of my good fortune in having a secretary, Clare Fallon, with the necessary skill and patience to decipher the resultant scrawl. When she had accomplished this I subsequently reworked her word-processed draft, typically three or four times, but for some chapters as many as five or six times, in order to produce a "final" draft for editing purposes.

I had always been conscious of the need for a good editor, having learnt over many years of journalism how beneficial the editing process can be—more especially in my own case as I have a tendency to over-write. And as work on the book proceeded it soon became clear indeed that because of the wealth of material available to me, and despite the physical discipline of handwriting that I had imposed on myself, the text was likely to turn out far too long. The publishers had originally envisaged a book not much longer than 200,000 words — and my first draft turned out to be well over twice this length, at 475,000 words.

As it gradually became clear in the process of writing that the text was going to be much longer than the publishers, or even I myself, had anticipated, I was moved in desperation to suggest that it be published in two volumes, but this was understandably greeted with a notable lack of enthusiasm by the publishers! It could instead be considerably shortened during the editing process, they suggested.

When, after about one third of the text had been completed, it came to the choice of an editor, Gill and Macmillan suggested that their hitherto anonymous reader, whose — happily favourable! — reports on the earlier part of the text I had by this time seen, should undertake this task. When I cordially agreed with this proposal I found that the reader was in fact someone I had known for very many years: Louis McRedmond, former editor of the Irish Independent newspaper and himself an author of some distinction.

His task was to reduce the manuscript by about one third. He proposed somewhat greater cuts, totalling about 175,000 words, which left room for me to restore some passages that I felt merited retention, either with a view to improve continuity or because of what I believed to be their intrinsic interest. As a result the net cuts made came to about 145,000 words, leaving a final text of 330,000 words, or 650 printed pages.

After writing a prologue to explain my family background, which was relevant to the development of my later career, and the first chapter on my childhood and youth, I was faced with the problem of organizing the subsequent material into coherent shape. For even in respect of the period preceding my entry into government, my multiplicity of careers was difficult to handle, especially after 1965 when I added the role of front-bench opposition politician to the three careers I had been pursuing for some years previously — viz., economic journalist, managing director of an economic and marketing consultancy company jointly owned with the Economist Intelligence Unit of London, and university lecturer carrying the load of lectures and seminars required of full-time members of staff.

Adherence to a strict chronological structure for this period would have made the text impossibly confusing for the reader; consequently there had to be a good deal of movement backwards and forwards between these four areas of activity, although, of course, for the period after my entry into politics, the main emphasis shifted to the newest, political, side of my career.

The same problem arose, however, in far more acute form when I moved on to my period in government. Because both of the government posts I held, with two breaks while in opposition, between 1973 and 1987 — viz., Foreign and Prime Minister — entailed considerable involvement in both European Community and other foreign affairs and in the Northern Ireland problem as well as in domestic affairs, it was clearly necessary to structure the book in such a way as to deal separately with each of these three aspects of my responsibilities.

For my period as Minister for Foreign Affairs from 1973 to 1977 I organized the material into three chapters on European Community and other foreign affairs, three chapters on Northern Ireland, and one on domestic political affairs in which, despite my other responsibilities, I played an active role during this period, especially in relation to social and economic policy; in the latter area I had a major part in shaping social welfare reforms and was the prime mover in the introduction of a wealth tax — which, however, did not survive the change of government in 1977.

I devoted a single chapter to my period as leader of my party — to which position I was elected unanimously, immediately after we lost office in 1977 — and consequently as leader of the opposition. Within this chapter, however, I structured the material once again so as to avoid confusion, interweaving sections devoted to foreign and Northern Ireland affairs with the main theme of domestic politics. And similarly with the following chapter, which covered my brief nine-month period as *Taoiseach* from June 1981 to March 1982, and my equally brief return to opposition from then until December of that year.

For my final four-and-a-quarter year period as *Taoiseach*, from December 1982 to March 1987, I reverted to the approach I had employed for my time as Foreign Minister, segregating the sections on Northern Ireland and European Community/Foreign Affairs into separate chapters. For this period, however, I decided I must both start and end with chapters on domestic affairs, "sandwiching" the external material between these two domestic sections.

Moreover, because of the complexity of the process leading up to the Anglo-Irish Agreement of 1985 on Northern Ireland and the desirability of helping readers to see the wood as well as the trees, I decided to introduce the three chapters devoted to this subject with a two-page summary of the main stages of this operation, which I entitled "Intermezzo".

I was reasonably happy with the outcome of this process of structuring my material to accomodate readers, although I was conscious of the fact that by segregating these three main themes of Irish political activity in this way something of the often hectic pressures encountered in real life while coping simultaneously with three such different streams of activity was inevitably lost.

More generally, in presenting the material I was conscious throughout of the need to ensure as much objectivity as is possible in an autobiographical work which of its very nature tends to be subjective and inevitably self-centred.

This pre-occupation led me to handle my documentary material with particular care. For example, in relation to Community or Foreign Affairs and to Northern Ireland, I was particularly careful when summarizing discussions with political leaders of other states — to preserve the balance of such exchanges as far as possible, and also to stick closely to the actual language of the reports upon which I was drawing. I applied this principle to all discussions of this kind that were relevant to the story, no matter whether I was, or was not, personally involved in them.

It is true that these reports were of their nature one-sided — being the Irish record of bilateral or, in the case of the EC, multilateral discussions. But as I mentioned earlier in relation to the Department of Foreign Affairs the tradition of the Irish civil service has been to make very full records of such meetings, often in dialogue form — records much fuller than those kept by civil servants from many other countries, including Britain. And since I completed the book the accuracy of the accounts I have given of some of these discussions has been privately accorded some external confirmation from other parties concerned. I believe, therefore, that when the relevant papers become available from the Irish and other Archives from the year 2003 onwards, the accuracy of the parts of my autobiography dealing with external matters will be demonstrated.

I should perhaps add that, in writing the book, I had the advantage of being able to draw on some records that may not be accessible even after thirty years, e.g., accounts of private ministerial or civil service discussions with people in Northern Ireland who might still be alive thirty years later and might be embarrassed, or perhaps put in danger, by disclosure of such contacts even three decades later. Drawing on records of such conversations I was, of course, careful to give no clue to the identity of the individuals concerned, describing several of these contacts merely as "Unionist politicians".

I should make it clear, however, that while the records of discussions on which I have relied are invaluable sources in relation to external matters, no similar material exists in the domestic area. Moreover, the archival material at my disposal does not include most Cabinet memoranda, which record the attitudes of ministers or in some cases of their departments to particular proposals.

In the absence of a contemporary record of many domestic matters with which I was concerned — and here a diary would have been especially valuable — I was forced to fall back on unaided memory, and I am extremely conscious of the fallibility of memory unsupported by any contemporary record. Many things that happen are subsequently altogether forgotten by participants, and, even in relation to matters of which one does have recall, the danger of getting events in the wrong order, or out of context, is considerable.

The domestic section of my autobiography is therefore less full and less satisfactory than those sections dealing with external events. Moreover, even in cases where I did have a clear recall of domestic events that was supported by contemporary material, I was still aware that it would be undesirable to disclose Cabinet discussions or mention positions taken up on particular issues by individual ministers, most of whom are considerably younger than myself and remain, and will continue for many years ahead to be, active politicians. Apart from possible damage to their individual political reputations, which I was concerned to avoid, such disclosure, for which there has been no precedent in Ireland, could have a negative effect on the operation of future governments. Members of such governments could be discouraged from speaking frankly to one another if they thought the positions they were taking up on various issues might be publicized a few years later in a colleague's autobiography.

Nevertheless, I did not seek to hide significant disagreements with or between colleagues where these were of historical importance, including some acute disagreements with my former party leader, Liam Cosgrave, in the years before the formation of the 1973–77 government in which he appointed me to be Foreign Minister.

I was also constrained, of course, by considerations of libel; Irish libel laws are stringent and the penalties for offending against them can be harsh. However, although the lawyer's report on the edited manuscript ran to over 100 pages, only a limited number of changes had to be made in the light of the advice it contained.

Subject to these necessary limitations I felt free to give a full account of the various events in which I was involved. Thus I saw no reason to withhold any details of the complex negotiations, at both ministerial and civil service level, that preceded the Anglo-Irish Agreement of 1985. True, if Margaret Thatcher had remained

Prime Minister I might, perhaps, in a final revision, have felt it necessary to make some adjustments to my full account of discussions with her, although I doubt that these would have been significant. However, her resignation at the end of 1990 relieved me of the need to consider such modifications.

The interaction of political and family life is an important element in a politician's career, and in the course of the book I endeavoured to trace the way, in which in my case, the two impacted on each other. Because of the fortunate proximity of my home, university, consultancy office in the period preceding my entry into government, parliament, and government offices — all within my compact constituency — my family life was much less disrupted by politics than is the case with the vast majority of politicians. Nevertheless, even in such favourable circumstances, public office has implications for family life, and the quality of family life can impact on a political career. I was remarkably fortunate in the support my wife was able to give me — despite her lack of enthusiasm for politics as a career — and I endeavoured to record in the book some of the debt I owe to her, including helpful suggestions she made in relation to some important appointments.

Nevertheless, although I thought that I was perhaps saying too much about the family side of my life — and one colleague who read a couple of chapters before publication suggested that I should cut out some of this material — after publication several reviewers commented on a certain reserve on my part which, so they had said, made the book more of a political memoir than a full autobiography. But that is for others rather than for myself to judge.

What is certainly true, however, is that in attempting to achieve as much objectivity as humanly possible I have been deliberately sparing with comments and reflections which seem to me to belong to another and quite different book that I hope to write in due course.

Finally, in the process of dealing with various mistakes I am widely perceived to have made I have tried to avoid the ever-present temptation to self-justification, confining myself to *explaining* why I did what I did in terms of my feelings and beliefs at the time.

Deformation of History
in Blasket Autobiographies

Cathal G. Ó Háinle

The Blasket Islands, where three remarkable autobiographies in Irish were written in the 1920s and 30s, are a group of tiny islands and rocks off the coast of the Dingle Peninsula in County Kerry. The largest of these islands, the Great Blasket, is a mere three miles by one in extent, and lies more than two miles from the mainland. From the early eighteenth century the population of the island was on a rising graph, reaching a total of about 153 persons just before the Great Famine of 1846–48. The decimation of the population by death in, and emigration from, the poorer areas of Ireland, caused by the failure of the potato crop in those years, was experienced by the people of the Blaskets also: in the period 1851–61 there were only ninety-five persons living there. But again the number began to increase, and by the 1890s had reached about 130 persons, comprising twenty families, and in the early years of the first World War had risen to 176 persons and twenty-one families.[1] However, by the late 1920s a pattern of emigration to the larger centres of population in Ireland and to the United States of America began to emerge, and the population of the Blaskets continued to fall until 1954, when the last remaining family moved to the mainland.

Of the total area of the large island a significant part was rough hill land and commonage, and the remainder was divided into tiny holdings which sustained a bare subsistence economy. Potatoes were grown, one or two cows and their calves and some hens, pigs and sheep were reared on each holding. Fish was an important element of diet and also a vitally significant source of income. Wreck, flotsam and jetsam were also an extremely valuable source of materials and of income. This fragile structure of existence was easily disturbed. Persistent bad weather and/or disease could lead to the failure of the potato crop and famine conditions resulted. This happened not only in the middle of the nineteenth century, but also in 1879–80 and in 1890–91. When the price of fish collapsed due to marketing factors, or when stocks became depleted or shoals no longer appeared in the area, hardship resulted from the consequent loss of income required to purchase other commodities. In such circumstances, only the intervention of charitable individuals or societies staved off disaster on a number of occasions.

The fact that from such a hostile environment, from a people living in so remote a place and in such harsh circumstances, three significant works of literature should emerge, requires some explanation. The people of the Blaskets, whose language was, of course, Irish, were the inheritors of a rich oral tradition of story, song and lore; but the transition from the oral to the written and from the traditional forms to that of full-length autobiography needed some dynamic. The education provided by the island school, which was opened in 1864, can hardly have been a significant factor, for its main aim was to provide the youth of the island with a competence in English, and the reading and writing of Irish were not taught at all. Tomás Ó Criomhthain (1854–1937), the author of the first of our autobiographies, acquired the ability to read Irish and to write it (in a highly individualistic, non-standard orthography, be it said) only after he had left school and through his own efforts. Even before he had done so, he was able to write, in some kind of English-based spelling, the verse of the island poet, Seán Ó Duinnshléibhe, at the latter's dictation. This fact is significant. Ó Duinnshléibhe had inherited the tradition of verse composition (and indeed the traditional view of the poet's role as recorder and satirist); he was also aware of the value of writing, as against memory, as a means of ensuring the survival of his compositions; but since he could not write, he had to depend on an amanuensis. When Ó Criomhthain himself came to compose, he was no longer dependent on memory since he could commit his compositions to writing.

Tomás was a highly intelligent man, was well-versed in the traditional lore, had a sophisticated command of the Irish language and could read and write Irish. Still, it is utterly unlikely that he would have undertaken the writing of his autobiography, had he not been almost driven to it. It was, however, his intelligence, his stock of lore and his linguistic sophistication which drew to him the people who provided the impetus towards committing his life story to writing. In 1907 the Norwegian linguist, Carl Marstrander, came to the Blaskets to learn Irish and spent several months being taught by Tomás Ó Criomhthain. Although, in spite of his best intentions, Marstrander never returned to the island, soon after his departure he wrote to Tomás asking him to set down on paper all the names of animals, birds, fish and plants that he knew and send them to him in Norway. Subsequently, Marstrander advised an Englishman, Robin Flower, to go to learn Irish from Tomás in 1910. Flower did so, and returned frequently to the island up to the time of Tomás's death in 1937. He in turn got Tomás to write brief accounts of aspects of life on the island and to set down traditional anecdotes. Thus when Brian Ó Ceallaigh, a young man from Killarney, came to the Blaskets to learn Irish in 1917, Ó Criomhthain was already accustomed to providing material in writing for those who came to learn from him. It was Ó Ceallaigh, however, who was ultimately responsible for the production of Ó Criomhthain's autobiography.

In the first instance Ó Ceallaigh prevailed on Tomás to write brief pieces on island life. He ultimately produced a great number of these, and a selection of them was published in book form in 1928 under the title *Allagar na hInise*. The second edition, published in 1977, contained an even larger selection.[2] In writing these pieces Tomás was, in many ways, serving his apprenticeship for the writing of his autobiography, and the title of this book, which I would translate as *Island Repartee*, highlights an important facet of this preparation, for many of these pieces consist of direct speech, often of great force and vigour. The ability to write passages of direct speech assumed great importance when he came to write his autobiography. Tomás was not yet willing to undertake this work, in spite of Ó Ceallaigh's promptings. But Ó Ceallaigh was determined to succeed. He now sent to Tomás the first two volumes of Maxim Gorki's autobiography in English translation, *My Childhood* and *In the World*. Tomás read them and was won over. At last he understood that his life story was worth telling. His son, Seán, with typical spice, reports what had happened: 'When Tomás saw that these gomerals had come out to tell their life-stories, he said: "Yerra, if they are gomerals, I'll make myself a gomeral too. I'll take a shot at it." '[3]

The result was *An tOileánach* (*The Islandman*), which Tomás wrote in longhand and sent in short sections to Brian Ó Ceallaigh. The text was edited by Pádraig Ó Siochfhradha, Ó Ceallaigh's former Irish teacher who had sent him to the Blaskets, and the book was published in 1929. A second, somewhat more generous edition was prepared by Ó Criomhthain's grandson, Pádraig Ua Maoileoin, and published in 1973. An English translation of the first edition was made by Robin Flower and published in 1937.[4]

An tOileánach was the first significant autobiography in Irish and is unquestionably a remarkable document which would have deserved to have been published in any language. Tomás Ó Criomhthain spent the whole of his long life on the Great Blasket and, apart from one occasion when he travelled to Cahirciveen on the neighbouring peninsula, never went further from home than Dingle village on the mainland. His contact with the scholars in the later part of his life no doubt extended his geographic and intellectual horizons; but the greater part of his active life was that of a farmer-fisherman, engaged in the humdrum existence of scraping out a living in a remote and harsh environment. Up to the time the scholars began to come to the island, his was an anonymous existence without any involvement in public life or any part to play on the national, not to speak of the international, stage. Thus, though his story follows the outlines of his own life from birth to late manhood, there was so little that was truly eventful in his life that it was necessary to flesh out the account by making it a record of the life of the island community as well as an account of his own. Or to put it another way, since his own life was in all essentials identical with that of each one of his neighbours, since his life was inextricably bound up with theirs, the record of his life is of necessity also the record of the life of his community.

This record offers many insights into Ó Criomhthain's mind and personality. It also lays bare the qualities of character that enabled the islanders to survive: heroic courage and endurance, qualities which classical scholars and critics have identified as being those which inform the poetry of Homer. It is Ó Criomhthain's great merit that he has successfully portrayed those qualities of his people in his book, and, without undue boastfulness, has represented himself as possessing them in a high degree. This is particularly true of his account5 of a hunting expedition which involved swimming under water through a narrow passage of extremely turbulent sea into a cave in order to kill seals with clubs. Seals were much sought after by the islanders for their flesh, for their skins and for oil for lamps. Those involved in the expedition ran the risk of being attacked and severely wounded by the seals, or of death by drowning. Hence Tomás categorizes the event as being a 'truly remarkable action', observing, however, that 'there is no limit to human resources when called on'.[6] His own involvement was peripheral at first, since he was relatively young, and only more mature men had the skill and experience required. However, when a rope broke and Tomás's uncle, a nonswimmer, was left stranded in the seal-cave, Tomás leapt into the water to rescue him. His quick thinking on this occasion is typical of the man, and Tomás is clearly and justifiably proud of his calm competence in an emergency.

This kind of episode was undoubtedly exceptional. Nevertheless the determined will to survive, and the courage and skill which were involved, came into play in many aspects of everyday island life, so that, as I have suggested, these qualities become a leitmotif in Tomás's book. Towards the end of his narrative he suggests that there will never again be people like his people. He means, of course, to express his awareness that the island may soon be abandoned, but also his conviction that the island people, his people, were unique: 'I have written a minute account of many of our affairs, so that they should be somewhere remembered, and I have tried to describe the character of my people so that a record of them would endure after us; for the likes of us will never again exist.'[7]

An tOileánach was soon followed by two other Blasket autobiographies, that of Muiris Ó Súilleabháin (1904–50), *Fiche Blian ag Fás (Twenty Years A-Growing)* (1933, 1976), and that of Peig Sayers (1872–1958), *Peig* (1936). The intervention of outsiders was again necessary in both cases, but their task must have been made easier by the fact that Tomás Ó Criomhthain had published his book and that it had been widely acclaimed. It was the Englishman, George Thomson, a noted Greek scholar, who urged Muiris Ó Súilleabháin to write his story, who edited it and collaborated in making the English translation (1933).[8] Similarly Máire Ní Chinnéide was instrumental in having Peig Sayers dictate her life story to her son, Mícheál Ó Gaoithín, and it was she too who edited the book. An English translation was not published until 1973.[9] Like Ó Criomhthain's book, the other two are as much concerned with the life of the community as they are with their own personal stories. There is, therefore, a basic similarity between all three books; but there are also fundamental differences which derive in part from differences of personality, but also from varying personal circumstances.

A former teacher of mine has accurately characterized the three books as follows: 'Tomás's story is that of an aged hero; Muiris's is that of a lighthearted young man; Peig's is the sad widow's tale.'[10] It must also be pointed out that, of the three, only Tomás spent all his life on the island. Peig Sayers was born on the mainland and only came to live on the island when she married an islander, Pádraig Ó Gaoithín, a circumstance which must have strongly influenced her view of life on the island. Indeed two thirds of her book are about her years before she married and only one third is concerned with her married life on the island. It is important to remember, of course, that apart from the added sense of isolation involved in living on the island, life on the mainland for those of Peig's social background would not have been materially different from the life of the island. Muiris Ó Súilleabháin, on the other hand, left the island in his twenties to join the police force and had already completed his course in the training college and been assigned to duty in Connemara in West Galway when he set about writing his book in 1929. He returned to the island only on vacation. He never experienced as an adult the rigours of island life so that his autobiography, which covers only his youth and early manhood, is indeed the story of a lighthearted young man, and a highly romanticized and nostalgic version at that, since it is narrated by one who has escaped from the island and dwells there only in memory, and who, furthermore, on his holiday visit to the island sees clear evidence that the place is being abandoned and is now occupied by an ageing and dwindling population.

These comments on Muiris Ó Súilleabháin's book bring me back to Tomás Ó Criomhthain, for there is much in his book too that is lighthearted; and it is with his and Peig Sayers's books that I wish to concern myself in what follows. George Thomson's influence on Muiris's life and on the production of his autobiography was so pervasive as to render an analysis of the book too complex a matter to be conducted here.[11]

As already mentioned Tomás's autobiography covers a long span of life from birth to late manhood. The book falls into two quite distinct halves: his life before marriage and after marriage, the first being a pleasant, carefree existence like that of Muiris Ó Súilleabháin, the second being characterized by a sense of care and responsibility. Tomás was not unaware of this distinction. Towards the end of the first section he remarks: 'Youth is beautiful. There is nothing so wonderful. I thought at that time that no earl or lord in Ireland was as satisfied as I. I hadn't a care in the world.'[12] He was only in his early twenties when he married. Nevertheless, having given an account of his wedding, he comments: 'Till that day I had known little of the responsibilities of life, but from that day on they came upon me. . . . Marriage makes a great change in a man's life. His disposition and his view of all sorts of things changes . . .',[13] and he goes on to synopsize the remainder of his life, describing the unceasing toil, and how emigration and death due to accident and illness took his family and his wife from him. In stark contrast, the first part of his narrative is full of *joie-de-vivre*, of music, song and dance, of courtship (including some quite frank accounts of sexual encounters with girls), till eventually he falls deeply in love. This idyllic experience was not to lead to marriage, however, for the girl in question lived, not on the Great Blasket, but on one of the smaller islands, and Tomás's sister convinced his parents that he would be better advised for good social reasons to marry the daughter of a neighbour on the main island. And so it was arranged. Of course, the made match (in Irish *cleamhnas*) was the norm, and Tomás acquiesced.

On the face of it, Tomás does not record any feeling of resentment. He does state, however, that at his wedding he sang one song, the words of which he sets down.[14] It is the song of a girl who complains of the faithlessness of her lover who has abandoned her. Several years ago James Stewart and Máire Mhac an tSaoi pointed out the impropriety of this song being sung by Tomás on that occasion: the girl whom Tomás had jilted could make the same complaint against him as the girl in the song makes against her lover.[15] Neither Stewart nor Mhac an tSaoi went on to draw the conclusion which I did in a more recent essay, namely, that Tomás could not have sung that song at his wedding, and did not. To have done so would have amounted to a gross insult to his newly wedded wife, an admission that he had been forced to marry her when he really wanted to marry another whom he loved. The facts would have been public knowledge: for Tomás to have rehearsed them on that occasion would have been in extremely bad taste. I suggest, then, that Tomás did not sing that song at his wedding and that his statement that he did so is purely a literary flourish, introduced into his autobiography when his wife was long dead and could not be hurt by his account of his deep love for another girl, nor by a reference to the fact that her own marriage to him was based on social convenience and was not an affair of the heart.[16]

We are dealing here, then, with an element of quite exquisite literary truth rather than historical truth in this detail of Tomás Ó Criomhthain's autobiography. Towards the end of his book Tomás asserted that his account contained 'nothing but the truth.' Truth here is not necessarily strict historical truth. Indeed his statement goes on to set truth over against 'fiction' rather than untruth; he has invented no part of the account of his life.[17] Tomás, however, was a product of a society whose records were a matter of memory rather than written documents. It is true that our age can stand amazed at the accuracy of those unwritten traditions: nevertheless we must also realize that the import of the narration of the traditional account of past events is much more important than the accuracy of historical detail. Account must also be taken of the likelihood that, when an event occurred in similar circumstances on different occasions, the details of the various occurrences could easily be confused. All of this is provided for in an understanding of the word *seanchas* in Irish which includes the areas of old tales, history and traditional lore. The need for strict historical accuracy would hardly be understood by one whose concept of past records was reflected by the word *seanchas*.

Thus Tomás would have felt free to improve the import or impact of his life-story in various ways while claiming not to have violated the truth in his record. I have referred earlier to his copious use of direct speech. Clearly, we are not to believe that Tomás is reporting the *ipsissima verba* used on any particular occasion, but rather that he is seeking to increase the impact of his account of various events by allowing the participants to speak for themselves. There is one event which I would like to highlight as a shining example of Tomás's awareness of the possibility of improving the imaginative impact of his account in this and other ways.

The Blasket islanders were tenants who were required to pay rent to a landlord. Like other members of the public they were also liable for public taxes or cesses. They frequently failed to pay either rent or tax, no doubt because they regarded them as a cruel imposition and also because they often did not have the wherewithal to pay. But it is clear, too, that they were happy to take advantage of the fact that their island home was a kind of fortress which could be defended against unwelcome visitors, including bailiffs and law officers.

Tomás has given two accounts of one such occasion, apparently in the early 1870s, when a gunboat full of bailiffs and police came to collect rent. In a collection of items of traditional lore, *Seanchas ón Oileán Tiar* (*Lore from the Western Island*), made by Tomás for Robin Flower, but not published until 1956 when both had been dead for several years, he records the event without much embellishment.[18] The women of the island, forewarned of the arrival of the bailiffs, had collected an arsenal of stones and rocks on the top of the cliff above the harbour, and, when a landing party from the ship approached the harbour in smaller boats, began to drop the stones and rocks on the boats. The landing party was forced to retreat and attempt to come ashore at another harbour, but the women got to that harbour before them and again forced them to withdraw. After a number of further futile attempts at both harbours, the party had no option other than to head for the beach and run the boats in on the sand and stumble ashore through the waves. They reached the high ground with great difficulty and then formed themselves into a rank threatening the village. Later in the day some gentlemen came ashore from the ship, and seeing the wretched circumstances of the islanders, decided that no rent should be collected. The bailiffs and police were ordered to return to the ship. As they left the island, the officer in charge of the police so angered the islanders by a remark he made that one woman, who had a child in her arms, attempted to throw the child at him and had to be restrained by another woman.

In Tomás's second account of this incident, given in *An tOileánach*,[19] the affair ends differently in that the women are represented as having succeeded in preventing the landing party from coming ashore. The effect is the same: no rent was collected. But in the second version of the story, the fact that the women repelled the invaders reflects even greater credit on them, a fact which is highlighted in Tomás's concluding remark: When the news spread that a ship came to the Great Blasket with armed men aboard and that they were *unable* to take rent or tax, the whole of Ireland was *amazed* (my italics).[20]

Tomás uses several devices to heighten the impact of this account. Not only by means of narrator's comments but also by the use of direct speech he demonstrates the anger, bravery and stoicism of the island women, and he also illustrates the mental state of the landing party. In various ways, too, he controls the action so as to increase its intensity. For instance, he omits mention of the second harbour and has the landing party approach the island and return to the ship several times. On the first approach only one boat is involved, on the second two and on the third three. On the women's part, their attack on the invaders becomes more frenzied, reaching a climax when the woman attempts to throw her child at them, exclaiming: ' "Damn me, I'll throw the child at them!" ', which elicits this response from her neighbour: ' "Yerra, you bloody fool, don't be insane; keep your child." '[21] This incident, barbarous as it is, now forms a natural part of the overall action and illustrates perfectly that the women's anger had reached boiling point; whereas in the earlier account it seems quite out of proportion to the insult offered, coming when a decision had been made not to collect any rent.

In these and other ways Tomás seeks to heighten the dramatic impact of the event. In doing so he shows himself well skilled in marshalling the devices of the creative writer and fully aware of the artistic significance of form. Clearly the event described in both accounts is the same, but in *An tOileánach* a fair degree of artistic licence is in evidence, and, while it does not destroy historical truth, it deforms it in the interest of imaginative truth.[22]

Humour imposes its own logic on the remembering and narration of an account of an actual event. In particular, it requires that aspects of the event that would lessen the humorous impact of the story be filtered out, and may entail the total separation of the humorous incident from the historical context to which it originally belonged. The likelihood of this happening was suggested, for example, by John M. Synge in *The Aran Islands*, when giving an account of evictions which he witnessed in Inis Meáin, Aran, in the early years of this century. Synge describes the anger and fear of the island men, and tells of the 'wild imprecations' uttered by a housewife who was seized 'with uncontrollable fury' on being driven from her home, and of her quiet grief and the 'mute sympathy' of the neighbouring women when the eviction had been carried out.

Then two pigs escaped from the bailiff's men, and as they raced up and down the narrow road, the islanders 'shrieked and howled to increase their terror,' so that when some of the accompanying party of police attempted to stop the pigs, 'there was a slight scuffle, and then the pigs continued their mad rush to the east, leaving three policemen lying in the dust.' Synge continues:

> The satisfaction of the people was immense. They shrieked and hugged each other with delight, and it is likely that they will hand down these animals for generations in the tradition of the island.[23]

That Synge's belief was well founded is confirmed by Tomás Ó Criomhthain's reference to a parallel event which occurred in the Blaskets in October, 1879.

> The potato crop having failed that summer, a severe famine followed, and by January 1880, the people of the Dingle Peninsula were in desperate circumstances, as reported by Father Egan, parish priest of Ballyferriter, in a letter to the Kerry Sentinel newspaper: It is with deep anguish I see the gloom and despair which are settling down on the vast majority of my people . . .
>
> In these times of dire destitution and distress, turnips and salt are the food of many of my poor people and are considered — well, I won't say a delicacy — but they are by no means despised; and those who possess a supply are esteemed lucky by some of their neighbours.

Referring to the Blaskets, he continued:

> Only the Great Blasket is inhabited. It contains about eighteen families, all miserably poor and in extreme want. About half of these have been recently put out of possession by Mr. Sam Hussey [the landlord's agent] for non-payment of rent.
>
> A gunboat and a posse of police recently invaded the shores of the Island for the purpose of seeing these evictions on the part of Mr. Hussey carried into execution, and for the purpose of levying Co[unty] Cess . . . [24]

In the midst of a cruel famine, this was indeed an utterly heartless exercise; it was also futile, however. Several families were indeed evicted, but, since it was impossible to find alternative tenants, were 're-entered as caretakers,' as the resident magistrate in charge of the enterprise reported to his superiors. So, too, the County Kerry rates collector, Bastable Hilliard, who had organized the expedition and had got permission for the use of a gunboat and posse of police, testified to the Grand Jury of Kerry in March 1880 that he had collected only five shillings of £97 due in rates and, by way of explanation, referred to the poverty of the islanders, which he illustrated by saying that during his visit to the island he had seen no stock apart from one mule.[25]

Thus neither Hussey nor Hilliard achieved anything by their 'invasion' of the island, other than to show their utter lack of concern for the islanders' plight and to demonstrate that the function of the law was to proclaim and defend the rights of the landlord and of the state.

In any case, famine and evictions were facts of island life, and, in his record of this event, Tomás Ó Criomhthain concentrates on the humorous aspects of what happened. Hilliard's report conceals the fact that the islanders had pulled the wool over his eyes and had made him the butt of their mockery, as is clear from Tomás's narrative:

> Some years after [the women's defence of the island] another [gunboat] suddenly appeared at anchor below the houses. There were small parties of civilians and armed men on board. The islanders had been informed that this was to happen and had been advised not to resist, but rather to drive what cows and sheep they had to the western end of the island.
>
> This was done. The youths drove them as far as they could. The chief rates collector and his underlings were aboard the boat. They were not obstructed in any way, but given ample scope to go about their business. Off they went up the hill, accompanied by the civilians who were specially chosen for the task.
>
> The chief collector went as far as the old Tower, but, if he had eyes, there was no sight in them. He sent others half-way back the island, but it was just the same. They found nothing but two old mules which were dead apart from their eyes and skin. The chief collector was asked whether he intended to take the mules with him.
>
> 'Surely the people would make fun of us,' he said.
>
> They went home as they had come, without cow, horse or sheep.[26]

In this rather spare narrative, Tomás does little to evoke the mirth of the islanders, though it is clear from his comments in passing on to another humorous event that they thoroughly enjoyed officialdom's discomfiture. It is likely that, when Tomás was writing, the mules, like Synge's pigs, had become part of the lore of the island, and that he would have considered it otiose to elaborate the story, as he was certainly capable of doing. The negative side of his treatment of the event is significant, however. Tomás has omitted all reference to the general context in which the event occurred, namely, a period of great suffering due to famine. And he is clearly at pains to eliminate any sense of fear or panic or threat caused by the incursion. There is no mention of evictions; the islanders are forewarned; the party aboard the gunboat is small; there is no confrontation. I would suggest that he has consciously removed from his account of the historical event those aspects that would hinder or diminish appreciation of the fact that what he was presenting was a humorous story, and that, in doing so, he has again deliberately departed from historical truth.

These instances of the liberty that Tomás Ó Criomhthain gave himself in dealing with the facts of his life story are by no means exceptional: there are many others in his book, though it is not always quite so easy to analyze the nature and extent of the distortion involved. And though I would suggest that Ó Criomhthain is the master in this regard, he is not the only one of the three Blasket autobiographers to treat historical truth in this way. There is evidence that Peig Sayers did not feel herself bound to narrate her story with absolute veracity either.

In 1970 Peig's son, Mícheál Ó Gaoithín, published a second volume based on his mother's reminiscences, *Beatha Pheig Sayers* (*Peig Sayers's Life*).[27] To a large extent it covers the same ground as that covered in the earlier book, Peig, but gives a somewhat different account of a number of events. In the first book, for instance, she informs us that her marriage to Pádraig Ó Gaoithín was the result of a made match (*cleamhnas*), just as Tomás Ó Criomhthain's was. While admitting that she was aware that marriage would introduce a welcome measure of security into her life, the purpose of her brief account of the making of the match is to emphasize her absolute obedience to, and trust in, her father. ' "Will you go to live on the Island?" ', asks her father. ' "I don't know the Island people," said I, "but you know them well, and what pleases you, pleases me too. I shall go wherever you tell me to go." '[28] In the second account she gives a very different reason for her willingness to go to live on the island: she had fallen deeply in love with Pádraig Ó Gaoithín some time previously and her love for him overcame the aversion she felt to island life: 'He was the first man whom I ever loved and therefore I would have gone anywhere with him.'[29] This may, of course, be a romantic fiction. On the other hand, love and a made match were not mutually exclusive; indeed they frequently enough coincided with one another. But if Peig's love for Pádraig is not a fiction, then she suppressed any mention of it in the first account, and this quite deliberate act of self-censorship was clearly designed to highlight her complete acceptance of her father's wish.

Both accounts cannot be accepted as being historically true, however. One of them must involve some degree of deformation of history, if not an element of fiction.

A more substantial element of deformation of history is involved, I am convinced, in Peig Sayers's accounts of personal hardship and tragedy in her first book. That she experienced a significant amount of hardship in her life is not at all in doubt. Clearly, too, her emotional reaction to it is firmly based on an unquestioning acceptance of God's will. She makes it abundantly clear that her upbringing and her continuing cultural experience tended strongly to confirm this, and one need not doubt that it greatly helped to soften the impact of the many hardships and tragedies that she had to endure. Her presentation of this attitude is, on occasion, dubious in the extreme, however, and this is particularly true of one of the greatest tragedies of her life, the drowning of her son, Tomás. The boy's body was recovered and brought home to Peig to be prepared for burial, a task for which she says she was psychologically ill-prepared. However, prayer and the proximity of a statue of the Blessed Virgin Mary enabled her to overcome her repugnance and her distraught feelings, so that she was converted, miraculously it seems, into 'an instrument in the hands of the Virgin and her Son,'[30] and performed the task without distress.

To admit to being overcome by crippling horror in face of a terrible ordeal would, for Peig Sayers, be tantamount to treason or rebellion against God, a denial of his goodness, a failure to accept his will. Rather than admit to such things, she converts the dreadful event into a striking illustration of God's goodness in that he provided her with the strength and presence to be calm in the face of her tremendous loss. Whether this actually happened or not is a moot point; at all events her presentation of the account is too facile to be convincing. But a more serious problem for the impact of her book in human terms is that, by presenting religious faith as a defuser of human emotions, she reduces it to the level of a tranquilizing drug, while at the same time she converts a deeply moving tragic event into one that is merely pathetic.[31]

In this last case, therefore, it is not possible to be sure whether we are faced with deformation of history or not, though I strongly suspect that we are. Peig's life, in any event, was indeed marked by the same confrontation of hardship, the same level of tragedy, as that which characterized Tomás Ó Criomhthain's. It is Tomás's great achievement that he has made his autobiography a remarkably challenging record of heroic stoicism, whereas Peig Sayers's story fails to rise above the level of pathos.

Notes

1 This information on population is based on the figures, derived from census records, quoted in Seán Ó Dubháin, 'Báillí agus Callshaoth' in Aogán Ó Muircheartaigh (ed.), *Oidhreacht an Bhlascaoid* (Dublin: Coiscéim, 1989), pp. 9–10; and in Mairéad Nic Craith, *An tOileánach Léannta* (Dublin: An Clóchomhar, 1988), pp. 98–99.

2 Tomás Ó Criomhthain, *Allagar na hInise*, ed. An Seabhac (Dublin: Muintir C.S. Ó Fallamhain, 1928); *Allagar na hInise*, ed. Pádraig Ua Maoileoin (Dublin: Oifig an tSoláthair, 1977).

3 Seán Ó Criomhthain, 'Agallamh a Dó', in Pádraig Tyers (ed.), *Leoithne Aniar* (Baile an Fheirtéaraigh: Cló Dhuibhne, 1982), p. 103. My translation. For a full account of Tomás Ó Criomhthain's contacts with the visiting scholars, see M. Nic Craith, *op. cit.*, *passim*.

4 *An tOileánach* (Dublin: Clólucht an Tálbóidigh, 1929; Dublin: Cló Talbot, 1973). Tomás Ó Crohan, *The Islandman*, translated from the Irish by Robin Flower (Oxford: Oxford University Press, 1951). The first edition of the translation was published by The Talbot Press, Dublin, and by Chatto and Windus, London.

5 *An tOileánach*, 1973 ed., pp. 104–07.

6 *Ibid.*, p. 106. My translation.

7 *Ibid.*, p. 256. My translation.

8 *Fiche Blian ag Fás* (Dublin: Clólucht an Talbóidigh, 1933; Maynooth: An Sagart, 1976). Maurice O'Sullivan, *Twenty Years A-Growing*, rendered from the original Irish by Moya Llewelyn Davies and George Thomson (Oxford: Oxford University Press, 1953, The World's Classics Series). The first edition of the translation was published by Chatto and Windus. Other editions by the Viking Press (New York) and Penguin.

9 *Peig* (Dublin: Clólucht an Talbóidigh, 1936). *Peig*: the autobiography of Peig Sayers of the Great Blasket Island translated into English by Bryan McMahon (Dublin: Talbot Press, 1973). Another edition by Syracuse University Press (Irish Studies Series).

10 Pádraig Ó Fiannachta, *Léas Eile ar ár Litríocht* (Maynooth: An Sagart, 1982), p. 252. My translation.

11 See Nuala Ní Aimhirgin, *Muiris O Súilleabháin: Saol agus Saothar* (Maynooth: An Sagart, 1983), *passim*.

12 *An tOileánach*, 1973 ed., p. 150. My translation.

13 *An tOileánach*, 1929 ed., p. 162, but omitted in the 1973 edition. My translation, based on Robin Flower's.

14 *An tOileánach*, 1973 ed., pp. 157–58, but omitted in the first edition.

15 James Stewart, 'An tOileánach — More or Less,' in *Zeitschrift für Celtische Philologie* 35 (1976), p. 245; Máire Mhac an tSaoi, 'An tOileánach by Tomás Ó Criomhthain (1856–1937)' in John Jordan (ed.), *The Pleasures of Gaelic Literature* (Dublin and Cork: Mercier Press, 1977), pp. 35–37.

16 In 'Tomás Ó Criomhthain agus "Caisleán Uí Néill"' in *Iris-leabhar Mhá Nuad* (1985), pp. 84–109. The treatment by the editors of Ó Criomhthain's manuscript account of his marriage is here analyzed.

17 *An tOileánach*, 1973 ed., p. 252. My translation.

18 Séamus Ó Duilearga (ed.), *Seanchas On Óileán Tiar* (Dublin: Comhlucht Oideachais na h-Éireann, 1956), pp. 131–35.

19 *An tOileánach*, 1929 ed., pp. 61–64; 1973 ed., pp. 59–61; *The Island-man*, pp. 52–55.

20 *An tOileánach*, 1973 ed., p. 61. My translation.

21 *Ibid*. My translation.

22 A full discussion of the two accounts of the event will be found in my essay 'Tóir an Chíosa' in Cathal Ó Háinle, *Promhadh Pinn* (Maynooth: An Sagart, 1978). A much expanded version of that essay, containing a full discussion of the historical background, literary comparisons with John M. Synge and Pádraig Ó Siochfhradha and some further examples of deformation of history in *An tOileánach*, is published as 'Stair agus Scríbhneoireacht Chruthaitheach i Saothar Uí Chriomhthain,' in Breandán Ó Conaire (ed.), *Tomás an Bhlascaoid* (Béal an Daingin: Cló Iar-Chonnachta), which appeared in 1991.

23 John M. Synge, *Collected Works: Volume II: Prose*, ed. Alan Price (London: Oxford University Press, 1966), p. 89.

24 These excerpts from Fr. Egan's letter of 13 January 1880 will be found in Thomas F. O'Sullivan, *Romantic Hidden Kerry* (Tralee: The Kerryman, 1931), pp. 242–43.

25 For the sources of these reports, see my essay in *Tomás an Bhlascaoid* referred to in n. 22 above.

26 *An tOileánach*, 1973 ed., pp. 61–62. My translation.

27 Mícheál Ó Gaoithín, *Beatha Pheig Sayers* (Dublin: FNT, 1970).

28 *Peig*, p. 178. My translation.

29 *Beatha Pheig Sayers*, p. 137. My translation.

30 *Peig*, p. 178. My translation.

31 For a fuller discussion of this aspect of *Peig*, see my essay 'Peig, Aonghus Ó Dálaigh agus Macbeth,' in Aogán Ó Muircheartaigh (ed.), *Oidhreacht an Bhlascaoid*, pp. 253–69.

Reading the Book
of Himself

The Confessional Imagination of
St. Augustine and Joyce

Dominic Manganiello

In an early essay, Joyce claimed that the 'artistic life should be nothing more than a true and continual revelation of [the] spiritual life.'
By seeking to realize or communicate the truth and integrity of the
self, the artist unites autobiographical and confessional impulses.
As one 'sufficient in himself,' he envisages individuation rather than
salvation as his ultimate goal; as a secular saint, he becomes the
spiritual focus of his time ('James Clarence Mangan', 184). In *A
Portrait of the Artist as a Young Man*, Joyce exploits the traditions
of Christian allegory and of the artist's coming of age, presented
as autobiographical narrative, to suit his own purposes. Among
the most significant of these, I suggest, is Augustine's *Confessions*,
which presents for the first time in Western tradition the literary
self-creation of an individual. John Henry Raleigh ('*Ulysses*: Trinitarian and Catholic', 117) has recently gone so far as to argue that
'there could have been, exchanging a few centuries, the Confessions
of St. James of Dublin . . . and Augustine's *A Portrait of the Artist as
a Young Man*.' Although Joyce bore the name of Augustine within
his own, it is difficult to imagine the two writers exchanging places
so easily. The protagonists of their respective writings do not, in
fact, lead parallel lives. What I want to examine is how their partial convergence illuminates the 'individuating rhythm' of Joyce's
confessional novel.

I/Thou

Augustine, who has been called 'the first novelist of the self' (Freccero, 'Introduction' to *Dante*, 5), unfolds his *Confessions* in three
stages: the confession of sin to confession of faith and, finally, to
confession of God's glory. The book's opening is the key to the
whole:

> *Can any praise be worthy of the Lord's majesty? How magnificent
> his strength! How inscrutable his wisdom!* Man is one of your
> creatures, Lord . . . The thought of you stirs him so deeply that

> he cannot be content unless he praises you, because you made us
> for yourself and our hearts find no peace until they rest in you.
> (*Conf.*, I.i.16)

The invocation taken from the Psalms forms part of a recurring feature of the writing. Augustine's words are continually glossed by the ineffable, divine Word. The verbal image of himself that Augustine limns is generated by the *Verbum caro factum est*. Through the Incarnation God speaks to the individual as human being, while enabling him to respond in human terms:

> He spoke, and we were made; but we are unable to speak of Him.
> His Word, by Whom we were spoken, is His Son. He was made
> weak, so that He might be spoken by us, despite our weakness.
> (*Enarrationes in Psalmos*, 99.6)

Augustine's quest for identity begins by acknowledging that he is made in the image and likeness of a Maker, and ends by identifying himself with the source of his existence, the very ground of being. What Martin Buber called an I/Thou relationship develops between creature and Creator, who engage in a conversation which is sustained throughout the volume. Interior transformation — the difference between 'what once I was' and 'what now I am' — provides the motive for a discourse in which 'I' is both subject and object. For Augustine, confessional writing, like receiving the sacrament of confession itself, was an act of self-liberation. He imagines the exemplary value of his story as contributing to the liberation of others, too, from the shackles of sin. Although the reader remains outside this primary dialogue, Augustine's narrative is written for his benefit, and invites response to the record of his pilgrimage. He does not speak in isolation but as one individual to other individuals in dialogic interaction. His 'dialogic imagination' springs from the Bible. In Bakhtin's terms (*The Dialogic Imagination*, 342), Augustine imbues his own word with awareness of the Other, with the 'authoritative word,' actualizing it into its dialogic tissue. The final community Augustine envisages — union with God — is open to all. The principle of referral in the *Confessions*, then, involves a text, Author, and authority other than the self.

Joyce cast *A Portrait of the Artist* in the confessional form of its prototype with some significant variations (Lanham 81–87). As the actual historical character writing about his own life, Augustine provides some distance between himself and his own words through the mediation of Scripture. The point of view in his autobiographical account remains primarily subjective, however. Joyce's fiction, of course, is mimetic, not overtly historical, and he intermingles third and first person narration in an effort to inject an element of objectivity into the narrative. In addition, he names the artist referred to in the title of his book Stephen Dedalus rather than James Joyce to weaken the link — biographical similarities notwithstanding — between real-life author and fictitious character. Finally, Joyce reinforces this crucial distinction through the much-advertised use of irony.

Despite these caveats, strong internal and external evidence suggests that the novel is a portrait of both Joyce and Stephen (John Paul Riquelme 51). The illusion of the author's total distancing of the self demonstrates how Joyce at once breaks with and rejoins his predecessor. He adopts the attitude towards his hero that he called, paradoxically, 'indifferent sympathy' ('Mr. Arnold Graves' New Work', 127) in order not to appear patronizing or sentimental. Although Joyce imputedly has 'a compulsion to make a self-image . . . with an eye to the approval of others,' as Rebecca West (11) claimed, he does not abandon Stephen, despite his narcissistic egoism, nor does he expect the reader to. His strategy, to which *Stephen Hero* (45–46) attests, is to combine 'an impersonal manner and . . . profound self-approval.'

Rather than address the reader directly, Joyce bends his verbal medium to fit the contours of Stephen's sensibility; his purpose is to achieve what Karen Lawrence (35–36) calls a 'stylistic sympathy' between narrator and character that enables us to view a double portrait of the artist and his style. Stephen enunciates a theory of impersonality, but the implied author is an ' "effaced narrator" only in that he never uses the pronoun "I" to tell his story' (Louis D. Rubin 146). He has forced himself into a subjective attitude to his material that is reflected in the autotelic realm of the protagonist's experience. Joyce provides a minimum of references back to the external world so that objective phenomena are displaced. The narrator probes Stephen's feelings at every stage of his development with such detailed consideration that it forestalls any suggestion of pervasive irony. The other characters are too little individualized, acting as a foil to the only character Joyce is really interested in (C.P. Curran 63). Stephen's mind imbues the style of the whole; he is, in short, the teller of his own tale (John Paul Riquelme 51).

Stephen's subjectivism is grounded in a modern philosophy which, as John MacMurray (31) notes, 'takes the Self as its starting point, and not the world, or the community, or God . . . the Self is an individual in isolation, an ego or "I," and never a "thou."' Rather than considering himself, like Augustine, a dependent being whose 'sufficiency is from God' (2 Cor. 3:5), Stephen severs the link to his divine origin and proudly proclaims the autonomous self. His Romantic theory of art focuses on the moment when 'the artist prolongs and broods upon himself,' and initially 'presents his image in immediate relation to himself' and subsequently to others (*Portrait*, 214). The 'godlike artist' replaces Augustine's metaphysical God in a way that recalls Swinburne's (726) creed in 'Hertha':

> What things does thou now
> Looking Godward, to cry
> 'I am I, thou art thou,
> I am low, thou are high'?
> I am thou, whom thou seekst to find him;
> find thou but thyself, thou art I.

Stephen follows Swinburne in reversing the central tenet of Western theological tradition by making the 'I' the ground of being.

Joyce no longer appeals to the universality of human nature but to the uniqueness and exceptional sensitivity of the artist-hero. Stephen accordingly cultivates the intense feeling that 'he was different from others' (*Portrait*, 65), and his self-image as 'a being apart in every order' (*Portrait*, 161). He makes his declaration of independence by shutting out the 'hollowsounding voices' of various causes (*Portrait*, 84), refusing to serve any cause other than his own. To foster a genuine self he must eradicate a false consciousness modulated by the opinions of Church, State, or friends. This radical position anticipates the secular scripture of contemporary self-theorists (Carl Rogers and Barry Stevens 9):

> In the beginning I was one person, knowing nothing but my own experience. Then, I was told things and became two people. . . .
> In the beginning was I, and I was good. Then came another I. Outside authority.

In this alternate Genesis, the subjugated 'I' overcomes its dividedness by self-assertion. Similarly, Stephen can be viewed as the modern fictional 'I' in continual conflict with other 'I's.' For Augustine sin divides the self; he considers himself, like Adam, solely responsible for his fall. Stephen blames the evil influence of institutions, as he experiences it in the pandybat episode, for the loss of his natural goodness.

Joyce bases his critique of Augustine's epistemology on libertarianism. One of his principal authorities, Max Stirner (182), had pushed Fichte's claim that 'the ego is all' to its philosophical extreme: 'To be a man is not to realize the ideal of *Man*, but to present *oneself*, the individual. . . . *I* am my species, am without norm, without law, without model, and the like.' Equally important for

Joyce was Oscar Wilde's (289) declaration about the sovereignty of the artist in a letter of 1897: 'The egoistic note is, of course, and always has been to me, the primal and ultimate note of modern art, but *to be an Egoist one must have an Ego*. It is not everyone who says, "I, I" who can enter into the Kingdom of Art.' If this pose strikes us as extreme, then it would be instructive to imagine Joyce replying, as he did to his brother Stanislaus, that the only possible modern novel was the 'egomaniac's' (cited in Richard Ellmann 265). It is perhaps more than an accident of literary history that *A Portrait of the Artist* was first serialized in *The Egoist*. After all, that individualist review was named in honour of Max Stirner.

Joyce turns Augustine against himself by making his own confessions those of a justified sinner: 'He was destined to learn his own wisdom apart from others or to learn the wisdom of others himself wandering among the snares of the world. The snares of the world were its ways of sin' (*Portrait*, 162). Recalling the motto of Milton's Satan, 'evil be thou my good,' Stephen can paradoxically only come to the knowledge of innocence through sin (*Portrait*, 222). Sin, in fact, becomes the principle of individuation. As he contemplates the meaning of his name and his return to his mythical father, 'a symbol of the artist forging anew in his workshop out of the sluggish matter of the earth a new soaring impalpable imperishable being' (*Portrait*, 169), Stephen's soul is 'in flight . . . in an air beyond the world,' moving towards self-directedness in the kingdom of art. Like the Neoplatonists, Joyce interprets the myth of Daedalus as a figure of the soul's journey to its heavenly *patria*: 'il faut que l'âme prenne son vol pour regagner sa patrie' ('the soul must take flight in order to regain its homeland': cited in Freccero, 'Dante's Prologue Scene', 12–19). The 'mind' of the artist ostensibly flies to Europe but not to the unindividuated 'mind of Europe' that T.S. Eliot discovered was 'more important than his own private mind' in 'Tradition and the Individual Talent.' When Stephen declares, 'My own mind . . . is more interesting to me than the entire country' (*Stephen Hero*, 248), he believes, like Milton's Satan, that the mind is its own country.

As a young man, Augustine had also been impressed by the ancient exhortation to seek wisdom: 'my heart began to throb with a bewildering passion for the wisdom of eternal truth. I began to climb out of the depths to which I had sunk . . . My God, how I burned with longing to have wings to carry me back to you, away from earthly things' (*Conf.*, III.iv.58–59). He describes his vocation as a philosopher, or lover of wisdom, metaphorically as a flight with wings and a liberation of the soul from matter. In this reinterpretation of the myth, Daedalus is an ancestor of the prodigal son returning home to his merciful Father from spiritual exile. To embrace worldly wisdom without reference to Christ and be dragged down by carnal passions in the process was to undertake an Icarian or fool's flight. The movements of Daedalus and Icarus in *A Portrait*, on the other hand, are ambivalent ones since, according to Blake's inversion of Dantescan wisdom, 'In Equivocal Worlds Up & Down are Equivocal' ('Illustrations to Dante's *Inferno*', 594). For Augustine freedom consists in one's subjection to the truth, whereas for Stephen it consists in one's subjection to 'error.' In Joyce's mind there was no substitute for 'the individual passion as motive power for everything—art and philosophy included' (*Letters*, 81).

Eros and Language

In the opening chapters of the *Confessions* consciousness begins in desire and in the growing need to express it verbally. Each of the successive desires of life — food for the child, sex for the adolescent, power and fame for the adult — are in fact desires for 'selfhood' which only find their ultimate fulfilment in *caritas*, or love of God. From the outset Augustine sketches his portrait, as Joyce was to do after him, with a consideration of the infant whose major characteristic is his speechlessness. As he struggles in these early years to express his desires through signs he finally masters verbal skills at the age of reason: 'I ceased to be a baby unable to talk, and was now a boy with the power of speech' (*Conf.*, I.viii.29). For Augustine and for Stephen, whose narrative opens in the babbling language of a small child, the features of infancy as defined by their linguistic contours hold as much importance as the features of adolescence in tracing the growth of a soul.

When Augustine reaches the age of puberty, this perspective is further widened to emphasize the link between love, in its dual dimension of *cupiditas* and *caritas*, and language. The search for the self in the things of the world is defined metaphorically as fornication, a turning away or '*aversio*' from God to harlotry (*Conf.*, I.xiii.34; II.vi.50). It is on frequenting brothels that the correlation between verbal and actual fornication becomes resounding, as evidenced in the famous prayer, 'Give me chastity and continence, but not yet' (*Conf.*, VII.vii.169). Significantly, Augustine interprets his moral failings as a perversion of language, a distortion of the faculty of speech to obtain selfish ends. To seek the self in the mirror of creatures, then, involves a kind of linguistic and sexual narcissism, an erroneous use of words which leads one to accept a false image of the self instead of the one originally fashioned by its Maker. It results at the same time in self-dividedness, for it is only by continence, according to Augustine, 'that we are made as one and regain the unity of the self which we lost by falling apart in the search for a variety of pleasures' (*Conf.*, X.xxix.233). This journey towards a new life, this turning towards God, or *conversio*, is described as a marital union with the heavenly bridegroom, 'Jerusalem, the chaste' *(Conf.*, X.xxxv.243): 'for unless he remained when we wandered in error, there would be none to whom we could return and restore ourselves' (*Conf.*, XI.viii.260). Augustine, like his model rhetorician Victorinus, who preferred 'to give up his own school of words than desert your Word,' accordingly renounces his linguistic prostitution as a vendor of words (*Conf.*, VIII.iv.163–164; VIII.v.164; IX.ii.182). He now experiences both linguistic and interior rejuvenation, asking that his tongue be cleansed: 'Circumcise the lips of my mind and my mouth. Purify them of all rash speech and falsehood. Let your Scriptures be my chaste delight. Let me not deceive myself in them nor deceive others about them' (*Conf.*, XI.ii.254). Having now wedded the Scriptures, Augustine understands his true vocation to be a preacher of the Eternal Word which will guide him in his 'journey through words to the translinguistic vision of God' (Marcia L. Colish 53). Augustine sees his own life, from physical birth to spiritual rebirth, as a witness or 'confession' of the continual unfolding of God's Word.

The relationship between eros, language and the emerging self plays an equally dominant role in *A Portrait*, but Stephen's life takes a different turn. Like Augustine, Stephen is initially depicted as a 'wandering soul' or *anima peregrinans* on his way back to his longed-for celestial homeland, a pilgrim who pleads with the Virgin Mary to '*guide us to Our Lord Jesus, guide us home*' (*Portrait*, 139). However, he eventually reverses this movement towards a spiritual destination, preferring instead to wander amid the snares of the world: 'There was a lust of wandering in his feet that burned to set out for the ends of the earth' (*Portrait*, 170). The vicious circle of his wanderlust is drawn every time he returns to the brothel district, where 'unspoken brutal words' articulate his fall into sexuality: '[it was] a cry for an iniquitous abandonment, a cry which was but the echo of an obscene scrawl on the oozing wall of a urinal' (*Portrait*, 99–100). Significantly, Stephen, too, considers his wandering away from God, literally and metaphorically, as fornication: 'evil, in the similitude of a distorted ritual, called to his soul to commit fornication with her' (*Stephen Hero*, 168). Lust fragments the self; only through confession can Stephen be 'at one with others and with God' (*Portrait*, 143). Violent temptations, however, soon mount against the 'citadel of the soul,' or what St. Theresa of Avila called 'the interior castle,' but Stephen manages to withstand the attack for a while: 'A restless feeling of guilt would always be present with him; he would confess and repent and be absolved, confess and repent again and be absolved again, fruitlessly' (*Portrait*, 153). These temptations, like those Augustine faces just before his conversion (*Conf.*, VIII.xi.175), pluck at Stephen's fleshly garment until he yields to nostalgia for his former sins. Confession seems to be a self-defeating exercise, and he doubts the sincerity of his interior conversion. Like Palamon in Chaucer's *Knight's Tale*, Stephen then decides to wage a perpetual war on chastity, on 'those foolish and grotesque virginities' (*Stephen Hero*, 198) as he calls his friends. Joyce translates his awakening to sexuality into a form of the 'resurrection' of the body:

> What were they now but cerements shaken from the body of death —the fear he had walked in night and day, the incertitude that had ringed him round, the shame that had abased him within and without—cerements, the linens of the grave?
>
> His soul had arisen from the grave of boyhood, spurning her graveclothes. (*Portrait*, 170)

In order to describe what Stephen is now compared to what he was then, Joyce radically alters St. Paul's presentation of conversion in the image of the burial of the 'old self,' human nature under the domination of sin, and the resurrection of the 'new self,' human nature restored by grace, a transformation in Stephen which is self-generated. The sensual and spiritual self are no longer in opposition as in St. Paul and St. Augustine, but form an allotropy.

This transfiguration process signals an increasing introspection on Stephen's part, especially as a manifestation of his eros-longing. Joyce draws our attention in this instance to the function of literature as a mediation of desire. *The Count of Monte Cristo* in particular exercises a veritable fascination over Stephen's imagination:

> He returned to Mercedes and, as he brooded upon her image, a strange unrest crept into his blood. . . . He wanted to meet in the real world the unsubstantial image which his soul so constantly beheld. He did not know where to seek it or how: but a premonition which led him on told him that this image would, without any overt act of his, encounter him. . . . They would be alone, surrounded by darkness and silence: and in that moment of supreme tenderness he would be transfigured. (*Portrait*, 64–65)

For Stephen, as for Roland Barthes (17), the text 'is a figure of the erotic body.' He reads 'literally,' that is to say, according to the flesh, mistaking the insubstantial shadows of the text for his own self. The literal knowledge of the text incites him to seek carnal knowledge of another; the book of Alexandre Dumas acts as a pander which inspires Stephen's so-called 'holy encounter' with a prostitute (*Portrait*, 99). The margin between textual and sexual pleasure is thereby blurred.

In *De Doctrina Christiana*, Augustine articulated the fundamental distinction between 'enjoying' a text 'for its own sake' and 'using' its literal sense in order to understand spiritual truth. The failure to distinguish between these two ways of reading results in carnal enjoyment, the kind illustrated by Augustine himself in the *Confessions* when he recounts reading the story of Dido. The pleasure of the text is so intense for him that he weeps for Dido when he has not yet wept for his sins, and for having broken his troth with God (*Conf.*, I.xiii.33–35). Such literal-minded reading is construed as a form of fornication. Augustine admonishes himself for indulging in the *Aeneid* for its own sake. Children's voices in a nearby garden saying, 'take it and read, take it and read,' point him to another text, St. Paul's epistle to the Romans, which converts his 'erotic' reading to a 'charitable' one (*Conf.*, VIII.xii.177). This, as T.R. Wright (96) observes, 'is an extremely intertextual conversion, the product of hearing a story about another conversion (that of Ponticianus) which itself was effected by another story (that of St. Anthony) whose conversion involved exactly the same personal appropriation of a biblical text.' Augustine's verbal epistemology rests on the principle that the reader should love the truth in words and not the words themselves (*On Christian Doctrine*, 136).

For Stephen, however, words turn inward, providing a kind of refuge in subjectivity. Increasingly aware that words are his passport to reality (*Portrait*, 62), he wonders whether he draws more pleasure 'from the reflection of the glowing sensible world through the prism of a language many-coloured and richly storied than from the contemplation of an inner world of individual emotions mirrored perfectly in a lucid supple periodic prose' (*Portrait*, 166–67). That he opts for the former is confirmed in a sentence from his diary entry for March 24: 'Crossing Stephen's, that is, my green' (*Portrait*, 249). The fusion of sign and signified indicates that the artist ultimately prefers his inner world to the communal or sensible world which he eventually rejects. As Marguerite Harkness (104–05) reckons, 'words . . . provide Stephen with vision and truth. But the truth he finds is his own truth: not by asking what the words mean does he discover the outside world, but by making them his own.' The attempt to appropriate words forces them to function as a mirror of the self.

Both reading and writing allow Stephen to luxuriate in the tantalizing glide of signs. When he hides his book of love verses dedicated to Eileen, for example, he gazes at 'his face for a long time in the mirror' (*Portrait*, 71), as if to legitimize John Fowles's (137) conviction that 'narcissism, or pygmalionism, is the essential vice a writer must have.' This principle can be seen at work when Stephen composes the villanelle sequence, where sexual and linguistic narcissism collide. The self-referential process Stephen engages in leads to the worship of man-made signs, words upon words, for their own sake. He delights in the exuberant dance of his temptress-muse, now an *interior* paramour, as much as he enjoys the rhythmic movement and textures of the words themselves until both text and writer explode in a *jouissance*: 'While his soul had passed from ecstasy to languor where had she been? Might it be, in the mysterious ways of spiritual life, that her soul at those same moments had been conscious of his homage?' (*Portrait*, 223). Stephen's homage is in fact autoerotic; like Pygmalion, he is aroused by the work of his own hands.

Stephen's autoerotic poetics exclude the realm of the ethical and invert the Augustinian analysis of desire. But ironically through them Stephen also undercuts his own aesthetic principles as well. His poem excites what he calls his 'kinetic emotions' rather than the 'static' or 'esthetic pleasure' he considers to be the product of a 'proper art.' According to his own definition, then, the villanelle stands as an example of 'improper art.'

Unlike Augustine, Stephen accomplishes his quest for identity by becoming his own *Verbum*: 'in the virgin womb of the imagination the word was made flesh' (*Portrait*, 217). His verbal universe revolves around autoreflexive signs which offer no mediation beyond the self. He is a priest of eternal imagination who preaches his own word. This act of extreme self-consciousness can be compared to the audacity of Dürer, who painted himself in the image of Christ, or of Nietzsche's autobiographical writing entitled *Ecce Homo*. *A Portrait of the Artist* has, as Kenneth Burke (241) puts it, 'all the accoutrements of a gospel, with Stephen as Logos, plus corresponding history and passion.'

Exegesis/Eisagesis

Reflecting on his own text, Augustine confides to his readers the hope that his *Confessions* will stir other hearts 'so that they no longer lie listless in despair, crying 'I cannot'' (*Conf.*, X.iii.208). In other words, 'he hopes that his text will shatter his readers' self-sufficiency as his had been shattered' (Geoffrey Galt Harpham 45). A useful reading, prompted by charity, would have the power to instil self-understanding for, as Hans-Georg Gadamer (57–58) stresses, 'to understand a text is to come to understand oneself in a kind of dialogue.' Reading Scripture, moreover, entails a 'loss of self' since it 'calls us to conversion.' We might be reading his book, but Augustine indicates that it is another Book that is reading us, reinterpreting us to ourselves according to the measure of the Logos made flesh. In imitation of St. Paul, who had begotten him through Scripture (1 Cor. 4:15; Gal. 4:19), Augustine proposes to beget others through the Incarnate Word (*Conf.*, XIII.xxii.332).

Not surprisingly, Joyce counters this textual strategy. Stephen recognizes no anterior Logos, no authoritative word other than his own. He posits, like Nietzsche (60), the 'creative, willing, evaluating Ego' as 'the measure and value of things.' Sanctioned by his attempt to discover a mode of life or art whereby he could express himself in unfettered freedom, Stephen emerges as the prime specimen of the self-sufficient individual whose ambition is to beget a new race in his own image and likeness: 'How could he hit their conscience or how cast his shadow over the imaginations of their daughters, before their squires begat upon them, that they might breed a race less ignoble than their own?' (*Portrait*, 238). He hopes the record of his apostasy in his own text will redound on others. Ironically, his inability to communicate with anyone in Ireland results in 'the internally persuasive discourse' (Bakhtin 342) of his monologic diary; he can only engage in what Matthew Arnold (445) had called 'the dialogue of the mind with itself.'

Stephen, then, acts as a dialogic counterpoint to the repentant sinner, refusing to play the role of Augustine to his mother's Monica:

24 *March*: Began a discussion with my mother. . . . [S]he said I would come back to faith because I had a restless mind. This means to leave church by backdoor of sin and reenter through the skylight of repentance. Cannot repent. (*Portrait*, 248)

Hardened in this Faustian attitude, Stephen deconstructs the key text of the prodigal son parable so that it effectively reads, 'you are not worthy to be my father.' The exclamation of Faustus's pride, 'I disdain to own any parents,' nourishes his Freudian desire to beget himself; he is both Dedalus and Icarus, is himself, as R.B. Kershner (618) says, the 'old father' whose aid he invokes at the end of *A Portrait*.

Can any man be his own maker? This overwhelming question continually haunts Augustine's imagination (*Conf.*, I.vi.26). The exegesis of Genesis with which he ends his book represents a final excursus on the subject, a figurative return to origins which is acted out in the *Confessions* at large. Augustine identifies himself throughout with the human race, considering himself no more than a type: a fallen Adam, a prodigal son on his way back to the Father. By acknowledging his derivation from the only One who can be conceived of as His own beginning, Augustine's personal narrative itself returns to its linguistic origins in the primal Word of Sacred Scripture.

The autonomous artist, on the other hand, considers himself an individual *sui generis* since, according to Stephen in *Ulysses*, paternity is nothing more than a legal fiction. From the earliest narrative time possible, the fairy-tale opening of *A Portrait* read by his father, to the personal diary ending read by himself, Stephen has the first and last word, acting as the ultimate interpreter of his own discourse. Whether as baby tuckoo or as a born-again Dedalus, he exhibits a need for influence which eventually compels him to personally appropriate and subvert biblical typology. Cranly can therefore be both John the Baptist and Judas, just as Stephen can be a Gnostic Christ who falls in love with his mirror image, Satan. Stephen's eisagesis of his secular scripture allows him to invoke his mythical father, but this return to origins leads not to solidarity with his race but to separation from it since he metaphorically returns to himself. As Robert M. Adams (114) noted some time ago, 'Narcissus presides over almost all phases of Stephen's career.' Or, to put it another way, he becomes the 'archetype, not of the poet as such,' to apply Auden's insight (214), 'but of the poet who loses his soul for poetry . . . Narcissus.'

During a moment of critical self-reflection in *Ulysses* (34), this poet hears a voice mocking his aspirations, 'Cousin Stephen, you will never be a saint.' Joyce's response to this kind of self-mockery was to paint, like Gauguin, a *Self-Portrait with a Halo*, or what might be called a hagiography of the sinner. For he knew that the modern writer whose life most resembled Augustine's was, as he once expressed it in a notebook (cited in Ellmann 495), 'Eliot: Bishop of Hippo.' And Joyce himself? I suggest it would be more accurate to think of him striving, as his brother Stanislaus (*Complete Dublin Diary*, 3) had predicted, to become 'the Rousseau of Ireland'.*

---

*Interestingly, Mary Colum (185), one of Joyce's friends, also linked the two writers: 'Like Rousseau, Joyce derived everything from his ego. . . . [L]ike Rousseau, he has a passion not only for revealing himself, but for betraying himself; like him also, he deforms everything he touches.'

Works Cited

Adams, Robert M. *James Joyce: Common Sense and Beyond.* New York: Random House, 1966.

Arnold, Matthew. Preface to *Poems* (1853) in *Criticism: The Major Texts*, ed. Walter Jackson Bate. New York: Harcourt Brace Jovanovich, 1970.

Auden, W.H. 'Poetry as a Game of Knowledge,' in *The Modern Tradition*, ed. Richard Ellmann and Charles Feidelson, Jr. New York: Oxford University Press, 1965. 209–14.

Augustine. *Confessions*, trans. R.S. Pine-Coffin. Harmondsworth: Penguin Books, 1984.

——. *Enarrationes in Psalmos*, quoted by Marcia L. Colish.

——. *On Christian Doctrine*, trans. D.W. Robertson Jr. New York: Liberal Arts Press, 1958.

Bakhtin, M. *The Dialogic Imagination: Four Essays*, ed. Michael Holquist, trans. Caryl Emerson and Michael Holquist. Austin: University of Texas Press, 1980.

Blake, William. 'Illustrations to Dante's *Inferno*' in *The Portable Blake*, ed. A. Kazin. New York: Viking, 1968.

Barthes, Roland. *The Pleasure of the Text*, trans. Richard Miller. New York: Hill and Wang, 1975.

Burke, Kenneth. *Language as Symbolic Action.* Berkeley: University of California Press, 1968.

Colish, Marcia L. *The Mirror of Language*, rev. ed. Lincoln and London: University of Nebraska Press, 1983.

Colum, Mary. 'The Confessions of James Joyce,' *Freeman*, July 19, 1922. Quoted in Marvin Magalaner and Richard M. Kain, *Joyce: the Man, the Work, the Reputation.* New York: Collier, 1962.

Curran, C.P. *James Joyce Remembered.* London: Oxford University Press, 1968.

Ellmann, Richard. *James Joyce*, rev. ed. Oxford: Oxford University Press, 1982.

Fowles, John. 'Notes on an Unfinished Novel' in *The Novel Today*, ed. Malcolm Bradbury. Totowa: Rowan and Littlefield, 1978. 137.

Freccero, John. 'Dante's Prologue Scene,' *Dante Studies*, LXXIV (1966): 12–19.

——. 'Introduction' to *Dante: A Collection of Essays*, ed. John Freccero. Englewood Cliffs: Prentice-Hall, 1965.

Gadamer, Hans-Georg. *Philosophical Hermeneutics*, ed. David E. Linge. Berkeley: University of California Press, 1976.

Harkness, Marguerite. 'The Separate Roles of *Language* and *Word* in James Joyce's *Portrait*,' *Irish Renaissance Annual IV*, ed. Zach Bowen. London: Associated University Presses, 1983. 94–109.

Harpham, Geoffrey Galt. 'Conversion and the Language of Autobiography' in *Studies in Autobiography*, ed. James Olney. New York: Oxford University Press, 1988. 42–50.

Joyce, James. *A Portrait of the Artist as a Young Man*, ed. Chester G. Anderson. New York: Viking, 1977.

——— . 'James Clarence Mangan' in *The Critical Writings of James Joyce*, ed. Ellsworth Mason and Richard Ellmann. New York: Viking, 1959. 73–83.

——— . *The Letters of James Joyce*, vol. II, ed. Richard Ellmann. London: Faber and Faber, 1966.

——— . 'Mr. Arnold Graves' New Work' in *The Critical Writings of James Joyce*, ed. Ellsworth Mason and Richard Ellmann. New York: Viking, 1959. 126–27.

——— . *Stephen Hero*. London: Jonathan Cape, 1969.

——— . *Ulysses*. Harmondsworth: Penguin, 1986.

Joyce, Stanislaus. *The Complete Dublin Diary of Stanislaus Joyce*, ed. George H. Healey. Ithaca and London: Cornell University Press, 1971.

Kershner, R.B., Jr. 'Time and Language in Joyce's *Portrait of the Artist*,' *ELH* 43 (1976): 604–19.

Lanham, Jon. 'The Genre of A Portrait of the Artist as a Young Man and "the rhythm of its structure," ' *Genre* 10 (1977): 77–101.

Lawrence, Karen. *The Odyssey of Style in Ulysses*. Princeton: Princeton University Press, 1981.

MacMurray, John. *The Self as Agent*. London: Faber and Faber, 1969.

Nietzsche, F. *Thus Spake Zarathustra*. Harmondsworth: Penguin, 1971.

Raleigh, John Henry. '*Ulysses*: Trinitarian and Catholic' in *Joyce's Ulysses: The Larger Perspective*, ed. Robert D. Newman and Weldon Thornton. Newark: University of Delaware Press, 1987. 98–122.

Riquelme, John Paul. *Teller and Tale in Joyce's Fiction: Oscillating Perspectives*. Baltimore and London: Johns Hopkins, 1983.

Rogers, Carl and Stevens, Barry. *Person to Person*. 1967. Cited in Paul C. Vitz, *Psychology as Religion: The Cult of Self-Worship*. Grand Rapids: Eerdmans, 1977.

Rubin, Louis D. *The Teller in the Tale*. Seattle: University of Washington Press, 1967.

Stirner, Max. *The Ego and His Own*, trans. Steven T. Byinton. New York: Dover, 1973.

Swinburne, A. 'Hertha' in *Victorian and Later English Poets*, ed. James Stephens. New York: American Book Company, 1949.

West, Rebecca. *The Strange Necessity: Essays*. Garden City, N.J.: Doubleday Doran, 1928.

Wilde, Oscar. *Selected Letters of Oscar Wilde*, ed. Rupert Hart-Davis. Oxford: Oxford University Press, 1979.

Wright, T.R. *Theology and Literature*. Oxford: Basil Blackwell, 1988.

No-Man's-Land
Beckett's Bilingualism as Autobiography

Ann Beer

In 1982 a London reviewer of the novella *Company* pointed out how strangely Samuel Beckett, an Irish author, had shaped his artistic life. Beckett wrote in both English and French, alternating, in his later years, between the two languages. The reviewer, George Craig, said:

> Even if French-speakers could read him only in French and English-speakers only in English, there would still be one person inescapably aware of his double venture: Samuel Beckett. . . . The signs are that he is exploring a verbal no-man's-land where neither French nor English holds sway. (921)

A verbal no-man's-land: what better description could there be for Beckett's refusal to take refuge in certainties of any kind, his construction in language of the painful and yet formative tensions of his Irish experience? The context for these tensions is clear: there must have been a wide gap between Beckett's early years as a privileged Protestant in Dublin and the existence of that city's many poor Catholic families. Beckett lived in an elegant suburb on the fringes of the city; they survived, or tried to, in decaying and over-crowded tenements. Self-definition, Beckett's career suggests, was a strange process for a sheltered adolescent in a world of tennis and tea-parties, surrounded by a city and country collapsing into civil war.

'A man's life-work is his fullest autobiography,' James Olney has said (3). In Beckett's case, to a remarkable degree, the life's work actually provides a direct meditation on the life, and even seems to shape the direction of that life. None of this writing, though, is explicitly called autobiography. Beckett blurs the line between fiction and personal history to such a point that distinguishing between them becomes impossible. 'Qu'y-a-t-il de vrai dans ce babil?' ('What truth is there in all this babble?') asks Malone in *Malone meurt*, one of the post-war trilogy of novels written in French (115). But he continues, 'Je crois seulement que je ne peux rien dire qui ne soit vrai . . . ' ('I simply believe I can say

nothing that is not true') (*Malone Dies*, 236). The translation is
Beckett's own. The English version, with its strongly Irish idioms
and rhythms, makes an equally 'true' fiction in another language, a
language Beckett abandoned and then returned to.

As Beckett shifted to and from French, and self-translated, did
he ever ponder the ironies of his position? Was he struck by the
paradox of an Irishman born into a country of two languages, English and the ancient Celtic tongue it had supplanted, making his
own oblique statement about Ireland's constant sense of Otherness? No doubt he did, though he refused to discuss it directly in
any depth. Instead, it emerges in his writing. 'There's no account-
ing for it . . . ,' says the speaker of *From an Abandoned Work*, 'with
a mind like the one I always had, always on the alert against itself' (131). Bilingualism and biculturalism, a sense of doubleness
or shifting perspectives, pervade every Beckett line. Each of his
fictional voices struggles with a distrust of language and yet con-
tributes, somehow, to one of many forms of truth.

John Montague evokes the ancestry of doubleness in *The Rough
Field*: 'To grow / a second tongue, as / harsh a humiliation / as
twice to be born' (39). Beckett's awareness of this Irish experience
pervades his drama, poetry and prose: language is both a snare and
a delight, never to be trusted and the only possible support. It can
be a very real form of suffering, as well as the means of articulating
suffering. Hardly surprising, then, is Beckett's remark in the 1960s
to Peter Lennon, 'I have never had a single untroubled moment in
my entire life' (22). Peter Hall, confirming this in a 1991 radio interview for the Canadian Broadcasting Corporation's program *Ideas*,
spoke of Beckett as a 'a troubled spirit.'

Beckett moved into a no-man's-land of his own making, his id-
iosyncratic response to the bilingual and bicultural tensions of his
native land. Although it may not have seemed deliberate at the
time, the pattern of his decisions, seen in retrospect, had a relentless clarity. He chose to study French at Trinity College, chose to
go to Europe, first for long visits and then permanently, chose even
to live in France in World War II rather than return to the safety of
the Irish Republic. He also chose, after the war, to write in French,
though the chances of gaining an audience in that language must
have seemed, at the time, remote. But later in his maturity he
felt free, finally, to use his native tongue, and even to revel in its
richness.

Beckett's no-man's-land can be explored in several ways. First,
the concept as it is used in time of war. War had a great impact
on Beckett's life, yet it is often ignored, even by the more bio-
graphically inclined of his critics. This is perhaps because Beckett

himself almost never refers to real wars explicitly. Yet his writing is full of injured, handicapped, and traumatized people. He shows a revulsion against the causes of war: nationalism, political and religious ideologies, territorial greed, colonialism. His commitment is to the victims of such conflicts, and has an almost medieval quality of fatalism and austere compassion. He worked to free himself from those loyalties that, in opposing each other, lead so easily to killing. Consistently he mocked complacency and pride — nationalist fervour in *Watt* and *Mercier and Camier*, bourgeois comforts in *Molloy*, the landed class in *Godot*, religious clichés in *All That Fall*. He himself lived for many years in self-imposed exile, poverty and even, in wartime, danger. Fame and prosperity came late to Beckett, well after his fortieth year. The pattern of needing privacy and simplicity had been set, as had the absolute refusal to be pulled back into the rhetoric of any one country or group.

A second perspective on no-man's-land is the space between ideological poles where so many Beckett characters live. Beckett's imagination led him to a vividly real landscape, a landscape of the human mind. It also, at times, resembles the bare, remote wastes and rocks of Ireland as they appear in the plays of Yeats and Synge: a good place for hermits and wanderers, for anyone seeking anonymity. By abandoning most of the co- ordinates, the superficial certainties, of the middle-class Anglo-Irish community he was born into, Beckett established a position from which he could travel through human experience directly.

A third and final perspective puts the emphasis in the term no-man's-land on *no man*. Beckett made an extraordinary contribution to questions of gender. In the 1990s it is at last becoming possible to gain a historical perspective on his appreciation of stereotyping (of men, as well as of women) and its effects. Androgyny and an escape from traditional sexual and social roles mark out a special kind of no-man's-land. With outrageous humour, energy and, at times, deliberate obscenity, Beckett's female and male characters insist on having a voice, on telling stories that construct their own truth. They also explore, as many writers on gender are now doing, a 'both-and' rather than 'either-or' approach to knowledge, leaving dualism behind. Gender polarization, as damaging as the polarization of class, race and religion, falls apart. No-man's-land becomes all people's land.

But the core and starting point remain what Thomas McGreevy, in a youthful phase of Left Bank enthusiasm, which he later disowned, called a 'strife-ridden, little town in the lesser of two . . . not very important islands off the coast of Europe and civilisation' (254). Ireland's marginalized, colonized and fragmented status has

often been seen as the key to its nurturing of so many major writers. Synge, Yeats, Joyce, O'Casey, Beckett, all bear the marks of the
impact of English as a colonizing language, invading a rich and profoundly different culture. This, too, can be seen in gender terms:
the extremely patriarchal culture of Beckett's Protestant ancestry
invading the more matricentric culture of a country that still had
links with a Celtic past.

Recently a Canadian poet of Caribbean background, Marlene
Nourbese Philip, has spoken of her relationship with the English
she was forced to learn at school in an evocative phrase: 'Queenglish
and Kinglish — the anguish that is english in colonial societies' (26).
In his self-determined exile from a privileged Protestant life in southern Ireland Beckett seems to have looked for an escape from the
Queenglish and Kinglish he was supposed to uphold.

Warring Certainties

I: 'No-man's-land: the area on a battlefield separating two com-
   batants.'

Wilfred Owen wrote: 'My subject is War, and the pity of War. The
Poetry is in the pity' (137). World War I, like the other wars of
this technological century, ripped away the superficial rationalism
of Western civilization. It exposed human brutality and pain in their
raw form. Beckett was eight years old when the so-called 'Great
War' began (as Paul Durcan says: 'O what made it Great? O save
us O Lord from Greatness' (99)). Beckett was ten at the time of the
Easter Rising in Dublin, and an adolescent and young man during
the Civil War years and their aftermath. His was a difficult, ambigu-
ous standpoint. As a product of Portora Royal School in Northern
Ireland, of Trinity College and the Church of Ireland, he should have
known clearly where he stood: a bastion of the dominant class, with
strong ties to mainland Britain. Yet he was Irish, not English. He
told Clancy Sigal that in London in the 1930s he was mocked and
called Paddy (because of his accent) by prejudiced Londoners who
assumed he was what they thought of as a typical Irishman. The
dislocation seems to have been extreme.

He had no nationalism which could be easily defined, and spoke
of one of his artistic idols, Jack Yeats, with a vehement refusal to
bring that artist and Irish nationalist fervour together: 'The Island
is not throttled into Ireland, nor the City into Dublin', he wrote of
Jack Yeats's novel *The Amaranthers* ('An Imaginative Work!', 90).
Later he claimed that 'The national aspects of Mr. Yeats's genius
have, I think, been over-stated' (*McGreevy on Yeats*, 96) when

reviewing his old friend McGreevy's highly patriotic discussion of Yeats as Ireland's national painter.

How much better, in such circumstances, for a young man to leave the dilemma behind altogether and move among the almost nationless expatriates of the Parisian artistic scene. The magazine *transition*, in which sections of *Finnegans Wake* were first published, symbolized the determination of youthful intellectuals of that time to get away from the nationalist excesses which they saw as having led to the war. *transition's* founder and editor, Eugene Jolas, who had a mixed French/American background, wrote:

> In the little border town of Lorraine, where French and German civilizations sought and fled each other in a ceaseless tension, I spent my childhood before the World War dreaming escape from the millenary struggle of languages and races. (243)

The answer to that millenary struggle seemed to be to bring languages and perspectives into a vortex, mingling them all. Joyce's multilingual masterpiece was hailed as the beginning of a new age.

Yet by the Second World War everything had, apparently, changed. Two of the countries whose literatures and cultures Beckett loved, Germany and Italy, had moved to Fascism and were suddenly on a distinctly 'wrong' side. France wavered and fell; the Irish Republic chose neutrality while the North was plunged into the British war effort. Beckett, by now living in Paris and with a French partner, who later became his wife, joined the Resistance and later escaped to the south when the unit was betrayed to the Gestapo. Many of his friends were Jews, others were Catholic French hostile to German dominance. In these years, without doubt the central influence on the direction of Beckett's post-war writing, he could at last live out a loyalty — to his friends — that demanded great sacrifices but in no way forced him to take sides in an Irish conflict.

The manuscript of *Watt*, now safely if somewhat incongruously housed in Texas, reveals this inner trouble vividly. The manuscript is more than twice as long as the printed novel *Watt*, and is dated like a journal over several years. It was begun in Paris in 1941, and accompanied Beckett on his escape to the southern town of Roussillon, where he spent the remaining years of the war. The manuscript is an outflowing of comic energy with a desperate edge, at times branching off into private reflection. It repeatedly returns to the characters who were eventually named Watt and Knott, but also reflects a good deal on 'Sam', who figures as the narrator, somewhat unreliably, in the printed text. The novel draws almost entirely on Beckett's Irish memories, and his responses to contrasting images of Irish life. From the Grants Committee, in what is obviously a comic version of Trinity College, to the prolific Lynch family and its endless children, and the ancient Irish speaker whom Louit finds in the Burren, it revels in the extremes of a divided culture which Beckett had to leave before he could see it whole. The darker elements, however, reflect more deeply on the horrors of war and civil unrest which never surface directly. The bewildered Watt, childlike and vulnerable, exists in a world where anything may happen when you step outside the walls of the home, the rigid patterns and routines of the Knott establishment. Out on the road, you are at the mercy of all comers.

At the end of the war, Beckett became part of an Irish Red Cross Hospital crew working in Normandy in the ruins of a town called Saint-Lô. In a radio broadcast for Radio Eireann in 1946 Beckett was at last able to use the pronoun 'us' about an Irish group that included both Catholics and Protestants. Irish doctors, nurses and support staff worked in unity to help in the reconstruction of a war-ravaged country. Beckett praises both the Irish and the French, working together in difficult conditions, and excuses any misunderstandings by adding, in a poignantly simple statement: 'It is only fair to say that many of us had never been abroad before' (75).

One of Beckett's most emotionally open poems of the period, 'Mort de A.D.' grieves for an Irish Catholic friend, Dr. Arthur Darden, who, as doctor, became the first terminally ill patient in the hospital Beckett had helped to provision. Beckett speaks of his friend 'devouring the lives of the saints, one life for each day of his life, (. . .) (who) died yesterday while I was living. . . .' (54, my translation). There is tremendous compassion for this devout Catholic's own approach to dying, however alien to the poet's own culture. Friendship, grief and love prove stronger than difference.

Waiting for Godot and *Molloy* spring from a realization of human vulnerability that is centred in physical awareness. During these years Beckett witnessed people dying, being wounded, losing everything they had, or taking to the roads in a vain search for safety. He saw severe physical pain and mental distress, and learned what it meant for whole towns to be destroyed and humans reduced to crawling, digging in mud for food. His most savage, and for many readers most difficult work, *How It Is* (1959–60), draws on this grim vision. Once again, a deeper historical level of reference is present, for someone born in a country where war and territorial expansion had led to so much famine, slaughter and pain.

His sense of combat focused, then, not on the self-belief and power of the opposing forces, but on the reality of those caught in between. Like Wilfred Owen, he wrote 'not about heroes.' His own uneasy position, between Irish and British life, his consciousness of the dividedness of Irish experience, make him an extraordinary kind of realist. Yet he dedicated the short play *Catastrophe*, in 1983, to Vaclav Havel, then a political prisoner in a savage ideological state. This gesture demonstrated that Beckett had not lost the idealism that can still exist beyond acceptance of 'how it is.' Havel's sudden elevation from prisoner to President, shortly before Beckett's death, is oddly appropriate to Beckett's almost medieval worldview. Like Pozzo and Lucky, anyone can change places in the game of power.

For Beckett, the polarizing tendencies of war and other conflicts, the oppositions of races and languages, could have only one solution: a retreat into an imaginatively defined inner space in which coherence was possible. As Malone, one of the most autobiographical protagonists, promises: 'I will not weigh upon the balance any more, one way or the other. I shall be neutral and inert. No difficulty there' (179).

The Space Between

II: 'No-man's-land: a tract or district to which no one can lay a recognised or established claim.'

When audiences or readers claim not to 'understand' Beckett, they are reacting with a healthy human impulse. Beckett is famous for his remark that he wanted to empty the theatre in which his drama was performed. Many people resist the extreme introspection which Beckett's characters indulge in; the reaction may also be a way of denying the menace of mortality, the tragicomic decay of a life, which Beckett insists on. His no-man's-land becomes a place in which only language, physical processes and memory hold sway. On one level it is full of a kind of religious seriousness, like that of Job or Bunyan's Christian. Yet Beckett's protagonists also laugh at themselves and at the world from their private, nameless space:

> That I am not stone deaf is shown by the sounds that reach me. For though the silence here is almost unbroken, it is not completely so. I remember the first sound heard in this place, I have often heard it since. For I am obliged to assign a beginning to my residence here, if only for the sake of clarity. Hell itself, although eternal, dates from the revolt of Lucifer. It is therefore permissible, in the light of this distant analogy, to think of myself as being here forever, but not as having been here forever. This will greatly help me in my relation. (*The Unnamable*, 297–98)

The Irish monastic tradition, the figures of legend and song who sought some absolute good in solitude, stand beside other traditions of introspection, English and French, in this relentless pursuit of self-awareness. What is remarkable in Beckett is that the search for solitude is a theme from beginning to end, though in deeper and deeper ways. It finds focus in his early years in a fascination with Dante and medieval Christianity, and reaches right through to *Company* and *Worstward Ho* fifty years later. In 'Dream of Fair to Middling Women,' Beckett's first, and still unpublished, novel, this is how the hero Belacqua finds temporary relief from both hetero- and homosexual difficulties, and from the problems with money and art that beset him:

> He moved with the shades of the dead and the dead-born and the unborn and the never to be born, in a Limbo purged of desire. . . .
> The mind, dim and hushed like a sick-room, like a chapelle ardente, thronged with shades; the mind at last its own asylum, disinterested, indifferent. ('Dream', 38–39)

Murphy, an Irish exile in London, sees his mind 'not as an instrument but as a place' (123). The speaker of *Le Calmant*, *The Calmative*, says: 'Nous sommes, bien sur, dans une tête' (57), 'we are, of course, in a head.' In *Endgame*, the entire stage can be seen as the shape of a skull, with its two high windows looking out on a devastated world. *Worstward Ho* actually seems to have descended to the level of the syntactic processes and the grey matter within the brain, the 'soft' or 'ooze' (46, 38).

Beckett's no-man's-land is a refuge from the world and a place from which to understand that world better. As his work expanded more and more into theatre and as he gained a large reading public, consequences of his sudden fame as the author of *Waiting for Godot*, he seems to have needed his mental refuge even more. Living in France, often in his country home that looked out on 'the Marne mud' where so many had died in World War I, he was able, from the 1950s, to revel in an increasingly austere French and a distinctive Irish English of his own making. His habit of evading certainties, undercutting definitions, began to move into the structures of language itself, with 'tattered syntaxes' moving his enquiry to ever more basic levels of expression.

He also began to play with his own critics and biographers. Deirdre Bair's controversial biography appeared in 1978. It aroused fury among many of Beckett's close friends, but provided his public with a vivid background and details that had not before been unearthed. In *Company*, Beckett responds to the threat, or the experience, of being misrepresented by deliberately using some of the

same well-known autobiographical fragments that Bair's biography
contains — such as the story of how he used to throw himself out of
a garden tree in childhood:
Here is Bair:

> One of Sam's favorite games was to climb to the top of one of
> the pine trees that towered over the house and to throw himself
> down, arms and legs spread-eagled, willing himself to fly, until
> the very end of his free-fall, when he hoped fervently that one
> of the broad lower branches would stop him before he slammed
> into the ground. (15)

And here is Beckett:

> You climb to near the top of a great fir. You sit a little listening
> to all the sounds. Then throw yourself off. The great boughs
> break your fall. The needles. You lie a little with your face to the
> ground. Then climb the tree again. (28)

Another dimension of the self comments:

> What with what feeling remains does he feel about now as com-
> pared to then? When with what judgement remained he judged
> his condition final. . . . (29)

He is outdoing his biographer at her own game, claiming back, in
a metaphorical, song-like prose of great beauty, the right to speak
of what is his. In his private realm, that of the voice in the dark,
he takes back what could only be distorted by being placed in a
sequential, speculative and external account of a so-called 'real' life.

Beckett's artistic retreat into an increasingly deep imaginative
space, his development in theatre of a stage more and more free of
props or worldly details, represent an apt response to the troubles
he was born to. He found a way to throw off the marked character of
his early Irish years in which his name, address, accent, education,
church and daily lifestyle all marked him out as one distinct side
of an 'either/or' kind of balance. Paul Durcan's poem, 'What is a
Protestant, Daddy?' captures the classification and the stereotype
from the side of a Catholic child brought up in the other camp:

> Gaiters were sinister
> And you dared not
> Glance up at the visage;
> It was a long lean visage
> With a crooked nose
> And beaked dry lips
> And streaky grey hair
> . . .

Protestants were Martians,
Light years more weird
Than zoological creatures;
But soon they would all go away
For as a species they were dying out,
Soon there would be no more Protestants . . .
O Yea, O Lord,
I was a proper little Irish Catholic boy
Way back in the 1950s. (59–60)

In *All That Fall*, written in 1956, Beckett finally gives a clue to the much changed historical position of Church of Ireland Protestants of his own kind. This radio play revels in a comic yet menacing sense of Irish culture in a south Dublin setting. It includes a character who, as a young Protestant in a more and more Catholic country, has retreated into religious isolation, 'Alone with (her) Maker' (20). Her name is Miss Fitt. As a misfit himself, Beckett was at last making a direct reference to his family's, and particularly his mother's, church. Miss Fitt retreated into religion, Beckett into exile and introspection. But language could bring both Miss Fitt and Beckett's word-obsessed protagonists, male and female, back to some level of community. By the time of the writing of *Company*, in the late 1970s, imagined journeys to 'Nowhere in particular' shift back to a precise piece of Ireland for which Beckett could at last show his affection, the road behind his Foxrock home:

> Nowhere in particular on the way from A to Z. Or say for verisimil-
> itude the Ballyogan Road. That dear old back road. . . . (30)

From the safety of no-man's-land naming becomes possible once again.

All-People's Land

III: 'No-man's-land: a region which is the subject of dispute between two parties; debatable land.'

Having considered Beckett's no-man's-land through the ideas of outer conflict and inner meditative space, I would like to finish with a third perspective: the no-man's-land between the 'cultures' of men and of women in the Irish context. Beckett anticipated many contemporary concerns that are surfacing in Ireland with the force of a subterranean river finally released, as the election of the Republic's new President, Mary Robinson, suggests.

His early work shows an uneasiness about women. They seem often to be threats to the sensitive consciousness of the retiring young hero who feels more comfortable with male friends, books and drink. For Belacqua and Murphy, almost all respectable women are horrors, on the rampage for sex, money and husbands. But in general male consciousness is central, and women are not shown in depth, with the notable exception of the loving prostitute, Celia, in *Murphy*. It had become almost a cliche of Bohemian life that prostitutes were the only sympathetic women, uninhibited and able to live for the moment. This was, of course, a decidedly male perspective.

In the middle period, women disappear from view almost altogether; *Watt, Mercier and Camier, Godot, Molloy, Malone, The Unnamable*, are almost entirely male in their voices and cast of characters. Yet these works explore a kind of character who exhibits few if any features of traditional masculine authority. On the contrary, the central figures are extremely androgynous, beyond the pale of middle-class patterns of behaviour.

From the 1950s, however, Beckett's curiosity about gender, or his sense of the artistic potential of a new direction, surfaced. For some critics and psychologists, the death of his own, apparently very dominant, mother in 1950 gave him a crucial release. His writing from then on illustrates an increasing sensitivity to gender-stereotyping as a powerful, because still unseen, form of dualistic control, a barrier to freedom. Although he was not close to Simone de Beauvoir, he did inhabit the same intellectual milieu in Paris in which her massive and influential work, *Le Deuxième Sexe* (*The Second Sex*), had appeared in 1949. He also met other women, artists and intellectuals, who challenged stereotypes of every kind.

In Beckett's own plays and prose, women begin to take on the role of central voice, defining and expressing love, jealousy, fear, and above all the urge to express. In *Happy Days, Footfalls, Not I, Rockaby* and *Ill Seen Ill Said*, a woman holds centre stage, and in each case her awareness, savage humour, stoicism or pain is remarkable. In *Not I*, for example, a red glistening mouth high on the stage frantically tries to make sense of a woman's life, struggling to speak in the third person. Neglected and traumatized in childhood, she has become one of those sad women of city streets. Here she recalls how she began to speak of her life at last:

> suddenly she realized . . . words were — . . . what? . . . who? . . . no! . . . she! . . . realized . . . words were coming . . . imagine! . . . words were coming . . . a voice she did not recognize . . . at first . . . so long since it had sounded . . . then finally had to admit . . . could be none other . . . than her own . . . (. . .) and now this stream . . . steady stream . . . she who had never . . . on the contrary . . . practically speechless . . . all her days . . . (219)

Not I is a devastating enactment of what can happen when a suppressed voice is finally heard. The history of colonized nations, as well as women's history, can be felt beyond this image.

Like two languages, two cultures, two religions, the two gender roles in Ireland have tended to be divided — at least in official rhetoric. Obviously everyday experience has never been so neat. But the Republic's position on contraception, abortion, and so-called immoral literature were for Beckett, who had written angrily about them in the 1920s and 1930s, symptoms of a profoundly imprisoning consciousness. So, in a sense, Beckett's readiness to understand recent gender studies had very early roots.

In the post-war works, sympathy extends to all who are at odds with patriarchal authority, or institutions that limit and control. The poor, the orphaned, artists, the old, those who fall foul of the police, all are in this sense part of a 'feminized' and dominated consciousness (women in official positions, of course, can also appear on the side of the patriarchs, upholding the values of authority). Androgynous qualities suggest a possible meeting in the centre.

In an exceptional passage in *Watt*, taken verbatim from Beckett's journal notebook, there is advance warning of this idea. He speaks of human consciousness as if even physical awareness may be shared between men and women, the 'prostate' and the 'ovaries' standing in for the whole body:

> To think, when one is no longer young, when one is not yet old, that one is no longer young, that one is not yet old, that is perhaps something. To pause, towards the end of one's three-hour day, and consider: the darkening ease, the brightening trouble; the pleasure pleasure because it was, the pain pain because it shall be. . . . And to decide not to smile after all, sitting in the shade, hearing the cicadas, wishing it were night, wishing it were morning, saying, No, it is not the heart, no, it is not the liver, no, it is not the prostate, no, it is not the ovaries. . . . (201)

The voice here is housed in a body that may be male or female. The pain it feels can be true for either.

The voice in *Not I*, that uncovers what had been repressed, has particular significance for Irish women writers today. As Eavan Boland, Medbh McGuckian and others are showing, female experience in Ireland has generally included significant considerable levels of silence or ambivalence. Real wisdom and experience were often shared only orally, with other women, if at all. In the public arena, women were not heard. Eavan Boland says of the idea of the Irish nation:

it has never admitted of women. Its flags and songs and battle-cries, even its poetry, (. . .) make use of feminine imagery. But that is all. The true voice and vision of women are routinely excluded. (54)

In a play like *Not I*, however, the voice sounds loud and clear.

Beckett's escape from an early life, shaped by polarized thinking in politics, gender and religion, gives force to his later assertions of freedom from these limits. In one of his late works, the wordless television play, *Quad* (1982), the four cloaked players, who move with ghost-like grace across the stage, can be either male or female. Beckett's directions include the lines: 'Players: As alike in build as possible. Some ballet training desirable. Sex indifferent.' This shows a further stage of the logic of no-man's-land. Having explored both male and female consciousness, he finally appeals to our imagination in a space between defined genders, allowing experience to be shared: Sex indifferent.

The tribalism that has often been noted in Irish history, from the Celtic period onwards, finds a strange response in Beckett's work. His restlessness, geographically, linguistically, and psychologically, marks the imagination of one who could not stay comfortably within tribal divisions of any kind. By constructing his no-man's-land, he could see the world and express it honestly. It is worth remembering that Beckett spent a total of less than thirty years of his long life in Ireland, and more than fifty years in France and elsewhere. Yet the Irish years are, of course, crucial because they were those of childhood, education and his self-definition as an artist. Moreover, Joyce, whom Beckett described as the central moral influence on his art, had shown Beckett a path he could follow; seeing Ireland whole by living beyond its borders. Through his long years as an expatriate his work shows a sensitivity to conflict, insisting that simply being human is more important than sectarian difference. The question of whether or not he can be 'claimed' by either Ireland or France — his status in each being based on the texts in that country's dominant language — is an insoluble one. Like so many in the Irish literary tradition, he drew deeply on European schools of thought and literary movements as well as those from the home tradition. I have met English and Irish people who are sure *En attendant Godot* was first written in English, and French-speaking people convinced that

Happy Days was written in French. Both are wrong, but under-standably so; Beckett has provided his own double texts and left us to puzzle out their implications.

It is fitting, for a man so determined not to be trapped, in his life or in his work, that he kept an Irish passport to the end. A passport has a satisfying ambiguity too. It is, for travellers, the document that allows you to get out of a country, something Beckett needed to do. But it is also the official text, the mark of identity, that insists that you still belong.

Works Cited

Bair, Deirdre. *Samuel Beckett: A Biography.* New York and London: Harcourt Brace Jovanovitch, 1978.

Beckett, Samuel. *All That Fall.* London: Faber and Faber, 1957/1965.

—— . *The Capital of the Ruins* (radio broadcast). Radio Eireann, June 1946. First published in *As No Other Dare Fail: For Samuel Beckett on his Eightieth Birthday.* London: John Calder, 1986. 71–76.

—— . *Le Calmant in Nouvelles et textes pour rien.* Paris: Les Éditions de Minuit, 1958. 39–69.

—— . *Company.* London: John Calder, 1980.

—— . 'Dream of Fair to Middling Women.' Unpublished. Corrected type-script in Baker Memorial Library, Dartmouth College, New Hamp-shire. Copy used: photocopy of this typescript in Reading University Library, England. Ms No. 1227/7/16/8.

—— . *From an Abandoned Work in Collected Shorter Prose 1945–1980,* London: John Calder, 1984. 129–37.

—— . *McGreevy on Yeats in Disjecta.* London: John Calder, 1983. 95–97.

—— . 'An Imaginative Work!' in *Disjecta.* London: John Calder, 1983. 89–90.

—— . *Malone Dies in Molloy, Malone Dies, The Unnamable.* London: Calder and Boyars, 1959. 179–289.

—— . *Malone Meurt.* Paris: Les Éditions de Minuit, 1951.

—— . 'Mort de A.D.' in *Collected Poems in English and French.* London: John Calder, 1977. 54.

—— . *Murphy.* London: John Calder, 1969.

—— . *Not I in Collected Shorter Plays.* London: Faber and Faber, 1984. 214–23.

—— . *Quad in Collected Shorter Plays.* London, Faber and Faber, 1984. 289–94.

—— . *Watt.* London: John Calder, 1976.

—— . *Worstward Ho.* London: John Calder, 1983.

Boland, Eavan. 'Outside History.' *Brick: A Literary Journal,* 39 (Summer, 1990): 48–57.

Craig, George. 'The voice of childhood and great age.' *Times Literary Supplement*, August 27, 1982. 921.

Durcan, Paul. *The Selected Paul Durcan*, ed. Edna Longley. Belfast and Dover, New Hampshire: Blackstaff, 1982.

Hall, Peter. (radio interview) for 'A Stain upon the Silence.' *Ideas*, C.B.C. Radio, Canada. February 28, 1991.

Jolas, Eugene. 'Response to "Inquiry into the Spirit and Language of Night".' *transition*, 27 (April–May, 1938): 243.

Lennon, Peter. *The Guardian* (Review section), February 1, 1990. 21–22.

McGreevy, Thomas. 'James Joyce at the Half-Century.' *transition*, 21 (1932): 254–55.

Montague, John. *The Rough Field*. Dublin: Dolmen Press, 1972.

Nourbese Philip, Marlene. 'The Absence of Writing.' *Brick: A Literary Journal*, 39 (Summer, 1990): 26–33.

Olney, James. *Metaphors of Self*. Princeton: Princeton University Press, 1980.

Owen, Wilfred. *War Poems and Others*, ed. Dominic Hibberd. London: Chatto and Windus, 1973.

Sigal, Clancy. 'Is This the Person to Murder Me?' *Sunday Times* (Magazine), March 1, 1964. 17–22.

The Circularity of
the Autobiographical Form
A Study of Seamus Heaney's 'Station Island'

Laura O'Connor

I want to open my discussion on *Station Island* with a quotation from George Gusdorf's essay 'Conditions and Limits of Autobiography':

> Every autobiography is a work of art and at the same time a work of enlightenment; it does not show us the individual seen from outside in his visible actions but the person in his inner privacy, not as he was, not as he is, but as he believes and wishes himself to be and to have been. What is in question is a sort of revaluation of individual destiny: the author, who is at the same time the hero of the tale, wants to elucidate his past in order to draw out the structure of his being in time. And this secret structure is for him the implicit condition of all possible knowledge in every order whatsoever — hence the special place of autobiography, especially in the literary spheres. (Olney 45)

One's life, one's life-narratives, and often one's work, are guided and shaped by one's 'secret structure' or characteristic mode of creating coherence. Drawing out this distinctive structuring mechanism, the matrix of personality, is the true subject of autobiography.

Like Gusdorf, Heaney's primary critical objective is to draw out the 'secret structure' of the poet's style. He traces his precursors' characteristic music to their 'instinctual ballast' and in a fascinating essay in *Preoccupations*, argues that Wordsworth's music of complaisance conforms to the rhythms of his rolling gait back and forth along the gravel path; that Yeats's music of control evolves from the deliberate selection of one amongst several possible assured voices; and asserts that 'certain postures and motions within the poet's incubating mind affect the posture of the voice and the motion of the rhythms in the language of the poem itself' (61). I wish to draw upon Gusdorf's and Heaney's critical insights to argue, as a brief review of Heaney's works attests, that the dominant motion in his 'incubating mind' is a circular one.

Heaney's synthetic-creative impulse is one of centring and pen-
etration. He recalls the magnetic hold exercised upon his childhood
imagination by a hand-water pump he identifies as an umbilical
omphalos, together with slimy wells, frogspawn, and bog-holes.
In 'Digging' (1966) he famously inaugurated his career with a re-
solve to dig such sources with his pen; in North (1975), he sank
shafts in the preservative bog to recover symbolic icons of tribal
warfare, reflecting the cylindrical shape of the enterprise in the ty-
pographical form of the poems: 'those thin small quatrain poems,
they're kind of drills or augurs for turning in and they are long and
narrow and deep' (Corcoran 108). *Fieldwork* (1979) yields domestic images of harmony — the holism of craftsmanship in a round
harvest bow, or the transformation by the loving gaze of a vaccina-
tion mark into 'the sunflower, dreaming umber'. *The Haw Lantern*
(1987), presents a rose-shaped concentric place of 'Mud Vision,' and
the principal sonnet sequence, 'Clearances,' represents his mother's
death as a space emptied into those around her to keep. The sift-
ing for circular shapes extends to an analysis of language, of the
dialects of rounded Republic versus angular Ulster speech — 'Our
tongue strikes the tangent of the consonant rather more than it
rolls the circle of the vowel' (*Preoccupations*, 45) — and one senses
a vigilant sorting operation in Heaney's mind where words, images,
and objects are savoured for roundedness, much as a cherry might
be rolled in one's mouth. Given the predilection for circular forms
it comes as no surprise to note that a Celtic pattern of spirals and
circular interlacings adorns the dust-jacket of this recent edition of
Selected Poems.

The penitential ritual dramatizes the confessional-autobiograph-
ical act. Essential to confession or autobiography is a divide over
which a present self (I as subject) looks back upon the deeds of
a past self (I as object), and Starobinski argues that this radical

change or conversion provides the motive for autobiography (Olney 78). Seen from this perspective, *Station Island* might be viewed as recording a midlife crisis that separates the early from the mature poet, and it devolves upon the reader to ascertain the character of that conversion. The pilgrimage provides Heaney with an opportunity to practise his faith and examine his conscience. He neither renews nor revokes a commitment to orthodox Catholicism. He confronts his responsibility for past choices and failures, but accepts that he cannot hold himself responsible for everything: 'as if the cairnstone could defy the cairn' (XI, 206). Through a liberating acceptance of himself as he is, he expiates early sexual guilt, guilt about his good fortune as 'a poet, lucky poet' (VIII, 202), and the crushing sense of the inadequacy of his response to the conflict in Northern Ireland.

Issues of conformity and nonconformity, insider and exile, are accentuated by the circumscribed space of the island itself. It is both a microcosm of the claustrophobic pressures that exist in the larger island, Ireland, and a symbol of the stoic endurance of Catholics in a country where, to quote Heaney, Catholic 'is almost a racist term'. A penitential pilgrimage to Station Island, or St. Patrick's Purgatory, Lough Derg, Co. Donegal, involves three days' privation of food and sleep. Pilgrims circuit the island, in prayer and reparation, by walking barefoot on the circular stone beds, which were made from the stones of eighth century monks' beehive cells. Each station of the circuit, traditionally the locus for repenting one's sins and contemplating Christ's passion, becomes a locus for Heaney's persona to encounter shades from his past and re-evaluate significant choices in his life.

Heaney was first attracted to the Station Island locus by Dante, and he adopts the interlaced *terza rima* form and circling procedure of *The Divine Comedy*. It's worth mentioning as an aside that the pilgrimage, of European renown since the twelfth century because the island contained a cave believed to be the entrance to the Other World, was the subject of a Tractatus that reputedly influenced Dante (Picard and de Pontfarcy 9, 33). Station Island is a subject in Anglo-Irish writing by Carleton, Kavanagh, Devlin, and O'Faolain, and guided by a Virgilian Dante, Heaney, the individual talent, confronts the literary tradition as he encounters the shades of Carleton, Kavanagh, and Joyce.

The stone bed circuitings remind us of Wordsworthian walks in iambic pentameter and this physiological motion, together with ascetic privation, might be expected to influence the poet's style. Does the circumambulatory rhythm cloak a self-comforting exercise in evasion, a 'walking around' painful issues of conscience? Or does it represent the unwinding procedure in the *via negativa* of asceticism, a self-forgetful concentration on the mystic source?

> I thought of walking round
> and round a space utterly empty,
> utterly a source, like the idea of sound; (III, 188)

The outer circles of the poetic sequence — the encounters with the hovering peripheral presence of Sweeney in the first poem, and with non-servitors, Carleton and Joyce, on his way to and from the island in the second and final twelfth poem — seem to undercut the legitimacy of the enterprise. Their straight, impatient exhortations to 'Stay clear from all processions!' (I, 183) and the encircling maternal pull of the island's rituals are registered in terms of becoming fork-tongued like Carleton or following Joyce's advice:

> Keep at a tangent.
> When they make the circle wide, its time to swim
>
> out on your own and fill the element
> With signatures on your own frequency, (XII, 212)

The implication seems clear. He is to abandon former habits and become a 'hard' man like them, leaving his curves for their tangential strikes into freedom, his sensual orotundity for their bitter terseness, his solipsistic reminiscences and self-justifications for their blistering critiques, and the well-trodden paths of tradition for a high new ground. This reading is confirmed by 'The First Gloss,' the next poem in the Sweeney Redivivus sequence, which rewrites 'Digging' as a non-serviam lateral thrust away from convention:

> Take hold of the shaft of the pen.
> Subscribe to the first step taken
> from a justified line
> into the margin. (*SI*, 97)

The radical departure is short-lived, however. Sweeney Redivivus then resurrects

> my head like a ball of wet twine
> dense with soakage, but beginning
> to unwind. (*SI*, 98)

and we are given a perfect image of the circular autobiographical form of Heaney's mode of coherence-making and poetry-making:

> So the twine unwinds and loosely widens
> backwards through areas that forwarded
> understandings of all I would undertake. (*SI*, 99)

One never retrieves any given moment from the unwinding twine of memory twice in the same way, so far from returning to a fixed point in the past and closing the circle, as it were, one's memory loosely widens in a spiral form. The child Heaney of the first poem, who peeked through the bushes at Sweeney, modified an unquestioning acceptance of his lifestyle as inevitable by registering an alternative to it. An older Heaney's recollection of the incident included a consciousness of Sweeney's ironic awareness of his 'First Communion face'; later still the memory incorporated the incident, subsequent recollections of it, and assigned a significance to it relevant to the present moment—in this case the division into a voyeuristic and conformist self necessary for the emergent poet and autobiographer. Each stage of the incremental spiral movement of autobiography represents a different narrative arrangement of his life to date. By following Joyce's advice to keep at a tangent and make the circle wide, Heaney shows that it is mistaken to regard hard lines and curves as opposed, since this tangential perspective creates a spiral form. The tangential distance represents one's increasing objectivity, yet one remains necessarily subjective, bound through a common identity to past selves. The 10-, 20-, 30-, or 40-year-old Heaney turns the interiority, or secret structure, of his life inside out in different ways and, as though to emphasize the multilayeredness and provisionality of the autobiographical enterprise, Heaney, in the ninth poem, represents the resolution of his crisis on Station Island as the implosion and reversion of the spiral form.

When at last permitted to sleep, the hungry, exhausted, footsore, and conscience-stricken Heaney dreams about an extreme figure of self-abnegation and personal/political conflict, the late hunger-striker, Francis Hughes:

> I dreamt and drifted. All seemed to run to waste
> As down a swirl of mucky, glittering flood
> Strange polyp floated like a huge corrupt
> Magnolia bloom, surreal as a shed breast,
> My softly awash and blanching self-disgust. (IX, 205)

The violent severance he makes to save himself from drowning in this vertiginous inferno is expressed in aggressive, priapic terms:

> Then, like a pistil growing from the polyp,
> A lighted candle rose and steadied up (IX, 205)

Again, a striking feature of this recovery is the indistinguishability of narrative and event. Was he sucked downward by self-disgust or by the nightmare image? Was his recovery an act of will or was it enabled by the grace of a new mode of creating coherence that gave him a lever on his despair? One's experience of events, after all, is determined by the coherence, or narrative, one imposes upon them. Autobiography attempts to create a narrative that 'fits' the self, a provisional fit subject to constant modification, and as the spiral unfolds, the life is modified to fit the narrative at least as often as the narrative is modified to fit the life.

Freed from preoccupation with the past, Heaney is concerned from now on with his craft and his future. The transformation of an estranged self into a new familiarity forms a paradigm for poetic composition and personal transformation that is represented as a process of translation. The kaleidoscopic series of transformations that comprise his conversion are described as translations, and the tenth and eleventh poems examine the conversion process of trans-lation. Autobiography, translation, and, we may assume, writing poetry, are represented as a turning inside out of hidden meaning to make its inner significance or secret structure visible.

In the tenth poem, a household mug used as a stage-prop is

> Dipped and glamoured then by this translation,

in the same way

> as the otter surfaced once with Ronan's psalter
> miraculously unharmed, that had been lost
> a day and a night under lough water. (X, 207)

Ronan's Psalter is an allusion to *Sweeney Astray*, Heaney's first major work of translation, although the miraculous resurfacing of a lost text unharmed may be understood as a metaphor for all trans-lated works. Like the candle-pistil, the fortuity of the resurfacing of this saving image is emphasised. This poem, first published in a different version in the Field Day programme for the world pre-miere of *The Communication Cord*, is undoubtedly included as a tribute to the playwright Brian Friel, and to their joint attempt in Field Day to effect some kind of cultural transformation in a local Irish context.

The translation of St. John of the Cross's 'La Fuente' in the eleventh poem is an attempt to plumb the depths of the most hid-den meaning, the ineffable source of bounty and regeneration. The inarticulable, inchoate source may be apprehended by translation into metaphor, and there is a striking similarity between Heaney's *omphalos* hand-water pump and John of the Cross's fountain. They both draw on the mystic tradition of water as regenerative, and of positing the source as the centre of a field of force around which the questing soul circuits:

That eternal fountain, hidden away,
I know its haven and its secrecy
    although it is the night.

But not its source because it does not have one,
which is all sources' source and origin
    although it is the night.

No other thing can be so beautiful.
Here the earth and heaven drink their fill
    although it is the night.

So pellucid it never can be muddied,
and I know that all light radiates from it
    although it is the night (XI, 208–09)

Translating the poem requires identification with otherness and self-forgetfulness, and this mystic path of *via negativa* draws attention away from multiplicity and remembering to unity and self-forgetting. At the core of the spiral is a void. The poem asserts that 'What came to nothing could always be replenished' and welcomes emptiness as resource, a fount for renewal of a plentiful and fortuitous supply of metaphor and narrative.

Heaney's translations of *Sweeney Astray*, Dante, John of the Cross's, and most recently, Sophocles, are attempts to transform his style by incorporating elements from the styles of precursors most unlike him, and most admired by him. Carleton describes the process in terms that recall the Yeatsian mask:

another life that cleans our element.

We are earthworms of the earth, and all that
has gone through us is what will be our trace. (II, 186)

The earthworm's trace forms a spiral and, as Eliot famously teaches us, tradition is formed by individual talents composing new syntheses of their precursors' traces. Heaney's confrontations with precursors' shades in *Station Island*, and the translation projects, acknowledge their contributions 'that forwarded / understandings of all I would undertake' and re-evaluates how he wishes his own trace to shape tradition in the future.

The locus of his autobiography, the living tradition of the pilgrimage, is itself a powerful alter ego from which he struggles to wrest a sense of personal destiny. Leaving aside other struggles, the un-Yeatsian metaphor of an earthworm reminds us that cleansing our element is a purgative process. Remembering Heaney's conviction that the physiological operations of the poet shape the music of the poem, we might expect that the asceticism of hunger, sleeplessness, and footsoreness would hone his style, and indeed, a contemporaneous interview reveals such an intention: 'I was devoted to a Keatsian, woolly-like, texture stuff, but now I would like to write a bare wire' (O'Toole). One might tease Heaney a little here, off to Station Island to purge his style of profusion and orotundity (and I might add in parentheses that shedding a few pounds is quite a common aspiration amongst contemporary worldly pilgrims). Yet it must be acknowledged that the spiralling purgatorial procedure is perhaps the best means for the poet to hone his style and, to quote Gusdorf, 'draw out the structure of his being in time'. One's trace, or autobiography, is a turning inside out of oneself to make such a secret structure visible. In that trace we find the poet, as Yeats describes him: 'he is never the bundle of accident and incoherence that sits down to breakfast; he has been reborn as an idea, something intended, complete' (Yeats 509).

The parallels here with Yeatsian masks and gyres are strong, and I would argue they are as essential and enabling for Heaney as they were for Yeats. Their differences, too, are marked, which I attribute to the fact that Heaney doesn't universalise his procedure as a cosmological phenomenon, but keeps it local and rooted in the concerns of his everyday life. It is also rooted in the circular 'motions and postures within the poets incubating mind,' and the genesis of the poet that wrote *Station Island* may be found in the young Heaney, attracted to a hand-water pump, bog-holes and secret 'Haunting the granaries of words like *breasts*' (VI, 195).

Works Cited

Corcoran, Neil. *Seamus Heaney.* London: Faber and Faber, 1986.

Heaney, Seamus. *Selected Poems 1966–1987.* New York: Farrar, Straus & Giroux, 1990. All quotations from *Station Island* are cited from this volume.

——— . *Station Island.* London: Faber and Faber, 1984. [*SI*]

——— . *Preoccupations, Selected Prose 1968–1978.* New York: Farrar, Straus and Giroux, 1980.

Olney, James, ed. *Autobiography: Essays Theoretical and Critical.* Princeton: Princeton University Press, 1980.

O'Toole, Fintan. 'A Pilgrim's Progress' (Interview), *Inside Tribune.* September 30, 1984. 2.

Picard, J.M. and Y. de Pontfarcy. *Saint Patrick's Purgatory. A Twelfth Century Tale of a Journey to the Other World.* Dublin: Four Courts Press, 1985.

Yeats, W.B. *Essays and Introductions.* New York: Macmillan, 1968.

Sean O'Casey

A Life in the Letters

Ronald Ayling

From the testimony of his early autobiographical sketches (as he called them) that are embodied in the first two volumes of his life story, Sean O'Casey as a child and an adolescent appears as an intensely solitary and introspective figure. His mother acted as sole protector for him within his family and, it seems, for some considerable time was his only sympathetic friend, listener, and comforter. Even later, in his autobiography, as a young man fervently committed to important social causes and, perforce, an active member of a number of popular and populous social groups and organizations, O'Casey still gives the fairly consistent impression of a lonely personality who, knowing many people and possessing a number of like-minded friends, seldom if ever had anyone with whom he was really intimate. Until the day he married, at the age of forty-seven—and even then with some qualifications, it might be thought—the dramatist was without a soulmate or true confidant. Of course, at different times there were individuals with whom he confided certain secrets or shared confidences of a limited kind—and those usually of a political nature. But such friendships, before and after his marriage, were rare and seldom long maintained. Towards the end of his life, seeking to console the aged George Jean Nathan over the loss of his friend, H.L. Mencken, the seventy-year-old O'Casey could say: 'I have no lifelong friend (fortunately, perhaps), and so will, at least, escape this kind of grief; although I feel very upset indeed at the passing away of G.B.S.' (*Letters*, 3 November 1950).

Even marriage never seems to have broken down an essentially solitary cast of mind; there were, in certain respects, areas of experience which Sean and Eileen seemed never to share and worlds in which they did not co-exist. (One should not be surprised; they came from vastly different backgrounds and had immensely different attitudes to, and expectations of, life.) He never had much time for the world of first-night parties and country house weekends which she (as a young actress and model) enjoyed, while his labour and nationalist sympathies inspired even less interest in her, though both liked friends and acquaintances from all these disparate worlds. There's no doubt that theirs was a long, close and happy marriage but there were important respects in which, as an artist and an activist, O'Casey was often a man apart — physically apart, that is, geographically apart, but not mentally or spiritually so, for, with his wife and with others, he conducted by correspondence a series of friendships that in some cases (as in that with Nathan himself) lasted for over twenty years until the latter's death.

O'Casey maintained epistolary contact with many people and, sometimes, these contacts became genuine friendships, even though most of them were marked only with an occasional meeting or a brief reunion. In the case of Nathan, while their friendship was strong and deep (and O'Casey's solicitude for him in his long last illness is indeed touching), it was conducted wholly by mail after an initial period of acquaintance during the dramatist's sole visit to New York. O'Casey had a true gift for friendship, as his prolific correspondence tellingly reveals: thoughtful of others, he was eager to encourage or console when necessary; helpful and (usually) tactful in giving advice and extending practical assistance, he was invariably loyal to old friends in adversity and (usually) able to absorb criticism from such friends — though seldom backward in counterattack when he thought such criticism unfair or unfounded. Writing letters was, moreover, an important means of keeping in touch with a larger world outside his own fairly restricted physical and human ambience (during a long life span he travelled relatively little): maintaining links with American life and culture as well as the contemporary New York stage, as in the case of his relationship with Nathan and by exchanging letters with Lady Gregory and Gabriel Fallon, retaining contact with his native land when in exile in England. O'Casey certainly lived a full and vigorous life in his letters and no more so than in his final two decades. His *Collected Letters*, indeed, open up for the reader a mutually enlivening two-way traffic of impressions, thoughts and feelings, criticism and gossip (two-way in that we can often observe the views and visions of his friends and acquaintances as reflected in his replies) from which eventually emerges a self-portrait worthy of hanging beside the more carefully delineated autobiographical picture that O'Casey created over more than two decades of self-examination from the late 1930s to the mid-1950s.

There are, indeed, good grounds for seeing O'Casey as a natural autobiographer, using his art — in plays and essays and even some polemical writings, as well as in the huge avowedly autobiographical narrative that eventually shaped itself into six hefty volumes with the collective title *Mirror in My House* — to make the world, and his own place within it, real to himself, recreating and re-evaluating his past in relation to his present. He sought to accomplish this by finding words and images that would both define his own nature and realize the world as it was (to his eyes, seen in relation to his own slowly evolving ideological conceptions of it) and also as it might be, ideally, given social changes and transformations that he envisaged and worked to bring about at different times in his life. As he grew older, he increasingly looked for the meaning of that life within himself as well as in arguments with that self, though persistently claiming in his letters that the individual was too often overvalued in the western world. Such apparent contradictions help create a flow of vivid and passionate life and an argumentative monologue that impel his life as a mature man and, inevitably, are often reflected in his extensive correspondence and in his autobiographical writings as well.

Learning slowly and painfully and in virtual isolation, there was little to guide O'Casey in coming to terms with the difficult conditions of a working-class man without formal education, trying to find himself as an artist and intellectual in a deeply divided, insensitive, materially philistine and snobbish world, in which he was disadvantaged in almost every single social, economic, and personal particular. Correspondence — particularly, to start with, letters for public consumption — seems to have been O'Casey's earliest (and almost certainly instinctively apprehended) means of finding his feet as a writer. In this respect he has something in common with Virginia Woolf, who as a very young woman likewise served a self-determined apprenticeship to the craft of writing by using letters to create varying moods and styles attuned to different correspondents, trying to make effective use of gossip for serious purposes and to describe people and places in a variety of ways, once again in accordance with what she conceived to be the desires and expectations of various recipients. Her letters were, mostly, personal and private experiences, primarily intended for the delectation of people she knew well. Becoming a novelist concerned above all to portray hitherto ignored states of mind and feeling, Woolf was the creator of a highly individualistic style which would realize, subtly and impressionistically, fine gradations of tone and inflection in the language of social intercourse and explore highly sensitive aspects of individual consciousness.

With O'Casey, the process was very different. He wrote very few (if any) letters in his youth and very early manhood and, almost certainly, none of a highly personal or intimate nature. The letters that eventually contributed significantly to his initial growth as a writer were of quite a different style and content: from his middle twenties (so far as we can tell) he began to write letters of a public nature on issues then often in the news in Ireland, though his own views on these matters were usually very much part of what was then minority, and often distinctly unpopular, opinion in Ireland. Subsequently, of course, certain minority opinions that he had held much earlier on nationality and nationalism were to become basic patriotic sentiment in the country, building blocks in the newly assembled national pantheon, as it were — but, by then, O'Casey's vision had moved far beyond such views.

In his correspondence on such themes, O'Casey honed one side (a significant part but only one side) to his craft as a literary artist: that of the polemical and often contentious political writer, who enjoyed public controversy and literary contention up to his dying day. Similarly, in his dramatic writings, he was to create several highly original characters (male and female alike) memorable for their pugilistic skills and ability at bar-room brawling (one thinks of Dolphie Grigson, Fluther Good, Bessie Burgess, the Young Covey and Sylvester Heegan) as well as others who exhibit well developed oratorical and debating skills — witness the platform orator in *The Plough and the Stars* and the various public speakers in *Within the Gates* and later plays. For himself as a playwright creating characters operating in the public arena (whether it be a tavern or a political meeting or, much later, a large public park), the overt rhetorical skills developed in O'Casey's early public letters can now be seen to have been aesthetically harnessed as, in another world altogether, Virginia Woolf's highly individualistic epistolary experiments were to be brilliantly exploited for her own vastly different fictional purposes.

Interestingly, both writers were later to develop and diversify their epistolary concerns, in quite opposite directions. Woolf's later letters, perhaps influenced by the rise of Fascism in Europe and the encroaching danger of another world war and also by her heightened awareness of gender politics, show a much more perceptible awareness of political and social factors that had to be taken into account in the late 1930s. The focus is on abstruse and impersonal forces to complement the private inner vision. O'Casey was to move quite otherwise; there are more often deeply personal dimensions within his later writings. Though the result was a fusion of the personal and the impersonal, the private and the public, the larger social issues are still as pronounced in his later letters as they are in his more formal writings. Yet he was always fascinated by the variety and multiplicity of human life and by the creation of often larger than life characters. 'The way to get life into letters, Virginia Woolf wrote to her sister Vanessa, 'is to be interested in other people.'[1] O'Casey's letters from the late 1930s onwards show him, increasingly, trying to keep in close touch with friends and former acquaintances he saw much less of in his retreat in rural Devon, by then relatively inaccessible. In addition he began to find a new audience, with many people from all walks of life writing to him, out of the blue in many cases, about his writings and his outlook on life; their reactions and criticisms he came increasingly to value as stage productions of his plays dwindled and he lost a theatre audience whose immediate spontaneous response to his work could be instantly understood and evaluated.

Earlier, however, after many years in his youth when he wrote few or no letters at all, O'Casey in his late twenties and early thirties used letter writing to keep in touch with many people in causes that he espoused, to work out his philosophical and aesthetic positions on paper and, often, to debate contentious issues in correspondence in the press and in polemical journals devoted to particular social interests. Letter writing and public debate were both essential components in O'Casey's self-education — and, often, the two could hardly be distinguished from each other: it was not uncommon for O'Casey as a young man to use jousting terms in his letters and to speak as though the letter he was writing was part of an ongoing public disputation — and sometimes it was, of course. Often, in his thirties, he issued challenges to letter writers with whom he was engaged in journalistic disputation to debate the self-same topic in public on a platform to be mutually agreed upon. The first section of the first volume of O'Casey's Collected Letters, covering the years from 1910 to 1919 (during which the playwright went from his thirtieth to his thirty-ninth birthday), provides a number of notable if often crude examples: in them we see O'Casey educating himself, by trial and (often) error, learning to write for public consumption and to give and take blows in literary disputation.

The first controversy in O'Casey's Letters is with A.P. Wilson (who wrote under the pen name of Euchan), a far more experienced adversary than O'Casey was at that time. It is the first public dispute involving O'Casey to be recorded in print, though earlier letters by him on nationalist issues had been published in Dublin journals. It is unlikely to have been the first such controversy in which the young Sean O'Cathasaigh (as he then signed his letters) participated, either on the public platform or in, say, the unpublished manuscript journals that were regularly read aloud to members of the various local branches of the Gaelic League. In the dispute with Euchan, O'Casey attacked an article by him in the Irish Worker, deriding his socialist stance because it failed to take into account Irish nationalist concerns (within a few months O'Casey himself was to adopt a pro-Labour position somewhat similar to that of Euchan, though he never failed to take nationalist considerations seriously even when differing from them). In the original argument O'Casey exhibits an overreliance on reiterated rhetorical questions and stilted, abstract (and ungrammatical) oratorical phraseology: 'How like is Euchan's words to those written long ago which the Gael has not forgotten: "The Gael is gone with a vengeance, Laus Deo!" The Gael is here still, Euchan, stronger to suffer than Hell can harm, and it is highly improbable that our hearts shall shake before the words of Euchan' (8 February 1913).

Characteristically, O'Casey's second letter to the editor of the *Irish Worker* in the same dispute starts with the words: 'Are you ready, Euchan? On guard, then!' Later, he says sarcastically but earnestly, picking up his opponent's points: 'Now Euchan of the logic and the intelligence, I challenge you to debate with me that "this is purely in Ireland a commercial age"; "that Home Rule will link Ireland with her commercial neighbours"; "that Ireland's past is past" and "that she can never be the glorious Nation she was" ' (22 February 1913). Obviously serious about a public debate, he asks his adversary to name a date, site, and appropriate chairman for such a combat; and as late as 20 December 1924, by which time he was the acclaimed author of *The Shadow of a Gunman* and *Juno and the Paycock*, he could still issue a public challenge in a letter to D.P. Moran, editor of the *Leader*, to debate publicly ('exclusively in Irish', he insists) whether or not the teaching of compulsory Irish to the children of Dublin workers (many of them unemployed and half-starved) be commendable.

By this time, already in his early forties, O'Casey had truly found his feet, as a man and an artist. Thereafter, he was never to question his vocation as a writer and, more particularly, a playwright. At different times he gave his time and attention to other literary occupations: for a brief while, in the mid-1930s, it was writing dramatic criticism for *Time and Tide*, and, later, book reviewing for the *Sunday Times*; subsequently, and more sustainedly, for two decades from the late 1930s, he devoted much creative energy to the construction of an elaborate autobiographical narrative designed to be a complex work of art rather than the memoir of a famous author. Playwriting was never far from his thoughts, however, and that professional concern was the vital and continuing link throughout his career. It is surprising how old he was before he fully found himself as a playwright and how long it took him to synthesize his economic and political views into an overall ideological stance, encompassing nationality and socialism, that was to become, for him, a viable practical philosophy. From then on, there was little or no appreciable change in his ideological outlook, though a maturing style and greatly increased self-confidence made for a more persuasive artistry.

Twenty-five years ago I brought out a posthumous collection of Sean O'Casey's occasional writings, choosing *Blasts and Benedictions* for its title. In a preface I explained the title's provenance and its relevance for that particular collection of essays and stories:

> Reviewing a volume of G.B.S.'s letters, Sean O'Casey exclaimed: 'What a man Bernard Shaw was for sending his blasts and benedictions everywhere, falling over the land like the thistledown from a blown-out dandelion.' As it was with Shaw, so was it with O'Casey. Both were prolific writers whose articles and reviews were published in periodicals and newspapers all over the world and who wrote copiously to unknown as well as famous people everywhere. Indeed, when O'Casey's correspondence is published, a further significant dimension to his personality as well as his writing will be revealed. Like D.H. Lawrence, it was virtually impossible for him to write a dull letter, whatever the subject; even his letters to the Inland Revenue, though containing more blasts than blessings, are no exception. O'Casey's concern for all sorts and conditions of men, his receptivity to all aspects of human experience, and his inexhaustible comic spirit make his letters . . . of absorbing interest. (ix)

That observation was made in 1965 and published in 1967. Since then three massive volumes of O'Casey's correspondence, totalling more than twenty-nine hundred pages, have been published and, though one final volume is still to come, it is now possible to give something like a considered judgement of the man and the writer as they are portrayed in his letters.[2] How then does that brief provisional assessment in *Blasts and Benedictions* stand up in retrospect a quarter century later?

Basically, I still stand by every word of the quotation. The particular virtues enumerated there still seem as vividly apparent throughout O'Casey's epistolary writings of the forty-eight years which have been encompassed in the printed record to date (that is, from 1910 to 1958, during which time the playwright progressed from his thirtieth to his seventy-eighth birthday) and even the analogies with Lawrence and Shaw, originally meant for provocative comparison, do not seem to be too farfetched. The considerable virtuosity in O'Casey's subject matter and style, though it may not fully match that displayed in those two superbly accomplished letter writers, still stands up well to examination, though it is assuredly fully stretched and severely tested by being exposed at such length in three huge volumes. One can now see that, while O'Casey's letters in general do not match the poetic intensity and vivid spontaneity of Lawrence's letters at their best or the genial good spirits and intellectual buoyancy of Shaw's (very few writers can, of course, match these qualities), many of them are beautifully written, possess literary and personal interest of a high order and raise considerably more pertinent issues and themes than have been acknowledged so far in critical reviews.

Perhaps the blasts and blasting, rather than the benedictions, are the more immediately apparent features in the three volumes of O'Casey's letters published to date; as with most explosive material, the sound and fury attract more attention and evoke (and provoke) the stronger emotional reactions. Much of the published commentary on the *Collected Letters* edition has been hostile; the vehement response of Denis Donoghue, first printed in the *New Republic* (26 April 1975) and then reissued in *We Irish* in 1986, is representative. The conclusion that he comes to is that 'O'Casey was the most quarrelsome writer in Ireland, a notoriously quarrelsome country' (*We Irish*, 226). Now it is true that Donoghue's article is a review of the first (and arguably the most contentious) volume of the three issued to date. Even so, I have to say that the longer one is acquainted with the three collections — and especially the second and third volumes — the more strongly one becomes aware of the powerful countervailing presence of benign and positive thought and emotion in O'Casey's letters.

Tender concern and solicitude is everywhere manifest, for friends and acquaintances and for writers and artists (ancient and modern) under attack or persecution or suffering from misunderstanding — much more than for himself, though he often defends himself and his work, publicly and privately. Indeed, O'Casey's correspondence salutes and celebrates as often as it criticizes and lacerates. Again and again, we encounter praise and encouragement as well as (or, often, instead of) blame and recrimination; moreover, when there is criticism, there is as much recognition of self-failings and personal limitations (and a fair share of self-criticism, besides) as there is of the faults and follies of others. To my mind, the benedictions often outweigh the blasts and maledictions and, usually, have a longer lasting effect.

Again and again, we encounter examples of O'Casey's kindness to, and consideration for, fellow-writers; in particular, young and struggling artists in all fields of artistic endeavour and, especially, in drama. He was assiduous, but tactful and discreet (so much so that his efforts were often unknown to those he sought to help) in putting in a good word for such artists, whether he knew them well or even hardly at all, with publishers, stage producers, theatre managers, drama critics, literary agents, anthologists, and academics. A list of writers, known and unknown, that he praised and encouraged throughout his long creative life would be a very extensive one. It includes orthodox mainstream novelists like Francis MacManus as well as more off-beat and personally difficult authors like Patrick Kavanagh, Flann O'Brien, Brendan Behan and many others whose work has either not survived or, in some cases, was never published or staged.

Denis Donoghue, in a perceptive and well balanced critique of D.H. Lawrence's letters,[3] has an especially perceptive passage on the novelist's seldom recognized capacity for tact and gentleness: 'Often in a most hostile and bitter letter, when the venom has expelled itself, Lawrence ends with a paragraph not of apology but of recognition; as if to say that beneath the flow of violence and rage there is another, of consanguinity and peace' (*England*, 289). I don't find a conjunction quite as astonishing as this in O'Casey's correspondence, but there is no doubt that, at times, the dramatist could be wonderfully tactful and diplomatic, as is evident in a letter to Leo Keogh, one of his old working-class butties from his early nationalist days. Writing more than forty years after their joint participation in the Gaelic League, O'Casey shows himself to be sensitive to an old man's ideals, for which (like O'Casey himself) he had worked unselfishly and made many sacrifices in early manhood, but which had become fragile and vulnerable in the light of subsequent defilement by cynical and manipulative national leaders.

At the time that the playwright wrote to Leo Keogh (12 October 1953), he was elsewhere conducting a vehemently critical campaign against the fear, oppression, and hypocrisy in Ireland, especially as it was manifested in its clerical and secular leadership. In his essays of this period, collected in *The Green Crow*, and in plays like *Cock-a-Doodle Dandy* and *The Bishop's Bonfire*, we can observe his honest and scathing dissection of many abuses, portraying contemporary Ireland as being, if anything, more reactionary than it was when he was a youth. Yet, in the letter to Keogh, after a detailed passage of personal reminiscence of the old days when 'we two met together under the rays from the Sword of Light,' O'Casey goes on to answer what must have been a query from Keogh juxtaposing the old days and the new. In doing so, he couches his response in terms that are quite different from those he would have used to answer the same question from, say, an interviewer for the *Irish Times*. Readers demanding consistency might well deplore the apparent evasiveness of his answer. 'I can't comment whether the ideals of the early days are in course of realization,' he begins, 'for it is twenty-eight years since I left the land, and many thousands more, apparently, have followed suit since then.' Of course, the criticism — so overt in his published writings — is still, implicitly, present: if past aspirations are being realized, why do the people leave the country? 'All the young, too, and the fittest among the young,' he continues: 'It is a dreadful drain on Ireland's virility and potential strength.' Referring to several history books on Ireland, he declares: 'Ireland's Story has yet to be written,' before going on to send best wishes to Keogh's wife and to other mutual friends. 'With us, new things have passed away, and all things have become old. Well, God be with the young,' he concludes — and, with him, this sentiment is no pious platitude but, rather, a faith in the future in which he genuinely believed.

By such stratagems — instinctively apprehended, no doubt — O'Casey avoids being directly contentious and possibly hurtful (or, at least, worrying) to an old man whom he may have thought was by then unable to change things or influence people and, above all, unable to find a new sustaining faith to replace the old Gaelic ideals which they had once held in common. Why unnecessarily disturb him? or, at least, unsettle him anymore than he was already, for his query in itself suggests that Keogh was uneasy about the way things were going in Ireland in the 1950s? Is it not better to pass over particulars, about which the dramatist had deeply pessimistic views which would, inevitably, have been deeply disillusioning for an old comrade? Whether or not these were O'Casey's thoughts on the subject, the question remains: is such evasion deceitful or dishonest? In this particular context I do not think so; the playwright's own views on Ireland in the nineteen fifties are clearly spelled out in his creative work at this time — there's no deception or even ambiguity in *The Green Crow*, *Cock-a-Doodle Dandy* and *The Bishop's Bonfire* — with characters in the latter two plays forthrightly arguing over the very issue raised by Keogh. O'Casey's attitude might be thought patronizing, I suppose, but the very length of the letter, and the intimate respect shown in it, surely counteract any such impression.

In his art as in his life, O'Casey enacted the authenticity of experience to which D.H. Lawrence once testified in a letter: 'All truth — and real living is the only truth — has in it the elements of battle and repudiation' (30 August 1926). As Donoghue demonstrates in his one-sided hostile response to the first volume of O'Casey's *Collected Letters*, there are many battles and frequent repudiations in the playwright's correspondence. He could be vicious, savage even, in his denunciations of his contemporaries, particularly politicians, artists, and critics in his native land and in the western democracies. Usually there are reasonable grounds for his onslaughts, and the reader can enjoy the vivacity engendered by his vehemence and the exuberance of style it produces. Far less justification can be found for the various defences he made for the policies and actions of the U.S.S.R. and its communist allies, and, though he honestly believed that humane and egalitarian ideals were realized in these countries in deed and not only by word of mouth, his various pronouncements on Soviet treason trials, cold war rearmament, and so on make for a sad spectacle unredeemed by recollections of how many other western intellectuals were likewise self-deceived.

It is true that, unlike most declared Stalinists, he could be firmly critical of communist theories and practice — though not of communism itself — especially in their actual manifestation in cultural and literary matters. There are, in the *Collected Letters*, several long epistles addressed to Russian editors and men of letters making quite clear his opposition both to official Soviet conceptions of Socialist Realism and to particular criticisms made of Boris Pasternak and other dissident artists in the U.S.S.R. In his published correspondence there are also several lengthy, carefully argued epistles to prominent Russian artists and important bureaucrats in the Union of Soviet Writers, staunchly defending the integrity of T.S. Eliot, James Joyce, Eugene O'Neill and other authors against charges of decadence and pessimism, charges with which he cannot wholly disagree but which he thinks less important than the authenticity of their artistic vision and (in the case of Eliot) 'his powers as a poet.'

It is important to put the playwright's pugnacity into proportion. While O'Casey could be wild and unfair occasionally, as most belligerents must be at times (and some too often), there is no doubt that he was often courteous and gracious in what he regarded as fair combat. Understandably bitter and incensed when engaged in what appeared to be unfair controversies, as in the 1928 Dublin dispute over *The Silver Tassie*, the 1935 Boston banning of *Within the Gates*, and the opposition to the staging of *The Drums of Father Ned* in Dublin in 1958, the playwright could be generous to opponents with regard to what he saw to be honest criticism.

The prevention of an important production of *Within the Gates* in Boston in 1935 was intolerable, because the ban was based entirely on the judgement of a single individual, the city's mayor, who had no expertise in literature or drama and whose personal decision was final, with no possible recourse to genuine arbitration or even debate on the issue. In such circumstances, the playwright's sense of outrage was reflected, understandably, in heated and offensive language of the kind that Donoghue has strongly condemned, when speaking of O'Casey's 'determination to keep himself exacerbated, outraged, violated,' without distinguishing (as a critic should do) between particular instances where such a reaction might be justified and others that could not be defended.

O'Casey's attitude to public criticism of the very same production — the New York première of *Within the Gates*, which had been scheduled to tour Boston and other New England cities — shows him, unlike Donoghue, to be sensitive to such distinctions. For instance, in a retrospective letter of 9 April 1935 thanking the *New York Times* critic, Brooks Atkinson, for his appreciative reviews of the play, the playwright also sent greetings to two of Atkinson's New York colleagues, saying: 'Give my good wishes to Messrs. Gabriel and Mason-Brown, hoping as I do, that they and I shall live to have another fight.' Both Gilbert Gabriel, in the *New York American*, and John Mason-Brown, in the *New York Post*, had written unfavourable reviews of the play as it had appeared on stage in that city. Thinking their critiques to be fair and honest, O'Casey respected both critics and regarded critical disputation with them as valuable intellectual debate, from which he as a pragmatic dramatist could learn and grow. In such ways, the playwright saw criticism, counterattack and public debate as potentially educational and creative.

Not all O'Casey's critics seem capable of similar discrimination between dishonest denunciation (often accompanied by open or covert censorship) and disinterested critical disagreement. O'Casey could so discriminate, even in the midst of a larger dispute over a play in production, in the course of which he lost money when he was desperately in need of funds (for *Within the Gates* was prevented from opening in Boston and its tour was subsequently curtailed though not abandoned). O'Casey also failed to get a full and well earned public hearing for a new experimental work over which he had toiled long and hard for many years.

It would have been understandable for him, in retrospect, to have lumped together all the hostile critics of *Within the Gates* in the United States as enemies of promise and censors of new thought; instead, he was careful to distinguish between the genuine critics and the thought-extinguishing moralists. In the same letter to Atkinson (of 9 April 1935) he makes his position on these matters quite clear, though it is obviously intended to be a 'thank you' letter rather than anything else. Visiting the United States for the first (and only) time to help with the play's première in New York, O'Casey had hoped to learn from seeing a theatrically intricate play in intensive rehearsals and in production. Talking to Atkinson of this experience, after he had returned to his home in England, O'Casey could yet write dispassionately: 'It was a bright time with a streak of bitterness in it, but there is no brightness so bright as the brightness that is slashed with a gleam of bitterness.' The dramatist went on to say that 'the controversy over the play' with 'a few of the critics' (as opposed to 'the ban,' which 'was another thing altogether') 'did me good, for a general and royal salute given to a play is a bad thing for the Dramatist to get — not that I am ever likely to get it, Brooks.' If we look objectively at many of O'Casey's critical essays and reviews as well as his letters discussing or embodying literary criticism, I think we shall see that a similarly mature and clear-sighted view informed much of his own polemical practice.

Of course, most of the playwright's critical writing was of an occasional nature and seldom fully explored or elaborately developed. He wrote reviews and short articles and commented fitfully but thoughtfully on immediate (and often practical) issues. Usually, he saw his role in this respect as an irritant satirical presence, when he was not defending his own writings or beliefs, and the title of his first book of dramatic criticism is apposite. *The Flying Wasp*, reprinting a number of his occasional reviews and critical commentaries with some asides on the state of dramatic criticism and of staged drama in the England of the time, was published in 1937. In it O'Casey saw himself as a reviewer (rather than a full-blown literary critic) stinging complacent drama critics as well as contemporary dramatists into controversy and re-evaluation, as well as into regenerative re-engagement with artists and critics ancient and modern whom O'Casey thought to be unjustly neglected in English-language theatre in the 1930s.

Though he downplayed his role as a formal critic, in letters and in his criticism itself, O'Casey certainly took critics and criticism very seriously. In this, he was unlike many creative artists who actively discount the value of criticism. The novelist William Faulkner is representative of this attitude; an interview he gave to Jean Stein in 1956 epitomizes his views on the subject. Asked about 'the function of the critics' for the writer, Faulkner replied bluntly:

> The artist doesn't have time to listen to the critics. The ones who want to be writers read the reviews, the ones who want to write don't have the time to read the reviews. The critic too is trying

to say 'Kilroy was here.' His function is not directed towards the artist himself. The artist is a cut above the critic, for the artist is writing something which will move the critic. The critic is writing something which will move everybody but the artist.

The interviewer interjected: 'So you never feel the need to discuss your work with anyone?' to which Faulkner responded:

No, I am too busy writing it. It has got to please me and if it does, I don't need to talk about it. If it doesn't please me, talking about it won't improve it, since the only thing to improve it is to work on it some more. I am not a literary man but only a writer. I don't get any pleasure from talking shop. (*A Modern Southern Reader*, 610)

It was quite otherwise with O'Casey, who often spoke appreciatively of the importance of criticism, in itself and for himself. In the very same letter to Atkinson that has been quoted earlier (9 April 1935), he conceives the art of the playwright and the drama critic to be in a kind of creative tandem: 'It isn't silly to expect the Theatre to be in advance of its time. If a man is a Dramatist then he must be in advance of his time; just as a man if he is a critic must be in advance of the Drama of his time.' Here, as so often in his life and letters, we can see that O'Casey practised what he preached. Years later, in a volume of collected articles and prose pieces entitled *The Green Crow*, he reiterated this belief in broader terms when he argued that

the critic and the playwright are fifty-fifties, of equal importance, both assigned to the hard, but enjoyable, task of keeping the theatre alive; of bringing before the [public] view the drama-blossoms of the past that have proved themselves to be everlasting in colour and perfume, and to select from the newer crowd of daisy and dandelion a blossom that has suddenly taken on the beauty of a lily or a rose. The drama critic, of surety, and the playwright, having the same quality, are one. . . . (19–20)

In the same article, prefacing as it does a book of robust and combative criticism, he declares: 'The critic who is afraid of a challenger is really afraid of himself; he hasn't got the gift of criticism, which is to shove the bad aside, make room for the good, lead it forth, and show it to the world' (20). Later, he goes further, arguing that 'Criticism is the guide, the defender of every lovely thing written in a book, picturing itself on a canvas, thrusting itself from stone or bronze, or strutting on a stage in finery of jewelled laughter or weeping in black over the grave of a lost woman or a lost cause' (21).

Elsewhere in the same collection of essays, answering a charge that he could not abide criticism (Donoghue was to make a similar observation years later), O'Casey asserted a large claim that can, I think, be substantiated by scrutinizing his reading and his writing and by concrete illustration from his letters:

> As a matter of fact, criticism is a part of my best-loved liter-ature, I have read as much of it as I have of story, poem, or play. A big amount—Atkinson, Nathan, Watts, Gassner, Emer-son, Matthiessen, Coulton, Coleridge, Dryden, Shaw, Yeats, Shel-ley, Read, Eliot—to mention a worthy few; criticism of philoso-phy, religion, of story, poem, and play; from Shakespeare's com-ments on life and love in the Sonnets to Yeats's sad comment on a young man's foolishness in his 'Down in the Salley Gardens'; for every poem, play, and story enshrines its own comment. . . . Good criticism is at times mistaken, but it is invariably interest-ing, and always leaves us to follow our own judgment. (126)

O'Casey's letters show him self-apprenticed to a tough and tur-bulent school of criticism, encompassing the school of street-corner evangelism and Hyde Park (or Liberty Hall) oratory as well as the more polite literary criticism he invoked in The Green Crow. In that sense he reveals himself as following in the footsteps of his evangelical father, who, as a Protestant missionary living and work-ing among Catholics in Dublin, must often have been involved in controversy and disputation in his day-to-day life as well as on an intellectual level. In a sneering conclusion to his review of O'Casey's letters, Denis Donoghue quoted lines from W.B. Yeats's bitter 'Re-morse for Intemperate Speech,' and claimed that O'Casey brought his 'fanatic Ireland' with him and 'held on to its rancour' wher-ever he happened to be. 'He was always the man who was sacked from his first job,' the critic concludes (*We Irish*, 229). I would ar-gue that this side to his personality is but one (and that an often finely controlled) aspect of a fascinatingly complex man. Rather than 'the man who was sacked from his first job,' O'Casey is the true son of a committed and resolute (but probably cranky) father, whose undoubted fanaticism is tempered by his mother's gutsy hu-mour and compassion and by the humanity learned in a lifetime's selfless devotion to humane causes embracing many creeds, classes and peoples.

Notes

[1] Nigel Nicholson and Joanne Trautman, eds. *The Letters of Virginia Woolf: Volume I, 1888–1912* (New York: Harcourt Brace Jovanovich, 1975), p. xx.

[2] The first volume contains 653 letters by O'Casey and 124 letters to or about the playwright; the second contains 807 letters by O'Casey; the third contains 506 letters by him.

[3] 'D.H. Lawrence in His Letters' appears in Donoghue's *England, Their England*, pp. 275–89.

Works Cited

Boulton, James, ed. *The Letters of D.H. Lawrence.* 6 vols. (September 1901 to November 1928). Cambridge: Cambridge University Press, 1979–91.

Donoghue, Denis. *We Irish: Essays on Irish Literature and Society.* New York: Knopf, 1986.

——— . *England, Their England: Commentaries on English Language and Literature.* New York: Knopf, 1988.

Forkner, Ben and Patrick Samway, eds. *A Modern Southern Reader.* Atlanta, Ga.: Peachtree, 1986.

O'Casey, Sean. *The Green Crow.* London: W.H. Allen, 1957.

——— . *Blasts and Benedictions: Articles and Stories*, ed. Ronald Ayling. London: Macmillan, 1967.

——— . *The Letters of Sean O'Casey: Volume I, 1910–1941.* New York: Macmillan, 1975.

——— . *The Letters of Sean O'Casey: Volume II, 1942–1954.* New York: Macmillan, 1980.

——— . *The Letters of Sean O'Casey: Volume III, 1955–1958.* Washington, D.C.: Catholic University of America Press, 1989.

III

STORIES OF
THE IRISH IN CANADA

Thomas D'Arcy McGee.

The Follies
of One and Twenty
D'Arcy McGee and Young Ireland, 1842–49

Robin B. Burns

In 1976 I thought I had laid D'Arcy McGee's ghost to rest. I had completed my thesis on his careers in Ireland and the United States, and I have not looked at him seriously since, except to reduce him for biographical entries in the *Dictionary of Canadian Biography* and the *Canadian Encyclopedia*. Members of the profession were also saying in 1976 that biographies, especially biographies of politicians, were not only passé but taboo. Then, all of a sudden, the Canadian Association for Irish Studies organized this conference on biography and the Centre for Canadian Studies at Edinburgh has called for papers on Irish and Canadian biography for this May. Last week, a publisher suggested a major biography of McGee. I am afraid that D'Arcy McGee's genie may be getting out of the bottle and his biographer may be coming out of the closet.

Under these circumstances, I found yesterday's sessions so stimulating and helpful that I began to question my approach to today's paper. Should I see this new interest in McGee as coming from a new political agenda in Ireland which now looks more favourably on what he was proposing 135 years ago? Should I begin with a public confession about my gene pool and boyhood so that the audience will be able to recognize my biases? Should I admit that I am a graduate of Cardinal Newman High School and Loyola College, taught by Christian Brothers and Jesuits, but tempered by a Presbyterian father from Glasgow who married a French Canadian Catholic whose great-grandfather came from Donegal? I will not. I will begin as I had intended, with an anecdote, delighted to have learned yesterday that this is the hallmark of historicism, my preferred philosophy of history.

The Effigy in the Car

Twenty-five years ago this March, D'Arcy McGee was still arousing passions among the Irish of Montreal. It was the year before the Centennial of Confederation, and Expo '67, and Madame Tussaud's decided to open a Canadian branch of its wax museum. It was

located in McGee's former Montreal home on St. Catherine Street
and one tableau featured his assassination. Shortly before Montreal's annual St. Patrick's Day parade, the museum approached
the United Irish Societies of Montreal, the association responsible
for the parade, and offered to lend it McGee's wax effigy for the
back seat of one of the open cars.

The proposal caused consternation. The United Irish Societies
began to divide. One faction objected and announced that they
would boycott the parade. The pro-McGee forces declared that
they would proceed. The anti-McGee group then tried the diplomatic route — not with their fellow citizens of Montreal but with the
Ambassador of Ireland to Canada. It was the decisive card. The ambassador announced that he would not review the parade if D'Arcy
McGee were in it. That brought Montreal's Irish Member of Parliament, Bryce Mackasey, on board. D'Arcy McGee stayed at home for
the 1966 St. Patrick's Day parade, amused perhaps at the continuing colonialism of Canada's Irish republicans (and here I might add,
after yesterday's discussion about the two Imperialisms in Ireland,
the British and the Roman, that from a Canadian perspective, there
is a third Imperialism, the Imperialism of Irish republicanism.)

The Irish Ambassador was asked for an explanation. The Montreal Gazette quoted him as saying, 'You may as well have [wax
figures of] Cartier and MacDonald [sic] in the parade.' 'D'Arcy
McGee may have been born in Ireland . . . he may have been a
great Canadian . . . and a Father of Confederation. But what has
that got to do with Ireland?'[1] What indeed! This paper is D'Arcy
McGee's revenge. The session may be entitled 'Stories of the Irish
in Canada,' but the paper has nothing to do with Canada, at least
not in the narrow sense that the former Irish Ambassador would
have understood it.

The hopeful years of D'Arcy McGee's youth in Ireland and the
United States had a lot to do with what he came to see as the potential of Canada, and his later years in Canada contributed to a
new vision of the future of Ireland. In 1865 he brought this point
of view to the town of his youth, Wexford. It had been seventeen
years since he had fled Ireland, with a price on his head, leaving behind a young wife expecting her first child. He had now just turned
forty years old and was a Minister of the Crown in the Province of
Canada. He gave a public address to the people of Wexford, and
referred to his earlier career in Irish public life between 1842 and
1849.

> I am not at all ashamed of Young Ireland. Why should I be?
> Politically we were a pack of fools. But we were honest in our

folly. And no man need blush at forty for the follies of one and twenty. . . . [2]

Many were not amused: some, like Gavan Duffy, were older; others, like the Fenians, were young.

Young Ireland in America, 1842–45

D'Arcy McGee's first departure from Ireland had been voluntary. The year was 1842 when 93,000 Irish left for America, the largest number before the Great Famine. McGee was about to turn seventeen, he and his younger sister disliked their stepmother, their late mother's sister lived in America and their brother worked on a timber ship between Wexford and Quebec.[3] Economically, the family was better off than most of the Irish, but not so well enough off it could have afforded formal schooling for the young McGee. Intellectually and culturally, D'Arcy brought a great deal from Ireland to the new world. He was a Catholic, intensely conscious of historic grievances. He was from a town which had been sacked by Cromwell, in which the ill-fated republic of 1798 had been headquartered and brutally suppressed, and where two stage coaches still operated to Dublin, one exclusively for Catholics and the other for Protestants. He belonged to the first generation after Emancipation, although the annual rent of three pounds fifteen shillings which the family paid for their cottage was not sufficient to qualify his father to vote.[4] Nevertheless, he was supremely optimistic about the future of Ireland. Daniel O'Connell would surely obtain repeal, Father Mathew was regenerating a temperate Ireland and the growing number of reading rooms was producing a more literate Ireland. By the time of his departure, D'Arcy McGee had taken the Father Mathew temperance pledge and was supporting repeal, in the words of his sister to their aunt before departure, '. . . for the good of Ireland — for the Repeal — his heart burns within him.'[5]

The young Irish immigrant arrived in America several months before the founding of *The Nation* by Thomas Davis and Gavan Duffy but he already shared their romantic nationalism. He had read about Ireland's Celtic past in the pages of *The Dublin Penny Journal* and was determined to bring his nationalist enthusiasm to the attention of the growing Irish community in the United States.[6] The publisher of America's largest Catholic newspaper, *The Boston Pilot*, was quick to recognize that this would sell newspapers. McGee had addressed an Irish audience in Boston celebrating the 4th of July, 1842. The speech was reported in The Boston Pilot, which also announced that McGee had been engaged as its travelling agent.[7] McGee now began to tour New England as if it were a province of

Ireland, giving speeches, publishing them in the Pilot, selling sub-
scriptions and trying to collect overdue accounts. One series was
called 'Irish Authors and Authoresses'. It was designed to prove
'. . . that Ireland is a nation, at least an intellect.'[8] It could have
been written by Davis or Duffy in The Nation; McGee wrote it a
month before the first issue of The Nation appeared.

D'Arcy McGee had brought something else with him from Wexford — an Irish preconception of the United States of America. It
was evident in his speech in Boston on the 4th of July, a day he
referred to as '. . . the birthday of freedom.'[9] Such a faith was rewarded, for in two years of travelling, speaking, and writing he had
been able to accumulate enough capital to contemplate a move to
Ohio and the study of law. But D'Arcy McGee and Irish nationalism
had been good for the circulation of The Boston Pilot and its publisher made McGee an offer he could not refuse — the editorship of
the newspaper. His first editorial was published on his nineteenth
birthday.[10]

Five weeks later, his faith in America was shaken to its foundations. He had undoubtedly encountered the anti-Irish and anti-
Catholic hostility of American nativism in the two years before he
became editor, but nothing had prepared him for the events which
now took place in the city of brotherly love. The Philadelphia anti-
Catholic riots of 1844 left thirteen people dead and two churches
completely destroyed. McGee visited the city in September and reported, 'We looked upon the ruins of the churches and our hearts
swelled almost to breaking.'[11] The scene was like a page out of the
history of seventeenth-century Ireland; it was not supposed to happen in the nineteenth century, and especially not in America. He
now described the United States as '. . . a land mocked by the fruits
of liberty, which . . . turn only to ashes.'[12]

His Irish nationalism now became a kind of Irish-American zionism. The Irish would never be accepted as equals in America until
the Irish recovered their homeland and became a nation among
equals in the world.

> For think you, banished children of Ireland, if there was a senate
> in Ireland — schools in Ireland — a national literature in Ireland —
> with her temperance and her piety, she would still be regarded by
> those foreigners who have not seen her, as the darkest and most
> wicked of countries? . . . Remember emigrants, until Ireland is
> free and respectable, you can never be but what you are.[13]

McGee had brought a second preconception with him from Ireland, an idea of what Canada was like; Canada, the British colony.
He may have arrived in America at Quebec, but his destination was

New England and his journey through Canada had been swift. As editor of *The Boston Pilot* he commented on the political situation to the north, and the issues for him were simple. ' "Repeal of the Union" is the Irish for "Responsible Government" '[14] he wrote in one editorial and endorsed the Canadian reform party of Baldwin and Lafontaine: '. . . its principles are those to which every Irishman is born.'[15] One Canadian reader objected and claimed that the Tories in that province had been much more tolerant of Roman Catholicism and its institutions. McGee, taken aback, exclaimed, 'The Tories! Well may the Catholics of Canada exclaim, "Oh, save us from our friends!" '[16]

The Return to Ireland, 1845–48

D'Arcy McGee had not gone unnoticed in Ireland. Within a year of becoming editor of *The Boston Pilot*, he was offered a position with Dublin's *Freeman's Journal*. His new American friends assembled in Boston to give him a farewell banquet. The main themes of the lengthy speeches were American democracy and the promise of Young Ireland. Michael Gallagher of Canton, Ohio, declared, '. . . he will bring amongst them, I say, practical experience of the country, of the excellence of democratic liberty over all systems of government ever invented by man.' McGee's predecessor as editor of *The Boston Pilot* added, 'He is of young Ireland; he will be with young Ireland.'[17]

Two months later McGee was with Davis and Duffy on an excursion to Wicklow to celebrate the publication of the first volume of The Library of Ireland. McGee was ten years their junior, not of their class, and without their education. To Davis, the Protestant, McGee had been '. . . spoiled, I fear by the Yankees.' To Duffy, the Catholic, he was '. . . too deferential for self-respect.'[18] After a holiday with McGee in September, Duffy wrote to Davis, 'McGee is full of original thought and will be a serviceable recruit.'19 In the spring of 1846 the publisher of the *Freeman* learned that McGee was contributing to *The Nation*. McGee was invited to leave the former and join the latter.

By the time of his move to *The Nation*, D'Arcy McGee's Irish world was crumbling. Thomas Davis was dead, the potato crop had failed, Daniel O'Connell had abandoned repeal and was offering support to the British Whig government. One hundred and forty-five years later, Young Ireland's bitter rift with O'Connell and its programmes for the creation of the nation of Ireland seem petty and naive. In the context of the Great Famine they seem irresponsible and absurd. An incident involving McGee is illustrative.

When he learned that Americans were organizing relief for Ireland, he wrote a public letter in *The Boston Pilot* urging Americans not to send aid. Conditions in Ireland should be allowed to deteriorate so that the British would be forced to act. The Irish priest who was presiding over the programme in America objected to '. . . the *hollow-heartedness, shallowness, absurdity, the want of prudence, patriotism, philanthropy and piety* [of the] writer.'[20] An American doctor added, 'It is all very well for the leading public men of Dublin, who have plenty to eat . . . to talk so dogmatically ignorant of our noble movement.[21]

To be fair, McGee estimated that Young Ireland's programmes to foster a public opinion 'racy of the soil' and to 'educate that you may be free' would take 50 to 70 years to accomplish. Under the circumstances of the famine, how could one wait that long? He soon admitted that his letter to Americans in which he advised them not to send relief was a mistake. '. . . I do, in my soul, believe that we are now, at this very hour, in process of being exterminated as a people,' McGee declared in April, 1847.[22] Self-government was more than a nationalist ideal; it now seemed necessary for survival itself.

O'Connell's Repeal Association had abandoned that objective when it allied itself with the British Whigs, and Young Ireland organized the Irish Confederation to take up the cause. It had all the forms of a major national and political organization: McGee served on two of its standing committees: 'Public Instruction' and 'Membership Cards.' The Irish Confederation also had a great deal of rhetoric, witness McGee:

> The dogma of our political belief is Ireland must be ruled by Irishmen. The only duty we require is, love to all men in this island, and hatred to all foreigners intruding here as masters.[23]

But there was not much of an audience for these words, especially after the death of Daniel O'Connell. A good example of the lack of support was provided when the leaders of the Irish Confederation tried to address a Catholic audience in Belfast in November 1847. As McGee, Smith O'Brien, John Mitchel and Thomas Francis Meagher tried to take the stage, the pro-O'Connell crowd would not let them speak. Some began to explode devices called 'Kentish Fire", a mixture of gunpowder and sulphur. The meeting became a riot. The police had to be called to restore order with fixed bayonets. Irish nationalists needed the constabulary to address an audience of Catholics in Belfast![24] News of the riot reached America, and *The Boston Pilot* reported, '. . . bruised heads and torn apparel bore testimony to the violent feelings of the opposing parties.'[25]

Every which way the Irish Confederation turned, the path was blocked. In the only election in which it ran a candidate, Meagher in the Waterford by-election, it finished third, behind a Whig and an O'Connellite. John Mitchel had already concluded,

> . . . that the 'legal and constitutional' shouting, voting, and 'agitating' . . . have made our country an abomination to the whole earth. [And that this] should be changed into a deliberate study of the theory and practice of guerilla warfare.[26]

Mitchel and his supporters were purged from the Irish Confederation for these views, but the revolution in France, combined with Meagher's electoral defeat, caused it to change course suddenly and to adopt his revolutionary policy in early 1848.

The men of Young Ireland were now prepared to pay the ultimate price for their love of country, the offer of their own lives. And the price would have been paid, had the British not been determined to avoid creating martyrs. After the fiasco at Ballingarry, the arrest, conviction and sentencing of the leadership, Parliament had to pass special legislation to allow the Crown to commute the sentences of death to transportation without the consent of the convicted. They had wanted to die for their country.

The Flight to America, 1848–49

D'Arcy McGee was not among them. Just prior to Ballingarry, he had been sent to raise volunteers from the Irish in Scotland. He returned to Sligo to direct operations, but the plan evaporated with the news of the humiliating defeat in the south. He decided to escape, back to the United States.[27] He landed at Philadelphia, issued a public letter on what had happened in Ireland and signed it defiantly, 'Thomas D'Arcy McGee (A Traitor to the British Government).'[28] Many concluded that this was not very manly. The real traitors were in prison, about to declare their guilt proudly before the court, refusing to beg the crown for clemency and demanding their right to be hanged. And when people asked, 'Where were you?' McGee had to keep his public silence. His young wife, pregnant with their first child, had remained in Ireland to give evidence at Gavan Duffy's trials. This member of Young Ireland, publisher of *The Nation*, and future Prime Minister of Victoria, Australia, would not plead guilty. He would challenge the Crown's evidence, and Mrs. McGee would have to testify that the editorials in *The Nation*, which the prosecutor claimed were seditious, were her husband's and not Duffy's. Duffy would have three trials over eight months, all of which found him not guilty. Mrs. McGee had to give her testimony and bear her child while her husband was an exile in America. Public statements by D'Arcy McGee in America about the activities of 1848 would not help Gavan Duffy. Many who did not know about his mission to Scotland became suspicious. Had McGee been a police informer or an agent provocateur?

D'Arcy McGee continued the public battle for Irish freedom in exile in New York for another year in the pages of his own newspaper, which he called *The Nation,* an exact replica of the now suppressed Dublin newspaper. A typical editorial began, 'Of all the enemies of man's liberty, the most insidious and artful is this hoary harlot Great Britain.'[29] His revolutionary enthusiasm also led him to embrace liberalism and an extreme form of anticlericalism. He blamed the clergy for the failure of '48 and rejoiced when Pope Pius IX was forced to flee Rome and a Roman republic was established. He now wrote,

> [Catholicism] has been made by saintly and immortal men compatible with barbarism, feudalism, the crusades, and monarchy. It has to be made compatible with democracy and social reconstruction.[30]

After Gavan Duffy was acquitted for the third time, the Crown gave up. Mrs. McGee was free to join her husband in New York with their infant daughter. McGee now wanted to return to Ireland and rejoin Duffy, but McGee had not been acquitted and the charges against him were still outstanding. He had to remain in America and he began to turn his attention to the condition of the Irish in the new world. By the summer of 1849 he had begun his retreat from revolutionary liberalism. It would lead him on the road to ultramontanism and constitutional monarchy, to Canada in 1857 and Wexford in 1865, to government office in 1862 and to a violent, premature death in 1868.

Epilogue

There is an epilogue to the story. Bryce Mackasey, having offended the pro-McGee faction in 1966, went on to campaign for a 'more-durable-than-wax' monument to McGee as an 1967 centennial project. Apparently he had never seen the magnificent bronze statue which the government of Canada had dedicated to McGee's memory in 1925, the centennial of his birth. It is easily seen from the Library of Parliament. Madame Tussaud's closed its Montreal branch shortly after Expo '67. Part of McGee's Montreal home is now a bar. I suppose he would approve, but I wonder what he thinks of the nude dancers? At least it's more lively than a wax museum.

And the United Irish Societies continue to sponsor the Montreal St. Patrick's day parade, which continues to arouse controversy. This year the organizers refused to allow any display commemorating the Easter Rising and its martyrs of 75 years ago. Perhaps they will be able to find McGee's wax effigy for next year's parade.

Notes

1 Paul Dubois, 'St. Pat's Parade Fight Flares Over D'Arcy McGee Effigy.' *The Gazette*, 11 March 1966. 2.

2 *The Nation*, 20 May 1865. D'Arcy McGee published a version of *The Nation* in New York between 1848 and 1850. When that newspaper is cited it will be as *The Nation* (New York). Otherwise, *The Nation* refers to the Dublin newspaper.

3 T.D. McGee to Mrs. Charles Morgan, 28 March 1842. Concordia University Archives, D'Arcy McGee Collection.

4 *Griffith's Evaluation*, 1853. National Library of Ireland.

5 Dorcas McGee to Mrs. Charles Morgan, 21 August 1841. Concordia University Archives, D'Arcy McGee Collection.

6 McGee recalled the influence of the *Dublin Penny Journal* in an article in *The Nation*, 22 June 1850.

7 *The Boston Pilot*, 9 July 1842.

8 *Ibid.*, 24 September 1842. The italics are McGee's.

9 *Ibid.*, 9 July 1842.

10 *Ibid.*, 13 April 1844.

11 *Ibid.*, 7 September 1844.

12 *Ibid.*, 18 May 1844.

13 *Ibid.*, 28 September 1844.

14 *Ibid.*, 29 March 1845.

15 *Ibid.*, 5 October 1845.

16 *Ibid.*, 18 January 1845.

17 *Ibid.*, 17 May 1845.

18 Charles Gavan Duffy, *Four Years of Irish History* (London: Cassell, 1883), p. 741.

19 Charles Gavan Duffy, *My Life in Two Hemispheres*, 2 vols. (London: T. Fisher Unwin, 1898), vol. I, p. 121.

20 *The Boston Pilot*, 7 February 1846. Italics in the original.

21 *Ibid.*, 7 March 1846.

22 'The Irish Confederation, April 22, 1847.' *The Nation*, 24 April 1847.

23 *Proceedings of the Young Ireland Party at Dublin, December 2, 1846*, (Belfast: John Henderson, 1847). 2.

24 *The Nation*, 20 November 1847 and D. Gwyn, *Young Ireland and 1848* (Oxford: B.H. Blackwell, 1949), p. 141.

25 *The Boston Pilot*, 1 January 1848.

26 *The Nation*, 8 January 1848.

27 'McGee's Narrative of 1848.' *The Nation*, 8 March 1851. Note that he published his narrative almost three years after the rising. The delay was probably due in part to Duffy's trials, but may also have been due to McGee's hope to return to Ireland and rejoin Duffy. He would not have wanted to incriminate himself. By 1851, the accusations by Irish republicans against McGee and Duffy for their role in the rising and their constitutional approach to Irish reform were becoming increasingly personal and virulent.
28 *The Boston Pilot*, 21 October 1848.
29 *The Nation* (New York), 25 November 1848.
30 *Ibid.*, 25 November 1848.

Ogle Gowan

Aspiring Statesman and Stage Irishman

Hereward Senior

Ogle R. Gowan, founding father of Canadian Orangeism, has not been popular with historians. This is not surprising as he was guilty of two cardinal sins: attempting to take Conservatism from the privileged classes, and attempting to take people from the Liberals. This is not to deny his sins of the flesh so ably catalogued by Professor Akenson.

Classifications are rarely satisfactory, but the category 'Popularist' seems to suit Gowan best. He was to the Conservatives what William Lyon MacKenzie was to the Reformers, an embarrassing ally who was often useful. While MacKenzie flourished for a decade before passing into folklore in 1837, Gowan remained a force in Canadian politics for more than a generation. Yet he never got beyond the margins of history and is not the stuff of which folk heroes are made.

Gowan was never a professed democrat, but, like MacKenzie, the chartist leaders in Britain, and Tammany Hall politicians in New York, Gowan was among those who helped transform democracy from an ideology into a reality. If democracy was to work, it could not remain the exclusive property of high-minded intellectuals.

At the opening of the 1830s both Gowan and MacKenzie were experimenting with democratic techniques. MacKenzie had one eye on Jacksonian democracy, and the other on British radicalism; Gowan drew inspiration from his observations of Daniel O'Connell's campaign for Catholic rights in Ireland.

Gowan's leaving Ireland in 1829 was the result of his quarrels with Irish Orangemen, but 1829, the year of his departure was also the year of O'Connell's triumph, which closed the door to aspiring Orange politicians in southern Ireland. This must have strengthened his decision to emigrate.

Gowan came to Canada with the idea of taking over the scattered bands of Orangemen in Canada, giving them a Grand Lodge or a central organization, and using it as a political base.[1] His ambition was manifest in the title he chose for his most successful venture in journalism, the *Statesman*, and in pursuit of that ambition, at the age of 26 he settled in the Brockville area, with a household of nine including two servants. The land he acquired was of little value, but lent some plausibility to his claim to be a kind of Canadian squire.[2]

In the pursuit of statesmanship, status was an asset, and if it was not self-evident, it had to be asserted. Gowan was in fact the son of Irish squire Hunter Gowan and the godson of George Ogle, an eminent Orange parliamentarian. This was useful in asserting status. Apart from this Gowan had acquired that essential element of democratic politics, the common touch. Against him were his illegitimate birth, a public quarrel about his father's will, which would plague him for the rest of his life, and an inability to live within his limited means.

He began well, calling a meeting of all known Canadian Lodge Masters, and organized a Grand Lodge on January 1, 1830. By skilful name-dropping and a genuine gift of eloquence, he induced the Canadians to elect him Deputy Grand Master, promising that the Duke of Cumberland would accept the office of Grand Master. As the Duke declined, Gowan eventually became Grand Master himself.

A general election called in the summer of 1830 provided Gowan with an opportunity to test his recently acquired status of Orange Grand Master. Like D'Arcy McGee over a generation later, Gowan decided to run as an immigrant candidate. Here he appealed to both the Orange and the Green. Local politics had hitherto been a monopoly of Loyalist families, the Reformer Buells and the Tory Sherwoods and Jones's. Gowan was rebuffed in his efforts to form an alliance with the Buells and in turn rejected an alliance with the Sherwoods.

He lost the election by a few votes, and proved himself a poor loser by attributing the defeat to a conspiracy. Yet he had at his disposal a large body of belligerent Irishmen, and with admirable restraint refrained from turning them loose at the polls and winning the election by force.[3]

With the election over, Gowan sought to create in Leeds County permanent political organizations under such names as Independent and Patriotic clubs, and accepted for a while the co-operation of the Tories. At the same time MacKenzie was seeking to build up a network of permanent organizations along Yonge Street. On one occasion, Gowan packed and successfully broke up a meeting organized by MacKenzie's followers in the Brockville area. MacKenzie does not appear to have been greatly upset, and by way of complimenting a fellow demagogue found Gowan's manner of speaking pleasing.

Although an Orange Grand Master, Gowan did his best to keep clear of 'Anti-Catholicism'; he nevertheless felt the need for an enemy. MacKenzie had invented 'The Family Compact' in his assaults on the office holders. Gowan at times borrowed from MacKenzie's vocabulary and also denounced 'The Compact', but he found a more suitable target in the 'Yankees.' As he announced, 'It matters little to me where a man is born'; if he expounds republican principles, 'I call him a Yankee.'[4] The epithet was often applied to the Reformers, who were his obvious target.

Democracy means organizing the people as they are. Appeals to xenophobia are often the tools of the trade. Reformers, including MacKenzie, denounced 'pauper Irish' Thomas Paine, and went so far as to denounce England as 'That hellish and barbarous power which has stirred up the Indians and Negroes to destroy us.'[5]

To the immigrant Irish, 'Yankee' meant the post-Loyalist American settlers who had entered the province either just before or just after the War of 1812. It was this group which made up much of MacKenzie's constituency. They were often well-established Methodist farmers who expected the newly arrived Irish to show some deference to the older inhabitants. The Irish, who considered that they were bringing civilization to the wilderness, were in no way disposed to defer to the 'natives'. The Tories, for their part, saw the immigrants as the means of shifting the political balance against the Reformers, but had no intention of sharing patronage with leaders of the immigrant community. Gowan instinctively understood this from the day he arrived, but was prepared to experiment with a Tory alliance. Drawing on his Irish background, he preached a 'Loyalist Ascendancy' as a counterpart of the Protestant ascendancy which he had once found in Ireland.[6] This ascendancy involved a monopoly on political office, the right to use violence against enemies of the ascendancy and a certain immunity from justice while doing so.

In 1832, Gowan sought to assert the Loyalist ascendancy by breaking up a Reformer meeting called to protest against the Clergy Reserves. The Reformers were duly chastised, yet Gowan's followers found themselves charged with assault, and the Tories made no move to save them from conviction and sentencing. Gowan then broke with the Tories, and in 1833 denounced the Family Compact and spelled out in no uncertain terms his demands for Militia commissions and other government offices for deserving Irish gentlemen. Loyalists had done a great service for the Canadas, but he felt they had been adequately rewarded.[7]

The following year, 1834, Gowan sought to bypass the Tories in the general election and establish an independent relation with the government. This appeared to be possible because the newly arrived Attorney General, Robert Jamieson, needed a seat in the Assembly. In those days the Executive Council was in theory composed of appointed civil servants, yet some offices like that of Attorney General could not be filled effectively without a seat in the Assembly.

Gowan persuaded Jamieson that he could offer him a safe seat. Gowan and Jamieson would run together as government candidates. As the Tories, being part of the patronage system, would not vote against government candidates, Gowan had compelled the Tories to vote for him. His problem, however, was that even with Tory support, he had no way of winning the elections in a fair contest.

As fair means would not work, Gowan decided to use foul, and had the means of doing so. He turned his followers loose, and they promptly blockaded the polls and prevented many Reformers from voting. He won the election, but it was a year of a Liberal landslide and his election was nullified by the Assembly. A second election was held which was, like the first, won by Gowan and declared invalid by the Assembly. Then, in 1836, after Lieutenant-Governor Francis Bond Head had called on the electorate to return loyal candidates, Gowan rode in on a Conservative landslide in company with Tory Jonas Jones. In this election, an alliance between the Orange and the Green, engineered by Gowan and the Roman Catholic Bishop Alexander MacDonnell, made a substantial contribution to a victory of government-approved candidates.[8]

Having at last obtained a seat in the Assembly, Gowan was soon able to acquire a second social and political asset: a military reputation. MacKenzie's rebellion and the subsequent raids along the frontier, brought Orangemen swarming into the volunteer militia. Gowan was wounded in action and was given the rank of Lieutenant-Colonel. In all, he saw at least as much action as Colonel Theodore Roosevelt saw at San Juan Hill in 1898.

By 1838 Gowan was in a position to attempt a conventional political career. He had used unconventional methods to secure a seat, but once in the Assembly he left the common touch behind him. His ideas were similar to those of Robert Baldwin and anticipated the Liberal-Conservatism of John A. Macdonald. He understood that the people, or at least his Irish constituents, were by instinct religious, patriotic, not much attracted by ideology, and would prefer Conservative politicians, providing their interests were protected. Orangeism offered a portable patriotism, in which loyalty was to tradition rather than to geography, in contrast to the nativism which was attractive to the older inhabitants. Nationalist historians have assumed that Gowan's type of patriotism would vanish with the colonial society, yet we are still in an age of folk wandering, in which Newfoundlanders often end up in British Columbia. Local landmarks are more likely to vanish than traditions and folk memory.

Gowan stood for tradition and folk memory but had no intention of placing them at the disposal of privileged office holders. His immediate difficulty was that the Crown's representatives in Canada were not in a position to grant patronage to the Orangemen.

In the United Kingdom, the Orange Lodge had been forced to dissolve. Bond Head, acting on instructions from London, requested that the Canadian Lodges dissolve. Gowan defied Head, and his successor Sir George Arthur, on this issue. By degrees, Gowan moved to the left, and by 1839 he was advocating responsible government.[9] He further estranged himself from the Tories by introducing a measure for dividing clergy reserves among all recognized denominations. By so doing he provoked a revolt of Conservative Orangemen against his leadership. He managed to survive as Orange Grand Master, but lost his seat in the election of 1841.

He won it back in the Tory landslide of 1844, and during the next few years came close to realizing his ambition to become a statesman. Like most Conservatives, he perceived the necessity of winning French support if the party was to survive in the United Province. Yet unlike most Conservatives, Gowan, as Orange Grand Master, was in a position to influence the largest and most militant and best organized Protestant Voluntary Society in the Canadas. Gowan was never to become a statesman, but at times he had a statesmanlike vision. He also had his gifts as a parliamentarian, which were fully recognized by his adversaries. LaFontaine found Gowan to be the most accomplished speaker of the House, while Francis Hincks declared that Gowan had more tact and general information than any man engaged in public affairs.[10] John A. Macdonald, who became a close associate of Gowan at this time, fully acknowledged his services to the party. Even MacKenzie acknowledged Gowan's abilities and liberalism.

In 1846 Gowan was approaching the frontiers of statesmanship,[11] but he lost control of the Orange Lodges in the same year and his seat in the House two years later.

After that he seems to have fallen into a state of despondency, foolishly insulting Lord Elgin because of his signing of the Rebellion Losses Bill, and consequently losing his commission of the peace and militia rank of Lieutenant-Colonel.

Yet Gowan still had important work to do. By the year 1858 the alliance between Upper Canadian Reformers and French Canada was breaking down under the hammer blows of George Brown of the Globe. A new bicultural party was needed, and that could only be brought about by an alliance of French Canadians and Upper Canadian Conservatives.

Under such conditions it was likely that the Orange Lodges, now under the innocuous leadership of Gowan's successor George Benjamin, would fall under the influence of George Brown. In 1853 Gowan, for purely personal reasons, had packed the Kingston Grand Lodge meeting and reclaimed the office of Grand Master. Benjamin promptly organized a schismatic Grand Lodge. When the schisms had taken place Gowan was in a position to swing most of the Orangemen behind the Conservative-French Coalition, which formed the government in 1854.

In the ensuing contest for control of the Orange vote, Benjamin's followers were no match for Gowan. Of the 563 Lodges in Canada only 106 followed Benjamin and all the Maritime Lodges supported Gowan. George Brown's denunciation of Gowan as an 'uncompromising adherent to the priest party while professing to be an Orangeman'[12] was a tribute to Gowan's influence.

At this time Gowan made efforts to re-enter Parliament which resulted in two defeats, but he finally secured a seat in his old territory, Leeds County. Yet this was an anticlimax: he was past his peak by the end of the 1850s.

Gowan's talents as a machine politician and parliamentarian never secured for him a high office or a place on the front pages of history. This can be explained partly by his private life. As Professor Akenson has pointed out, Gowan entered the Victorian Age with Regency morals. His relationships with young working-class women led to litigation which became public knowledge.[13] Apart from this he was conspicuously wanting in the arts of the courtier. Like MacKenzie he took particular delight in insulting members of the local elite. These faults were compounded by his permanent isolvency, a condition which he shared with D'Arcy McGee.

In essence, Gowan was a father of liberal conservatism who, had he achieved that elusive quality, respectability, might have become a father of Confederation.

Notes

[1] Hereward Senior, 'Ogle Gowan, Orangeism, and the Immigrant Question 1830–1833,' *Ontario History*, 66 (1974): 193–95.

[2] Donald Akenson, *The Orangeman* (Toronto: Lorimer, 1986), p. 121.

[3] *Gazette* (Brockville), 30 October 1830.

[4] *Ibid.*, 31 December 1830.

[5] Thomas Paine, *Common Sense*, ed. Philip S. Foner (New York: Citadel, 1945), p. 25.

6 Hereward Senior, 'A Bid for Rural Ascendancy: The Upper Canadian Orangemen 1836–1849,' in Donald H. Akenson, ed. *Canadian Papers in Rural History*, vol. V (Ganonoque, Ont.: Langdale, 1986), pp. 224–34.

7 *Antidote* (Brockville), 29 January 1833.

8 *Vindicator* (Montreal), 12, 17 June 1836; *Gazette* (Brockville), 21 June 1836; Hereward Senior, *Orangeism: The Canadian Phase* (Toronto: McGraw-Hill, 1972), p. 29.

9 *Statesman* (Brockville), 27 August 1839.

10 Hereward Senior, 'Ogle Gowan,' D.C.B., Vol. X (Toronto: University of Toronto Press, 1972), pp. 311–12.

11 *Colonial Advocate* (York), 29 July 1830; *Brockville Recorder*, 17 November 1831.

12 Hereward Senior, 'Ogle Gowan,' D.C.B., Vol. X (Toronto: University of Toronto Press, 1972), p. 313.

13 Akenson, pp. 295–307.

Isaac Weld and the
Continuity of Canadian Poetry

D.M.R. Bentley

The Editors and contributors have not joined in a chauvinistic hunt for 'the great Canadian novel' or even for 'Canadianism.' They wish to demonstrate, not to argue about, what and how much has grown up in Canada. . . . This book treats, not only works generically classified as 'literature,' but also . . . other works which have influenced literature or have been significantly related to literature in expressing the cultural life of the country.

—Carl F. Klinck, 'Introduction,'
Literary History of Canada

When the Irish poet Thomas Moore visited Canada in 1804 he evidently carried with him a book that had a seminal influence on the poetry written in this country between the turn of the nineteenth century and the onset of the Confederation period: Isaac Weld's *Travels through the United States of North America, and the Provinces of Upper and Lower Canada, during the Years 1795, 1796, and 1797.* '[S]hould you like to see a particular account of the Falls,' Moore told his mother in a letter of July 24, 1804 from Niagara Falls, 'Weld, in his Travels, has given the most accurate I have seen.'[1] Arguing that the 'language' of poetry as it then existed was inadequate to describe Canada's most sublime sight, Moore did not in this instance follow Weld's example and produce a poetic description of Niagara Falls. But apparently he did use Weld as a point of departure for at least two of his most influential 'Poems Relating to America,' the 'Ballad Stanzas' that he is reputed to have composed under a 'small tree'[2] on the north shore of Lake Ontario and the exquisite 'Canadian Boat Song' ('Faintly as tolls the evening chime . . . ') which declares itself to have been 'Written on the River St. Lawrence.'[3] At least part of the inspiration for the former, with its memorable 'silence' broken only by a 'woodpecker tapping [a] hollow beech-tree',[4] obviously came from Weld's description of a 'solemn silence' in a New York forest broken only by a 'woodpecker . . . now and then tapping with its bill against a hollow tree.'[5] For the latter, Moore probably drew similar inspiration from Weld's remark that '[t]he French-Canadians . . . have one very favourite duet amongst them, called the 'rowing duet,' which as they sing they mark time to, with each stroke of the oar . . . ' (*Travels*, II, 51). To observe that Moore's 'Ballad Stanzas' lie behind the opening lines of Adam Kidd's *The Huron Chief* (1830)[6] and that his 'Canadian Boat Song' is echoed in the opening stanza of Archibald Lampman's 'Between the Rapids' (1888)[7] is already to indicate the extent of Weld's reach into nineteenth-century Canadian poetry (and, indeed, beyond, for Lampman's poem is in turn echoed in Don McKay's *Long Sault* [1975]).[8] Who, then, was Isaac Weld, and wherein lay the appeal of his Travels?

'A descendant of learned and pious clergymen,'[9] who carried forward the name Isaac in memory of Sir Isaac Newton,[10] Weld was born in Dublin in 1774 and died in the Irish village of Bray in 1856. Upper middle class by background and English in orientation, he was 'rich' in Gibbon's sense that his income was superior to his expense and his expense was equal to his wish to pursue in a gentlemanly manner his scientific and topographical interests. In addition to his *Travels*, these interests issued in such works as *Illustrations of the Scenery of Killarney and the Surrounding Country* (1807) and a *Statistical Survey of the County of Roscommon* (1832) produced under the auspices of the Royal Dublin Society, an organization of which Weld was a long time member and, in 1849, vice-president. Of course, it was Weld's *Travels* that earned him a membership in the Historical and Literary Society of Quebec and an entry in the Literary History of Canada.[11] Written while Weld was touring the United States and Canada with the view of 'ascertaining whether, in case of future emergency, any part of those territories might be looked forward to as an eligible and agreeable place of abode' (I, iii), his *Travels* was first published in London in 1799. It was reprinted three times between 1800 and 1807 and translated during the same period into French, German, and Dutch. An Italian version appeared in 1819, and in our own day there have been two facsimile reprintings of the final English edition of 1807.

There are two primary reasons for the popularity of Weld's *Travels* in the early years of the nineteenth century. The first, as G.M. Craig points out, was a matter of historical timing: Weld gave an 'early, sometimes first, account of many aspects of North American life' (*DCB*) — life in a frontier environment that was of great and growing interest to Europeans. Moreover, and especially for people interested in Canada, Weld's *Travels* had no serious rival as a description of the country and its inhabitants until the publication in 1809 of John Lambert's similarly popular *Travels through Canada, and the United States of North America, in the Years 1806, 1807, and 1808.* (As Lambert's echoic title indicates, his book is partly a response to Weld's work, and, indeed, addresses it explicitly in several places.)[12] The second reason for the popularity of Weld's *Travels* lies, as Craig again points out, in its author's 'special skill' in describing the physical and social landscapes through which he travelled in the late seventeen nineties. Not only did Weld have the ability to portray scenes and people in an evocative manner, but he also had an eye and an ear for the small detail—the sound of a 'woodpecker . . . tapping . . . a hollow tree' and so emphasizing the uncanny silence of a North American forest—that gives to a description a convincing touch of authenticity. It is the success of his *Travels* in conveying vivid impressions of the sights and sounds of North America that puts Weld in the company of Thomas James, Jonathan Carver, Peter Kalm, and the other visitors to this continent whose prose has proved inspirational to poets.[13]

A third and more restricted reason for Weld's popularity in Britain, and particularily in British North America, is the political bias of his *Travels.* 'Like many other British travellers, then and later, Weld felt more at home in the provinces [of Canada] than in republican America' (*DCB*). As well as finding the treatment of the blacks and the native peoples in the United States abhorrent, he was repelled by the ugliness of American cities and the inefficiency of American agriculture. What was worse from an American perspective (and unforgivable to Washington Irving and many other Americans), Weld found the ordinary people of the United States rude, slovenly, greedy, and self-interested. In contrast, he saw Canada as a demi-paradise of attractive scenery, burgeoning prosperity, excellent roads, and friendly, tolerant, communally-minded people—in short, as a far better destiny for emigrants than the United States. Almost needless to say, these attitudes were bound to endear Weld to British North Americans, not least those whose Tory views predisposed them to relish alike his disparaging remarks about the United States and his enthusiastic endorsement of Upper and Lower Canada. Little wonder that Weld's earliest and greatest impact in Canadian poetry was on a young writer who characterized the United States as a traitorous and—wishful thinking—increasingly 'weak republic' controlled by 'despot *rabbles*'[14] and such poisonous snakes and Thomas Jefferson.

A deeply conservative and probably tubercular student from Christ's College, Cambridge, Cornwall Bayley arrived in Quebec about a month before Moore passed through the province on his way to Nova Scotia. It is tantalizing to imagine that the two met and, indeed, that it was Moore who introduced Bayley to Weld's

Travels, but it is more likely that this meeting of like minds occurred impersonally and earlier, and perhaps even lay behind the young student's decision to come to Canada. In any case, Bayley's *Canada. A Descriptive Poem* (Quebec, 1806) makes extensive use of Weld's *Travels*, drawing in its opening lines on the traveller's depiction of the view from the upper town of Quebec (the best for 'its grandeur, its beauty, and its diversity . . . in America, or indeed in any other part of the globe' [I, 354]) and reflecting in its closing paragraphs and footnotes the 'tender sentiments'[15] and quaint details of Weld's description of the Ursuline Convent in Trois Rivières.[16] In the body of *Canada*, Bayley relies on Weld for his treatment of a wide range of topics, from the winter amusements of the Lower Canadians to the growing settlements on the shores of Lake Erie. Here, for the purposes of comparison, is part of Weld's description of the 'stupendous Falls' (II, 112) at Niagara, followed by Bayley's rendition of the same sublime sight as seen by an elderly *voyageur*:

> No words can convey an adequate idea of the awful grandeur of the scene at this place. Your senses are appalled by the sight of the immense body of water that comes pouring down so closely to you from the top of the stupendous precipice, and by the thundering sound of the billows dashing against the rocky sides of the caverns below; you tremble with reverential fear, when you consider that a blast of the whirlwind might sweep you off the slippery rocks on which you stand, and precipitate you into the dreadful gulf beneath, from whence all the power of man could not extricate you; you feel what an insignificant being you are in the creation, and your mind is forcibly impressed with an awful idea of the power of that mighty Being who commanded the waters to flow. (II, 128–29)

> Wave upon wave it tumbles from its height;
> The rocks below receive th' incessant stroke,
> And back recoil a cloud of watery smoke. . . .
>
> Thus whilst he tells, the aged sire recalls
> His former thoughts of these stupendous falls,
> He feels how grand — how infinite the tale,
> Himself how little in Creation's scale;
> And still too low his maker's works to raise,
> Bids more expressive silence muse his praise!
> (*C*, 366–68, 373–78)

This is but one of several instances in *Canada* which show how Weld filtered Canadian scenes through the aesthetics of the sublime and the picturesque and then inspired Bayley to do the same thing. That the final line and much else of Bayley's description of Niagara Falls is borrowed from James Thomson conjures up a compositional setting for *Canada* that is typical of early Canadian poetry: Bayley, pen in hand at a desk far from Niagara Falls, with Weld's *Travels* open to his left and Thomson's *Seasons* open to his right. Indeed, so typical is this combination of poet, travel account, and poetic source that it can be described without exaggeration as the primal scene of early Canadian poetry—the verbal intercourse which, in Bayley's phrase, 'Gives birth to song' on Canada (*C*, 34).

Implicit in Bayley's conception of the 'aged sire' in the passage quoted a moment ago is his agreement with Weld that, in contrast to the United States and post-revolutionary France, French Canada has remained a deeply religious society in which traditional faiths are held and practiced with impunity. 'There are no animosities in Canada about religions,' says Weld, '[e]very religion is tolerated . . . and no disqualifications are imposed on any persons on account of their religious opinions' (I, 415; I, 370–71). Or, as Bayley puts it, 'in *these* cots afar from Atheist pride, / And bigot deceit allied . . . persecution tempts not from his door, / To seek a gentler rule the pious poor' (*C*, 379–80, 385–86). Bayley does not always agree with Weld's analysis of French Canada, however; on the contrary, he finds Canada freer than his predecessor did of the moral abuses of feudalism and capitalism, and he defends the French Canadians themselves against the charge of vanity levelled repeatedly against them in the *Travels*. 'Some of the lower classes of the French Canadians have all the gaiety and vivacity of the people of France,' Weld observes, '[but] vanity . . . is the ascendant feature in the character of all of them. . . . They are the vainest people, perhaps, in the world. . . . The spirit of the Canadian is excited by vanity. . . . The shape of [their carioles or sledges] is varied according to fancy, and it is a matter of emulation amongst the gentlemen, who shall have the handsomest one' (I, 338–39; II, 4, 9. I, 392). Bayley disagrees: 'His neat Calash (himself the artist) [is] made, / For use and pleasure—not for vain parade . . . ' (*C*, 404–05). As these examples show, Bayley did not follow Weld slavishly but responded to him, relying upon the reader to recognize points of agreement and disagreement. By articulating a position to which readers and writers could respond on the basis of their own firsthand experience of Canada and its inhabitants, Weld both prepared a readership and opened up imaginative spaces for Bayley and others. Especially when the response to him is corrective or tinged with pique, it is clear that Weld has provided the occasion for the exercise of an emotion that is surely essential for the development of any regional or national poetry: local pride.

Two native-born Canadian poets whose long poems contain a spectrum of responses to Weld based on local pride are Adam Hood Burwell and Oliver Goldsmith. Born and raised in what is now southwestern Ontario, the former draws heavily on Weld in *Talbot Road: A Poem* (1818) to depict the Lake Erie area and to describe the creation of the Settlement from which his poem takes its title. In October, 1796 the 'dangerous storms' (II, 296) that Weld regarded as characteristic of Lake Erie had forced the vessel on which he was travelling 'to lay at anchor for three days' before sailing east towards Buffalo Creek by way of some islands 'which had the most beautiful appearance imaginable. The woods with which the shores were adorned, now tinged with the hues of autumn, afforded in their decline a still more pleasing variety to the eye than when they were clothed in their fullest verdure; and their gaudy colours, intermingled with the shadows of the rocks, were seen fancifully reflected in the unruffled surface of the surrounding lake' (II, 297). As Burwell's repetition of the word 'unruffled' indicates, this picturesque description and the events surrounding it provided the pretext for the following passage in *Talbot Road*:

> Uninterrupted roves the careless eye
>
> . . . where the lake its billowy surges pours,
> And round the beaten cliffs tremendous roars;
> Or, mirror-like, smooth and unruffled lies,
> And seems to mingle with the distant skies,
> Where oft the vessel glides with swelling sails,
> Or waits impatient for the fav'ring gales.[17]

But while Burwell follows Weld closely here, he carefully places his emphasis, not on the violence of the storm, but on its placid aftermath. Elsewhere in *Talbot Road* he contradicts Weld's extremely low opinion of the harbours on the Canadian shore of Lake Erie. 'On its northern side there are but two places which afford shelter to vessels drawing more than seven feet . . . and these only afford a partial shelter' (II, 159–60), asserts Weld; on the contrary, writes Burwell proudly (and, very likely, in an attempt to lure pioneers to the Talbot Settlement by emphasizing its water privileges), Otter Creek near St. Thomas provides both a safe harbour from the 'rough lake' and a 'broad highway' to the Talbot Road itself, 'whence they transport with ease,/Provisions, furniture, or what they please' (*TR*, 199–204). In dialogue with Weld, Burwell thus emphasizes the present amenities and the future prospects of an area which, twelves years earlier, Bayley had seen mainly through

Weld's eyes as a 'wild' region where 'the scatter'd cot/But proves the former deserts of the spot . . . ' (*C*, 351–52).[18]

Perhaps Burwell's most subtle and patriotic use of Weld in *Talbot Road* occurs in his account of the firing of fallen timber during the clearing of land in the Talbot Settlement by a newly-arrived 'Woodman.' While visiting Virginia in the spring of 1796, Weld witnessed a dangerous 'conflagration' which he attributes to 'the negligence of people . . . burning brushwood to clear the lands' and describes as a 'sublime sight' complete with a 'terrible whirlwind,' a cloud that darkens the horizon, and a 'prodigious column of fire' (I, 160–61). 'When these fires do not receive a timely check,' Weld writes, 'they sometimes increase to an alarming height; and . . . proceed with so great velocity that the swiftest runners are often overtaken in endeavouring to escape the flames' (I, 161). Obviously taking his cue from this portion of the *Travels*, Burwell provides the reader of *Talbot Road* with a similar description of 'Wide flashing fires' surmounted by a 'dense mantle' of dark 'clouds,' and heightens the sublimity of the spectacle with echoes of the opening books of *Paradise Lost*.[19] But whereas Weld attributes blame to negligent Americans for the kind of fire that he witnessed in Virginia, Burwell characterizes his typical Upper Canadian settler as responsible and 'assiduous.' Only after he has worked his way among the 'raging fires' to 'trim the heaps, and fire th' extinguish'd brands' (*TR*, 289–93) does the 'Woodman' wend his weary way homeward to his wife and family. In the United States there is slovenliness and bad planning, but in Canada there is 'morality and good order' (I, 416).

Like Burwell and Bayley before him — and in a manner which, again, signals the emergence of local pride and a local perspective — Goldsmith agrees with Weld on some matters in *The Rising Village* (1825, 1834) and departs from him on others. At several points in the *Travels*, Weld snobbishly comments on the tendency of the 'lower and middling classes of people . . . in the country parts of Pennsylvania' and elsewhere to pester travellers with unwelcome questions. 'On arriving amongst the Americans,' he says in one letter, 'a stranger must tell where he came from, where he is going, what his name is, what his business is; and until he gratifies their curiosity on these points, and many others of equal importance, he is never suffered to remain quiet for a moment. In a tavern, he must satisfy every fresh set that comes in, in the same manner, or involve himself in a quarrel . . . ' (I, 124–25). And in another letter he continues: 'A traveller on arriving in America may possibly imagine, that it is the desire of obtaining useful information which leads the people, wherever he stops, to accost him; and that . . . particular enquiries . . . are made to prepare the way for questions of a more general nature. . . . [B]ut when it is found that these questions are asked merely through an idle and impertinent curiosity, and that by far the greater part of the people who ask them are ignorant, boorish fellows . . . the traveller then loses all patience at this disagreeable and prying disposition . . . ' (I, 134–35). Goldsmith concedes that pointless questions are disconcerting to the 'traveller' or 'stranger,' but puts them in the mouth, not of the settlers whose hard work has built the poem's typical Nova Scotia settlement, but of the well-meaning keeper of the village tavern:

> Where some rude sign or post the spot betrays,
> The tavern first its useful front displays.
> Here, oft the weary traveller at the close
> Of evening, finds a snug and safe repose.
> The passing stranger here, a welcome guest,
> From all his toil enjoys a peaceful rest;
> Unless the host, solicitous to please,
> With care officious mar his hope of ease,
> With flippant questions to no end confined,
> Exhaust his patience, and perplex his mind.[20]

In their defence of the settlers of Nova Scotia in particular and North America in general from Weld's charges, the ensuing lines in *The Rising Village* recall Bayley's protective attitude to the French Canadians in *Canada*.

> Yet, let no one condemn with thoughtless haste,
> The hardy settler of the dreary waste,
> Who, far removed from every busy throng,
> And social pleasures that to life belong,
> Whene'er a stranger comes within his reach,
> Will sigh to learn whatever he can teach.
> To this, must be ascribed in great degree,
> That ceaseless, idle curiosity,
> Which over all the Western world prevails,
> And every breast, or more or less, assails;
> Till, by indulgence, so o'erpowering grown,
> It seeks to know all business but its own. (*RV*, 141–52)

At once protective and, to a degree, disapproving of the behaviour of the settlers, Goldsmith here exhibits two of the psychological hallmarks of the colonial: an embarrassed sense of the inferiority of the colony in relation to the mother country, and a truculently defensive attitude to criticisms of colonial life by condescending visitors from the imperial centre. Perhaps such ambivalence is inevitable in a poem written to celebrate the social and material advances of Nova Scotia by a man who in 1818 had very reluctantly returned to the province after setting his heart on living in England.[21]

If one portion of Weld's *Travels* stands out as making a repeated and enduring impact on early Canadian poetry, it is the traveller's description of the birds of North America. Basing his remarks on Mark Catesby's *Natural History of Carolina, Florida and the Bahama Islands,* Weld observes of the birds in Virginia, and of North American birds generally, that they are 'much inferior to those in Europe in the melody of their notes, but . . . superior in point of plumage' (I, 195). By way of illustrating this observation, he mentions several European song birds (the blackbird, the skylark, and the nightingale) and he singles out the American 'blue bird' and 'red bird' as being especially 'remarkable for their plumage' (I, 195). He also notes that 'many other birds' in North America such as 'jays, robins, larks, [and] pheasants . . . were called by the English settlers after birds of the same name in England . . . though in fact they are materially different,' and he concludes by describing a bird that would become iconic in pre-Confederation Canadian poetry: 'the whipperwill, or whip-poor-will, as it is sometimes called, from the plaintive noise that it makes . . . ' (I, 196). '[T]o my ear,' he writes, the bird's call 'sound[s] wyp-o-il. It begins to make this noise, which is heard a great way off, about dusk, and continues it through the greater part of the night. The bird is so very wary, and so few instances have occurred of its being seen, much less taken, that many have imagined the noise does not proceed from a bird, but from a frog, especially as it is heard most frequently in the neighbourhood of low grounds' (I, 195–96).

While Bayley describes another bird mentioned by Weld, the humming bird (I, 196; *C*, 269–70), and Burwell insists on both the 'mellow song' and the bright 'plumage' of Upper Canadian birds (*TR*, 52–54), neither of them so much as mentions the whip-poor-will, the reason probably being that the Romantic vogue for birds had little impact in Canada in the first two decades of the nineteenth century. By the eighteen twenties and thirties the influence of Byron and Scott (not to mention Moore) had been firmly transplanted, however, and may even have had an impact on the stalwartly Georgian Goldsmith, who, nevertheless, need not have read anything more recent than Weld and Pope to generate his lyrical account of the whip-poor-will in *The Rising Village*:

> The note of the Whip-poor-Will how sweet to hear,
> When sadly slow it breaks upon the ear,
> And tells each night, to all the silent vale,
> The hopeless sorrows of its mournful tale. (*RV*, 477–80)

Goldsmith's note to these lines confirms that, whatever their poetic influences, their prose source was Weld's *Travels*. 'The Whip-poor-Will . . . is a native of America,' reads the note; '[o]n a summer's evening the wild and mournful cadence of its note is heard at a great distance; and the traveller listens with delight to the repeated tale of its sorrows' (*RV*, 477n.).

Between the publication of *The Rising Village* in England in 1825 and in New Brunswick in 1834, another native-born Canadian writer, John Richardson, included a reference to 'the wild plaining of the Whipperwill' in *Tecumseh; or, the Warrior of the West* (1828) and glossed the bird in a decidedly post-Romantic expansion of Weld that must be quoted at length: 'The notes of [the Whipperwill], seldom seen, and scarcely ever caught, even by the Indians, are singularly wild and melancholy. I have never met with it but on the banks of Lake Erie and adjoining rivers. Its plaining is to be heard only at night, and always more distinctly when the canopy of heaven is unclouded, and the pale moon-beams, playing on the motionless bosom of the waters, attest the calm of universal nature. It pronounces the word whipperwill . . . in so extraordinary a manner, that the most interesting impressions arise to the mind; and the heart naturally attuned to the enjoyment of solitude, may linger on those sweet banks, forming images of happiness, and indulging in every voluptuous sentiment of the soul, until the star of morning, in discontinuing the blended magic of the scene, awakens to miserable reality, and demonstrates but too faithfully that our fairest perceptions, and most exquisite sensations in life, are but the fleeting visions of a faithless dream.'[22] It is almost as difficult to doubt that when he wrote this Richardson had Keats's 'Ode to a Nightingale' in mind as it is to deny that he must have had a copy of Weld's *Travels* to hand.

To give many more examples of Weldean whip-poor-wills in early Canadian writing would be tedious and redundant. One more example must be given, however, if only to illustrate the endurance of Weld's impact on Canadian poetry. It comes in the third chapter of Alexander McLachlan's *The Emigrant* (1861), at the end of what is obviously a versification and elaboration in the Ontario woods of Weld's observations on the birds of Virginia:

Lovely birds of gorgeous dye,
Flitted 'mong the branches high,
Coloured like the setting sun,
But were songless every one;
No one like the linnet gray,
In our home so far away;
No one singing like the thrush,
To his mate within the bush;
No one like the gentle lark. . . .

*   *   *

Some had lovely amber wings,
Round their necks were golden rings;
Some were purple, others blue,
All were lovely, strange and new;
But although surpassing fair,
Still the song was wanting there;
Then we heard the rush of pigeons,
Flocking to those lonely regions;
And anon when all was still,
Paused to hear the whip-poor-will;
And we thought of the cuckoo,
But this stranger no one knew.[23]

The fact that Weld also mentions the European 'thrush' (I, 195) and the 'wild pigeons of Canada' (II, 42) merely confirms that the *Travels* was one of the books that McLachlan had to hand when he wrote this passage (and, indeed, several other portions of *The Emigrant*).[24] And the fact that some of the other books on McLachlan's writing desk — most notably Moore's *Poems* and Catharine Parr Traill's *The Backwoods of Canada* (1836)[25] — also reveal the impact of Weld once again emphasizes the seminal and multifarious nature of his influence on Canadian writing. When Weld 'depart[ed] from this Continent' in January, 1797 he did so 'without a sigh, and without entertaining the slightest wish to revisit it' (II, 376). As far as early Canadian poetry was concerned, however, he did not really leave at all.

On September 29, 1804, in his last letter before leaving Nova Scotia for England, Moore wrote as follows to Joseph Dennie in Philadelphia: 'I have seen . . . the chief beauties of upper and lower Canada, and they have left impressions upon my heart and fancy which my memory long shall love to recur to. If the soil be not very ungrateful, the new thoughts it is scattered with, will spring up, I hope, into something for your hand to embellish by *transplanting.*'[26] In his graceful assurance to Dennie that he will send him material for publication in *The Port Folio*, Moore uses a botanical metaphor — poems as transplantable organisms — that is rich in resonances for early Canadian poetry and useful, too, in assessing the rôle of Weld and other travellers in the development of writing in and on Canada. As a work that played an important part in preparing the ground for similar and different species of writing — Moore's lyrics, the long poems of Bayley, Burwell, Goldsmith, Richardson, and MacLachlan, Lambert's *Travels*, and the settler narratives of Traill, Susanna Moodie, and others — Weld's *Travels* is the equivalent of a pioneer plant, an early arrival in an environment that makes later transplantings possible in various ways, most notably by breaking up the soil and by leaving an accumulation of fertile organic matter. The first effect of Weld's *Travels* and similar works was to penetrate and divide North America into micro environments — Niagara Falls, brush fires, taverns, birds — that were hospitable to various species and subspecies of English poetry such as the topographical poem and the picturesque *tableau*. Their second effect is almost invisible because it springs from the residue — the humus — left by the pioneer plant/travel account in the literary soil from which successive species grew and have continued to grow. Just as *The Huron Chief* sprang from ground broken and fertilized by Weld, so too in their use of the works of Traill and Moodie do Margaret Laurence's *The Diviners* (1974) and Margaret Atwood's *Journals of Susanna Moodie* (1970). And how many contemporary works of Canadian fiction and poetry have, in their turn, been influenced by the works of Laurence and Atwood? If it is true that we each have within us one atom from the body of Cleopatra, then, by the same laws of survival and dispersal, it can hardly be doubted that in a great many works written in Canada from 1799 to the present there is at least a trace of Isaac Weld's *Travels*.

Notes

My thanks to Beth McIntosh for transforming my scrawl into typescript.

1 *The Letters of Thomas Moore*, ed. Wilfred S. Dowden (Oxford: Clarendon, 1964), I, p. 77. For references to Weld in 'Poems Relating to America,' see *The Poetical Works of Thomas Moore*, ed. A.D. Godley (Oxford: Humphrey Milford, 1915), pp. 117 n. 1 and 3 and p. 120 n. 1. See also my 'Thomas Moore in Canada and Canadian Poetry,' *Canadian Poetry: Studies, Documents, Reviews*, 24 (Spring/Summer, 1989), pp. [vii–xiii].

2 This 'tradition' is recounted by John Galt in *Bogle Corbet; or, the Emigrants* (London: Henry Colburn and John Bentley [1831]), III, p. 3.

3 *Poetical Works*, pp. 124-125.

4 *Ibid.*, p. 124. Galt refers to 'Ballad Stanzas' as Moore's 'Woodpecker poem.'

5 *Travels through the States of North America, and the Provinces of Upper and Lower Canada, during the Years 1795, 1796, and 1797*, 4th ed. (London: John Stockdale, 1807), II, p. 320; hereafter cited as *Travels*.

6 See *The Huron Chief*, ed. D.M.R. Bentley (London: Canadian Poetry Press, 1987), p. 5: 'Nor heard a sound, save wood-doves cooing,/Or birds that tapped the hollow tree. . . . '

7 See *The Poems of Archibald Lampman* (*including At the Long Sault*), intro. Margaret Coulby Whitridge, Literature of Canada: Poetry and Prose in Reprint (Toronto: University of Toronto Press, 1974), p. 36. Both 'A Canadian Boat Song' and 'Between the Rapids' find voyageurs nearing rapids at twilight, and both contain references to bells, the shore, and the stream.

8 *Ibid.*, p. 37 ('And where is Jacques, and where is Virginie') and 'Wolflip,' *Long Sault* in *The Long Poem Anthology*, ed. Michael Ondaatje (Toronto: Coach House, 1979), p. 137 ('and/where is Jacques and where is Virginie . . . '). See also Charles Sangster, *The St. Lawrence and the Saguenay*, ed. D.M.R. Bentley (London: Canadian Poetry Press, 1990), pp. 125–26; 'I expected to see the Rapid (St. Anne's) which Moore has immortalized in his "Canadian Boat Song," somewhat deserving the honor with which Erin's gifted Bard has covered it; but I was sadly mistaken. . . . At the present time it is a mere ripple. . . . I fancy that many tourists, approaching the Rapid with book in hand . . . have felt very much as if they had been hoaxed. . . . Notwithstanding this, the ground is sacred, one of the "green spots upon memory's waste" dedicate to Moore, and it will continue such. . . . '

9 This and subsequent details of Weld's biography are taken from the entry on him by G.M. Craig in the *Dictionary of Canadian Biography*, VIII (Toronto: University of Toronto Press, 1985); hereafter cited as *DCB*.

10 See Martin Roth, 'Introduction,' *Travels*, 4th ed. (reprint New York: Johnson Reprint Corporation, 1968), I, p. xix.

11 See *ibid.*, I, p. xx and James J. and Ruth Talman, 'The Canadas 1763–1812,' *Literary History of Canada*, ed. Carl F. Klinck (Toronto: University of Toronto Press, 1965), pp. 88–89.

12 See, for example, *Travels through Canada . . .* , 3rd ed. (London: Baldwick, Cradock, and Joy, 1816), I, pp. 17 and 469–74.

13 See the 'Explanatory Notes' in my editions of Thomas Cary's *Abram's Plains: A Poem* (London: Canadian Poetry Press, 1986), *passim* (Carver) and J. Mackay, *Quebec Hill or Canadian Scenery. A Poem. In Two Parts* (London: Canadian Poetry Press, 1988), *passim* (Kalm), and — for Coleridge's use of Thomas James — Miller Christy, 'Introduction,' *The Voyages of Captain Luke Foxe of Hull, and Captain Thomas James of Bristol, in Search of the North-West Passage*, in

1631–32, Works Issued by the Hakluyt Society, No. 88 (London: Hakluyt Society, 1894), I, pp. clxxxix–cxciii.

14 Cornwall Bayley, *Canada. A Descriptive Poem*, ed. D.M.R. Bentley (London: Canadian Poetry Press, 1990), pp. 13–15; hereafter cited as *C*, with line numbers.

15 Lambert, *Travels*, I, 473.

16 See the Explanatory Notes to *C*, pp. 1–28 and 485–96.

17 *Talbot Road: A Poem*, ed. Michael Williams, intro. D.M.R. Bentley (London: Canadian Poetry Press, 1990), forthcoming (ll. 69–76); hereafter cited as *TR*, with line numbers. Weld also refers to a 'favourable' wind, 'tremendous' waves, and a 'gale of wind' (II, 297–98).

18 *Cf.* Weld, II, 326: "Settlements are now scattered over the whole country. . . . "

19 Such phrases as 'dubious maze' and 'eternal night' (*TR*, 287–88) have a distinctly Miltonic ring. See the 'Introduction' and 'Explanatory Notes' of Williams' edition of *Talbot Road* for the presence and significance of other echoes of *Paradise Lost* in Burwell's poem.

20 *The Rising Village*, ed. Gerald Lynch (London: Canadian Poetry Press, 1989), pp. 13 and 15; hereafter cited as *RV*, with line numbers to the 1834 text.

21 See *Autobiography of Oliver Goldsmith: a Chapter in Canada's Literary History*, 2nd ed. (Hantsport, N.S.: Lancelot, 1985), p. 38.

22 *Tecumseh; or, the Warrior of the West: a Poem, in Four Cantos*, with Notes, intro. William F.E. Morley (Ottawa: Golden Dog, 1978), pp. 25 and 86. See also *Travels*, II, pp. 18 and 86 and *Tecumseh*, pp. 21 (I, p. vii) and 84 (n.1) for Richardson's use of Weld's accounts of Indian canoes and torch-fishing.

23 *The Emigrant*, ed. D.M.R. Bentley (London: Canadian Poetry Press, 1990), forthcoming (III, pp. 93–116).

24 See, for example, the 'Explanatory Notes' to *The Emigrant*, III, pp. 5–92.

25 See *ibid.*, V, pp. 4–36 for the use made by McLachlan of Weld, Moore, and Traill in 'The Log Cabin.'

26 *Letters*, I, p. 81. Moore continues the metaphor in his next sentence: 'Indeed, my dearest Dennie, I cannot speak half my acknowledgements to you for the very cordial interest you feel in my reputation, and for the truly beautiful *frames* of eloquence in which you take care to *set* all my little miniatures.'

Theory and Fiction
The Author Comments on
At Face Value:
The Life and Times of Eliza McCormack/John White

Don Akenson

That's right. It is not truth or fiction, but truth and fiction. I don't mean 'truth' in the woolly sense that used to be spouted by the person who said, 'There's more *truth* in Dickens than in any book of nineteenth-century history,' but rather in the limited sense of accuracy. As professional historians, we have been indoctrinated in a set of false identifications, namely (1) to be as accurate as possible in factual matters, and (2) to present our factual information in a particular and narrow scholastic mode — namely the German-derived research monograph.

Now, in fact, it is perfectly possible to present accurate fact in a wholly different series of forms which are slightly less deadly to the human soul than the research monograph — polemics, personal essays, novels and poetry have all been used successfully. This is not to be cavalier about the traditional monograph (and I include most political and military biographies in this category), for it serves well in presenting information on a wide variety of topics. But it is a bit of a sausage machine, and no matter what you put into its maw, out comes link after link of mass-produced historical sausage.

So, when my colleagues in the historical business are brought to ask about *Eliza*, 'Is it truth or fiction?', what they really mean is, 'I am made uneasy by a package that looks a bit different — by a novel, in fact — and I want to know before I start *if I should believe it or not.*'

Well, like everything ever written about anything, you should believe parts of it and not others. And, actually, that is the way it is with any piece of writing that an historian deals with. Do you really believe that there is anything written that is purely fictional? Certainly not. Pure fiction is like 'absolute zero,' an ideal point that in the real world cannot be encountered under natural conditions. This is so by definition of the human condition. Even the inwardmost private poetry can be fashioned by the poet only out of stored neurological experiences of historical events, however private. Fact, then, always slips in, however transmogrified. And, at the other end of the scale, is there such a thing as perfect accuracy? Equally, no. Even that great Canadian equivalent of the historical telephone book—the *DCB*—while admirably accurate as to fact, has in each article a narrative structure, implied causalities, an entirely imaginative creation that is anything but merely factual. In that sense, truth is as difficult a goal and as unachievable as is fiction. A given piece of work will lie closer to one pole than the other, perhaps, but inevitably it partakes of both.

This sort of tiresome clarification would be unnecessary were it not for the industrial categories that we continually have to fight if we are to maintain our intellectual integrity. Academic departments are perhaps the greatest single threat, but consider such a seemingly innocent exercise as the Governor General's awards. Juries manage to split fiction and non-fiction, as if they were distinct species of vegetables that grow in different climates and never interbreed. And their judgements are solemnly received.

Eliza is, therefore, real history, just of a different sort. This is not to deny that it is subversive, and intentionally so. In the first place, I reject as unnecessary the point of view from which almost all Canadian history is written: the modest omniscience of the Almighty. Historians—and here I include most traditional biographers—play God. By virtue of their knowing how, in a limited time period, things turned out, they then presume to explain how that happened. Of course, they are just guessing, and creating and writing a form of fiction. (Let me emphasize that I am not bad-mouthing guessing. The best definition of intelligence is 'the ability to guess right.')

So, if I have written the first one-third of *Eliza* in the traditional omniscient historical third person, it is to gain the confidence of the traditional reader, but, thereafter, the story is told from within Eliza's head, from inside her consciousness, not mine and certainly not God's. That is one way that a novel differs from traditional history, but that does not make it necessarily any the less accurate. (Incidentally, I fully realize that it is possible to write a novel as if the author is God, and sometimes that works wonderfully, as in the Pentateuch.)

A second subversive point is easily stated. By attempting to break down the barrier between academic and non-academic history, I am refusing to accept the historical convention that those who are not professional historians are in some way second-class citizens in the observation of the past. It is an amazingly blind profession that could believe this, but, alas. . . .

And, thirdly, I am trying to rock just slightly our conventions about gender. Even very 'progressive' sorts are frequently unsettled by gender blurring. Almost always, observers of human behaviour assume gender as a fundamental category and judge everything within it; and that has never been more true than in the present stage of the women's movement. My point is the opposite: do not assume anything about the gender-styles of any human being or any group of humans. Let them decide.

So, how does *Eliza* work? Pretty simply, I think. It obviously is a rewriting of *Moll Flanders*. The clues to that are clearly set out: Eliza is stimulated, in several ways, by Defoe's work on female pirates — mannish, sensual, active, and very unrestrained by conventions. Of course it is *Moll Flanders* with a difference. My brief — self-assigned, to be sure — was to rewrite *Moll Flanders* as if it had been done by a politically informed, progressive, and (God help us) politically correct, late twentieth-century historian. So, of course, it had to be set in the nineteenth century, with the eighteenth-century original as a subtext. And what kind of woman would Moll have been in that setting by that sort of narrator? Why, a self-empowering, robust, subversive female; but, being Canadian, secretive in her anarchy. And, of course, in equal parts Tory and transvestite.

I am convinced that the phenomenon that is dealt with in *Eliza* will be found by the next generation of archives-burrowers to have been quite common. In a world in which women had little power, a perfectly sane way to get it was to become a man. Irving Abella's new book on the history of the Jews in Canada reveals that the first young Jewish male to arrive in Quebec, one Jacques La Forge, who landed in 1738, turned out to be a nineteen-year-old girl. She spent a year in jail because of her Jewish religion, not because of having falsified her gender. Julie Wheelwright's *Amazons and Military Maids* documents, with occasional inaccuracy the lives of a score of women who dressed as males in pursuit of military honours, of adventure, and, so it seems, of their selves. Betty T. Bennett has just followed a paper trail left by one of Mary Shelley's close friends, an illegitimate daughter of the fifteenth Earl of Morton, who spent much of her adult life as not one, but, successively, two men, one of them quite unhappily married. Fraser Easton has just completed a Princeton Ph.D. on eighteenth-century female husbands. And, going back to our religious origins, it is worth remembering that in the early ninth century we may have had a female pope, and, as Harold Bloom perhaps tells us, the 'J' behind Jahweh in the books of Moses well may have been female.

This leads us into one of the questions that vexes modern historians, anthropologists, and especially writers of biography and novels. It is the question of 'right' and of 'appropriation' of culture and of history. It is frequently held that whites do not have the right to deal with non-whites, non-natives with natives, and so on; that men should not write about women, or women about men; and, in fact, no one should write about what they themselves are not.

That gives the historian a particular problem. The one thing all our subjects have in common — and this holds for most biographers as well — is that our subjects are dead and we are not. So, a huge leap into another world is required, no matter what.

One aspect of the 'right' question, it is argued, is that sometimes authors (biographers, historians, novelists, poets) do not have a right to write about something other than themselves and their own culture because they cannot by the nature of the exercise do it well. This is a sadly vulnerable argument, for, although a lot of writers make a mess of things (including writing about themselves and their own cultures, let alone about other people and other peoples), it is capable of direct empirical disproof. Here is Nadine Gordimer and one particular example:

> By and large, I don't think it matters a damn what sex a writer is, so long as the work is that of a real *writer*. . . . After all, look at Molly Bloom's soliloquy. To me, that's the ultimate proof of the ability of either sex to understand and convey the inner working of the other. No woman was ever 'written' better by a woman writer. How did Joyce know? God knows how and it doesn't matter.

Whether or not I had a right to write about Eliza is a matter for you to judge, not me. Be it said, however, that there were not a lot of dead Irish female transvestites queuing up to do the job.

Ultimately, I hope you come to know Eliza, not so much as history but as an evocation of possibility, and that, therefore, in your own lives, you recognize that you possibly have met Eliza, and that she is the man that lives next door.

Dressing up History

A Critic Comments on Don Akenson's
At Face Value

Roger Martin

Reviewers of Don Akenson's *At Face Value* fall mainly into two camps. The first camp is a camp of allies, and I suspect that it is composed largely of friends of (or possibly even of debtors to) the author — a suspect and inevitable group that Robertson Davies might refer to as an author's 'claque.' For whatever reason, these reviewers fall prey to enjoying the book and are often at pains to describe their own bemused reactions to its suggestion that a prominent, nineteenth-century Tory backbencher may in fact have been a woman named Eliza McCormack. These reviewers come to see the book as a novel, and the measure of the work's success is the extent to which it entertains the reader.

The second camp is a camp of hostiles: these readers espouse, to varying degrees, feelings of suspicion and/or outright hostility toward the work. Reviewers here are characterized by their concern that the book's admittedly tenuous premise should be presented as anything other than an exceedingly remote possibility. *At Face Value*, then, is read as using a number of academic conventions (for example, its thirty-nine pages of notes, or the familiar authoritative tone of its omniscient third-person narrator) dishonestly: these legitimizing devices are thought to be deployed as a means of turning the worst kind of speculation into a plausibility — and this with the apparent intention of dressing up the whole mess as History!

Reviews of this kind often take issue not only with the unusual claim of the novel but also with the methodology by which the narrative attempts to stake that claim. Noteworthy too is the latent or, on occasion, the overt vehemence of these analyses. Akenson is not alone in confronting this tensile presence of readerly suspicion. George Bowering, Robert Kroetsch and Rudy Wiebe are just a few of the many contemporary Canadian writers whose historical writings must face a considerable distrust of the historicity of certain kinds of narrative endeavour. In Akenson's case, it is apparent that the threat of this hostility was sufficient to motivate the author to undertake the practice, made infamous by the likes of Defoe and

Wordsworth, of writing a preface as an apology for the work which ensues.

Prefaces or other defensive strategies notwithstanding, reviewers still distrust this book and others like it, and their reviews fall into a recognizable pattern: they discount the claims and the methodology of the work and often proceed to suggest, as in a gesture of unprofessional largesse, that if the book is to be found on sale, it might prove a good investment for a buyer anxious to pack off yet another 'light' historical fiction to an ailing distant relative.

By repackaging the work as either an 'entertainment' or, still worse, as an 'historical fiction,' each of these camps responds to the historical ambiguity of the narrative by devaluing its claim to historicity. In either case there is evidence of our persistent desire or need to impose an ontological dichotomy between history and fiction. And we all know which of these two discourses is to be considered the more authoritative. Two questions, therefore, present themselves here: First, why does our culture apparently feel a need to dismiss or devalue certain kinds of historical investigation? And secondly, can fiction, or, perhaps better, *will* fiction allow itself to be the object of so cavalier a disdain?

Looking at the first question, I suspect that it would be possible to argue that capitalism has a vested interest in fostering various kinds of historical ignorance in the constituent members of its social organizations. To impose a dichotomy between history and fiction is to preserve a mythology of the inaccessibility of history. This mythology in turn becomes one of many pillars upholding a temple of consumerism: if history is essentially indecipherable, and if its relations to present circumstances are so inscrutable, then perhaps we are somehow justified in reaching for *products* as a means of resolving complex problems which confront us. In part, the Bush administration's eagerness to reach into America's technological arsenal as the primary means of resolving the Gulf crisis may be a consequence of just such an impatience with the longwinded processes of history. Is it possible that a change in our culture's valuation of historical discourse might begin to jeopardize a whole society's unexamined faith in technology? After all, the myth of technological progress is a culturally indispensable mythology; it is an invisible engine both of consumerism and of the reckless optimism we seem to have concerning our ability to continue present industrial and commercial practices without incurring any material consequences for our planet.

How does our sense of history fit into these frighteningly durable myths? These speculations may seem to stray a long way from John White, who may be East Hastings' most famous transvestite. My contention, however, is only that our responses, as individuals and as a culture, to books like *At Face Value* are implicated in many cultural structures and processes, and that these interrelations merit further inquiry.

Turning to the second question as to whether fiction will allow itself to be devalued as an instrument of historical knowledge, I would direct our thoughts to the genre of historical fiction. What is historical fiction? Joseph W. Turner wryly notes that 'aside from the tautology of common sense (all historical novels are novels about history), . . . all we can say in general about the genre is that it resists generalization.'[1] The elusive quality of the genre, however, does not dissuade Turner: he proceeds from this tautology to attempt to distinguish between the documented, the disguised and the invented historical novel. For Turner, a documented historical novel is one that involves actual historical characters. The use of these characters generates historical expectations within the reader that the author can then exploit in any number of ways. Turner realizes, however, that 'having actual people in a novel raises the problem of the ontological status of "real" as opposed to "invented" characters' (337). Further, he argues that the author should not draw any attention to this ontological problem:

> The farther you keep actual and fictitious characters apart, that is, the more you remind the reader of the difference, and the more you deprive yourself of one of the great advantages of documented historical fiction — the tendency for the novelist's intentions to accrue historicity from their very proximity to historical events. . . . If his fiction is to carry the weight of history, the novelist does well to distract any attention from himself or the artifice he has created, to gesture through his text to the past he seeks to recapture. (350)

For Turner, then, this kind of historical fiction acquires its power by imposing and manipulating an illusion of continuity between invented and actual events. To draw the reader's attention to this machinery of illusion is radically to compromise the peculiar historicity of the narrative.

At Face Value is clearly what Turner would describe as a documented historical novel. Akenson freely uses actual historical people as characters: John A. MacDonald, MacKenzie Bowell, Egerton Ryerson, even Ogle Gowan, to name but a few, are all personages that will be more or less familiar to a great many readers. But if Akenson is interested in maintaining a seamless continuity between actual historical events and the machinations of his narrative, he has most miserably failed.

It may be telling to look closely at this failure. To begin with, how should the reader approach the irony of the title? Viewed literally, the title asks us to reconsider the traditional gender representations of Eliza McCormack and John White. Considered in relation to the intrusive rhetorical strategies of the book, the title prompts us to determine what kind of truth value we might be prepared to associate with this historical fiction and others like it.

A second peculiarity of the book is its narrative structure: this is one of the few autobiographies I know that is written by someone other than the central character. The most obvious structural feature of the book is that its narration moves from the third to the first person. This book changes from biography into autobiography. This kind of transition is difficult to ignore.

Besides these structural features, the book contains a number of disconcerting encounters. One of these involves an appointment between Eliza and Egerton Ryerson. Buffeted somewhat mercilessly by the death of her father and her experiences in a strange new world, Akenson's Eliza enters what she describes as 'the most exclusive echelon of the world's oldest profession'[2] under the watchful eyes of an avuncular figure called the Faithful Retainer. She goes on to describe her encounters with Mr. Ryerson:

> He called on me twice a month, on average, when he was not travelling in the countryside or in Europe on business. Each of his visits followed the same pattern. He would have the Faithful Retainer accompany him to my room, as if he were being shown it for the first time. The Retainer would knock, and when I opened the door he would introduce me to Mr Ryerson. Each time there had to be a formal introduction. After taking off his coat, Mr Ryerson would suggest that I be seated on the bed. Meanwhile he took a seat on the overstuffed chair and, exhaling heavily, uttered this sentence: 'Many people have asked me to describe to them the course whereby I became a Methodist minister and a lifelong servant of God. . . . ' (105)

This passage brings together one of the more august historical personages in the book and circumstances of absolutely farcical proportion. And in this iconoclastic clash of history and fiction what emerges? The autobiographical discourse of Egerton Ryerson: a discourse which flagrantly exploits its fictional context while reminding us simultaneously that Victorian figures do indeed have sexual identities and also that any character's sexual constitution plays a role in historic events, even if that character is Egerton Ryerson.

This scene dramatizes in miniature the conflict between historical and fictional discourses that is the foundation of the work as a whole. But why should Akenson choose to foreground this conflict, rather than to conceal it?

At Face Value is a metafictional text. Patricia Waugh defines metafiction as 'writing which self-consciously and systematically draws attention to its status as an artefact in order to pose questions about the relationship between fiction and reality.'[3] Linda Hutcheon, pursuing the theoretical speculations of Hayden White, has examined a range of contemporary Canadian texts which, like this one, foreground the historiographical dilemmas of their own production. She observes that reading metafictional texts has specific implications for the reader:

> We, as readers, make the link between life and art, between the processes of the reception and the creation of texts: the act of reading participates in (and indeed posits or infers) the act of textual production. The focus here is not on the reader and author as individual historical agents, but on the processes involved in what in French is called the *énonciation*, the entire context of the production and reception of the text.[4]

If Hutcheon is right, metafictions are subversive texts that position themselves not to throw history into disrepute but to challenge the authoritative presumption of certain kinds of historical discourse. Metafictions re-empower readers in two ways: first, by tempting them to become aware of the processes by which history is narrativized, and second, by encouraging them to become active participants in these processes.

In an essay 'On Science Fiction' C.S. Lewis comments on the way in which book reviewers' predispositions can affect their reviews:

> It is very dangerous to write about a kind [of writing] you hate. Hatred obscures all distinctions. . . . Many reviews are useless because, while purporting to condemn the book, they only reveal the reviewer's dislike of the kind to which it belongs. Let bad tragedies be censured by those who love tragedy, and bad detective stories by those who love the detective story. Then we shall learn their real faults. Otherwise we shall find epics blamed for not being novels, farces for not being high comedies, novels by James for lacking the swift action of Smollett. Who wants to hear a particular claret abused by a fanatical teetotaller?[5]

Metafiction is not a common term; it denotes a complex contract between reader, writer and text that is not as familiar to readers as it might be. James and Smollett notwithstanding, I must confess my own penchant for metafictions, and my own view of *At Face Value* is that it finds in Eliza/John's transvestism a perfect metaphor for the uneasy commerce between history and fiction which lies at the very centre of this form of narrative. Eliza's story, and its telling, act in concert to remind us of our tendency to respond to persons and events in terms of how they happen to be dressed. Its historical referents aside, this book is very much a product of our times in that it points to the attempts we make, or don't make, as readers, as individuals or as a culture, to mobilize tolerance when confronted by difference. As metafiction, *At Face Value* asks us simultaneously to re-examine our latent gender prejudices and to extend a measure of a spirit of tolerance towards what may at first appear to be an ill-dressed substitute for historical inquiry. If in the meanwhile we learn, for example, to re-evaluate the role that sexual identity plays in the determination of character and event, perhaps we will move, at that point, from observing a mere disguise of facts to a place where we may begin to apprehend the flesh and blood of times long gone, but not forgotten.

Notes

1 Joseph W. Turner, 'The Kinds of Historical Fiction: An Essay in Definition and Methodology,' *Genre*, 12 (Fall 1979): 335.

2 Don Akenson, *At Face Value: The Life and Times of Eliza McCormack/John White* (Montreal and Kingston: McGill-Queen's University Press, 1990), p. 105.

3 Patricia Waugh, *Metafiction: The Theory and Practice of Self-Conscious Fiction* (New York: Methuen, 1984), p. 2.

4 Linda Hutcheon, 'Canadian Historiographic Metafiction.' *Essays on Canadian Writing*, 30 (Winter 1984–85): 228.

5 C.S. Lewis, 'On Science Fiction' in Walter Hooper (ed.), *Of Other Worlds: Essays and Stories* (London: Geoffrey Bles Ltd., 1966), p. 60.

"They Are Treating Us Like Mad Dogs"

A Donnelly Biographer's Problem

James Reaney

So far as I am concerned, no biographer of the Donnellys has quite done them the justice they deserve in certain areas of their lives no matter how favourable (e.g., the Orlo Miller books) they may seem to them. Let's review, rapidly, three authorial viewpoints on this tormented and, some would add, tormenting, family.

First of all we have Gothic novelist Thomas P. Kelley, whose *The Black Donnellys* ('black' meaning cruel, heartless) sums up his viewpoint with:

> Oh all young folks take warning,
> Never live a life of hate,
> Of wickedness or violence, lest
> You share the Donnellys' fate. . . .[1]
>
> Six ringleaders were put on trial,
> But they were all set free.
> It was said men deserve medals,
> Who will kill a Black Donnelly.[2]

Because this Harlequin Book was first in the field, the *Maria Monk* of its era, this attitude is more or less the public attitude to the Donnellys even unto Peter Gzowski on Morningside, although Edith Fowke wrote in to remind him of other viewpoints, e.g., that, whatever it is, of my dramatic trilogy.

Now the Donnellys were aware of their terrible reputation and tried to counteract it with letters to the newspapers, after they had been called 'the Donnelly Tribe,' pointing out that there are 'two sides to every story.' Old Mr. Donnelly's remark quoted above in my title is such an attempt, as is another famous utterance of his: 'Sure, if a stone fell from heaven, they'd say Donnelly done it.' And, despite those who still consider it a moral duty to extirpate Donnellys, there has arisen a folk-saying in Ontario which goes like this: 'The Donnellys didn't do all the things they were accused of.'

Ray Fazakas, secondly, brilliant researcher, in his *Donnelly Album* puts his case thusly:

> The massacre has forever linked the name Donnelly with Biddulph and Lucan. Instead of being endured as just another family of hooligans and forgotten with their passing, the Donnellys have become folk heroes. . . .[3]

As you shall see, I disagree with 'just another family of hooligans.' Their story, because of sudden flashes of Donnelly nobility and ability to endure, seems, to me, a tragedy rather than a comedy without laughter. I find it far easier to dismiss the grandeur films try to give such psychopaths as Jesse James and Billy the Kid, than I do to outlaw genuine concern and terror at the way this family was treated:

> There can equally be no question that they did not merit the savage punishment meted out to them by their neighbours. I consider their unavenged deaths an unexpunged blot on the Canadian judicial system.[4]

But still Orlo Miller (*The Donnellys Must Die*) fails in certain key instances, all near the end of the story, to support his case with certain obvious, at least to me, supporting facts.

The first fact is that the whole story is not just one set of hooligans fighting another gang of the same; it's a vendetta, as Albert Hassard notes in his *Famous Canadian Trials* (Toronto, 1924), a really rare phenomenon in Canada though not in Sicily or New York. The Donnelly image promulgated by the Vigilantes is a concoction designed to cover up a murderous dispute over land between the Donnelly and Maher families, evidently cousins of each other, even first cousins. This comes out, not in Miller's book where it would have helped, but in the Orlo Miller Papers, where a letter written by Mrs. Clay, William Donnelly's California daughter, proposes this hypothesis, and thus makes for a darker story, a more worthwhile one, than 'hooligans' or 'saints' or 'to the sky the wild flames flew.'

Also, one other feature needs emphasis here; why, if the Donnellys are so monstrous, are they such good friends with the Crown Attorney Charles Hutchinson? When I first opened the Sheriff's Daybook for those times and looked at the index, the scores of Donnellys gave me the signal — ah yes, *Donnelly crimes*. Yes, but most of them refer to payments to the Donnelly stage line for delivery of a great number of subpoenas to the Biddulph and McGillivray areas.

I mention Charles Hutchinson, the Crown Attorney. He put his finger on the one loose cannon the Donnellys had amongst them — Robert Donnelly, later confined to an asylum — as responsible for his parents' deaths. Responsible, of course, in atrocities that made them an easier mark for the Vigilantes? Apparently. One of Hutchinson's first reactions to news of the massacre is to point out that the reputation of the Donnellys is terrible. But are they *themselves* terrible? The overtones I receive from the Donnelly associates — the Sheriff, the Mayor of London, the Crown Attorney, Grits all, is that they knew the other side of the story — not just Bob, but also the vendetta aspect which brings in the Maher family and their nephew, James Carroll.

Just to refresh your memory on the land controversy with regard to the Donnellys and the Mahers: in 1857, Michael Maher bought the whole of the Biddulph farm the Donnellys had cleared for their landlord, John Grace, and threatened to evict them; the next documents show the Donnellys buying the north half of Concession VI, Lot 18 for 50 pounds while the Mahers pay 750 pounds for the south half. Shortly afterward, the inflated land values of the Crimean War collapse into depression and the Mahers move away to Iowa. In the late seventies, the next generation produces the psychopathic James Carroll, landless, brooding over his father's second marriage in which a Stephen township farm went to a stepmother, and . . . James Maher is reported to have killed James Donnelly Sr. in the attack on the Donnelly house in February 1880. What few people realize is that the Donnelly heirs next rented the farm to the Feeheley family, who had been close friends; what William Donnelly did not realize was that this family had changed sides, betrayed his mother and father as a matter of fact for a promise of $500. The next tenant of the north half of Lot 18 is Jack Kent, a close Protestant friend, but at least for a year the Maher faction must have felt somewhat closer to regaining what they evidently considered *their* farm. John Grace, the Donnellys' landlord during the forties and fifties, has a lot to do with the intensity of the vendetta since nothing can have been more infuriating than for the Mahers to have been promised the whole 100 acres, then be palmed off with just 50 acres, then learn the mortifying fact that the Donnellys paid so much less than they did, then see the end of the Crimean War, the depression, and financial failure. Similarly, on the Donnellys' side, I can think of nothing more irritating than watching enemies plowing land *they* had cleared, land forever severed from its first possessors. I've never been satisfied with the usual explanations as to how Farl and his death at Mr. Donnelly's hands fit into all of this, but I wonder if it cannot be traced back to Dunkerrin in North Tipperary where Farl turns out to be born in the same diocese as Mrs. Donnelly.

One other letter in Reverend Miller's file I wish he had used is from a Biddulph correspondent who claims that the Donnelly family were some special sort of Irishman who paid no attention whatsoever to what their priest and church expected of them with regard to obedience, decorum, church attendance, etc. A relevant document came to view when William Butt discovered at Kingston an interview James Donnelly Sr. had with the warden just as his sentence ended. When asked about attendance at chapel, he replies — only at Christmas and Easter. Having been surprised at the many, many secret societies in Ireland during the 1830s, the thought does cross my mind that given this intricate swarm of peculiar sectarian and factional cross-webbed fighting cocks, could it be possible that there was a group of Irish secularists, non-pious anti-feudals? As an example of this in Quebec, a province not noted at one time for its lack of filial piety towards Mother Church, there is a recent play by Christian Bédard called the *Grand Schisme au Rang du Gravel* in which a whole parish, dissatisfied at its priest's choice of a new church site, advertise for a Protestant pastor to come up from Montreal and take over. The Donnellys' marked preference for Protestant neighbours may be relevant here, as well as the boys' marriages to Protestants.

One other thing that I am dissatisfied with in my three Donnelly authors is the way they handle the dynamics of what became known as the Cow Case which took place in the fall of 1879. It seems to me that when a mob of eighty-five farmers come to the Donnelly door in broad daylight with rifles and demand entry to search for a lost cow, the onlooker is anxious to see how the Donnellys react.

Kelley denies them any heroism at all, but I find both father's and son's and mother's reaction rather thrilling. Donnelly Sr. opens the door and says: 'I am not in the least afraid of you. I would see you all in hell first.'[5] Mrs. Donnelly's reaction is to ask her son John to hitch up the cart and let her drive by another road than that taken by the Vigilantes over to Whalen's Corners where she arrives at William Donnelly's house just before the Vigilantes arrive. Does William reach for a rifle? No, he decides that a fiddle will do, and as James Carroll and others approach his front yard he suddenly comes out his front door playing *Boney over the Alps*, along with, in some versions — satirical songs about those present. The mob turns tail and runs away. Now that, as Huckleberry Finn would say, shows 'real sand.' Fazakas and Miller don't underline the scene as much as they could: 'Ho hum, another defiance of a mob.' Surely not.

Moving ahead into 1880, I want some different nuances wrung from the Fire Trials at which Mr. and Mrs. Donnelly are accused of burning down Grouchy Ryder's barn.

As you remember, this occurred when all the remaining Donnelly boys save Robert and Patrick were at a wedding dance at the Keefes'. Without much ado, James Carroll simply stroked out their names from his warrant, and substituted the names of their sixty-year-old parents.

First of all, you have to read the depositions of two young girls present with Mr. and Mrs. Donnelly that night and agree that they are not lying. This seems fairly easy to do unless you have Vigilante-Kelley fever; Kelley's untruths spring up like dragon's teeth as the last days approach. But you have to underline something else too, and that is the fact that Grouchy Ryder's barn is burnt down by the Vigilantes themselves in an agreement with him or with his son; no animals are injured, and the barn is rebuilt for him by Vigilantes within two months. The whole scenario is: 'the Donnellys haven't committed any atrocities lately — get me an atrocity.'

'All right,' says James Carroll, 'damn it, the boys have an air-tight alibi, get me the mother and father and we'll keep changing the preliminary enquiry locales until we wear out their resistance. Also, we'll keep them in the township.' Mrs. Donnelly tried to run away to her daughter in St. Thomas but was dragged back by Carroll. Again, underline the genuine horror and pathos here. Suddenly the Vigilantes realize that they have overplayed their hand, the senior Donnellys will now sue them for false arrest, and so — the end is inevitable. 'They burned down the barn,' is backfiring; get rid of them before they yet again outwit us with their powerful Grit friends literally at court in London.

And too I would emphasize the domestic Dutch interiors we get in the testimony of Bridget Donnelly and Bridget O'Connor as to what an evening Chez Donnelly was like: hemming handkerchiefs, quilting petticoats, and baking teacakes for a ten o'clock tea party does not sound like the Gothic grotesques Kelley is dishing out, nor the commonplace hooligans Fazakas lets barely by, although to give him credit he does quote Jack Donnelly as saying in Detroit: 'Why did they kill us? Aw, we had fine clothes and beautiful horses — they were jealous of us.'[6]

In the case of Miller, I want him to get rid of Kelley's hypnotic influence: Mr. Donnelly did not slay Farl with an iron spike, but a wooden handspike. Also, Mrs. Donnelly did not run over to Whalen's Corners; that lines her up for Olympic endeavours the night of the Ryder barnfire. No, no — it says quite clearly in the documents that she drove over.

Why am I so careful of these nineteenth-century wretches who enraged their neighbours so?

Well, I hope you can sense that, as William Porte once said at Maclean's Hotel, 'I'm a Donnelly man'; once you get addicted to their astounding situation, you cease not to admire their will, in spite of all, not to be afraid, but to go on living—despite all the mobs and gossip and hatred that furiously marshal themselves against them. And go on living, they have!

Notes

1 Thomas P. Kelley, *The Black Donnellys* (Don Mills, Ont.: Greywood, 1972), p. 158.
2 *Ibid.*, p. 153.
3 Ray Fazakas, *The Donnelly Album* (Toronto: Macmillan, 1977), p. 282.
4 Orlo Miller, *The Donnellys Must Die* (Toronto: Macmillan, 1962), p. x.
5 James Reaney, 'James Donnelly,' in Marc La Terreur (ed.), *Dictionary of Canadian Biography*, vol. X (Toronto: University of Toronto Press, 1972), p. 235.
6 Fazakas, p. 50.

A Donnelly Biographer Creates

A Selection of Four Poems and an Excerpt from the Puppet Play *Sleigh without Bells,* with an Introductory Note by James Noonan

James Reaney

The following brief texts are the work of one of Canada's finest poets and playwrights—James Reaney. They show how the extensive biographical research of Reaney has been transformed into literature while retaining the essential truth Reaney gained from his research. Some of it indeed may be called metafiction in the modern sense of that term, for Reaney has his characters coming back from the grave to set the record straight for his readers.

The excerpts contain both published and unpublished material by Reaney on the subject on which his paper in this volume is written, and which has preoccupied him for so many years—the story of the Donnellys of Biddulph township, Ontario. Four of the selections are poems; the other is an excerpt from his unpublished puppet play *Sleigh without Bells.*

'Ballad' is an unpublished poem which recalls many of the events in the life of the Donnellys, mainly through the activities of Mrs. Donnelly shortly before her murder in 1880. It contains much of the imagery that was developed in Reaney's trilogy of plays *The Donnellys*, including the imagery of wheat and of the Donnelly sons' shirts hung on a line to dry. Like many ballads, the story is told in a simple and straightforward fashion.

'Entire Horse' is a suite of three poems, each a monologue by a different person. The poems were first published in the anthology *Un Dozen* (Windsor: Black Moss, 1982). The suite takes its title from the second poem, 'We were horsemen', narrated by Tom Donnelly, the youngest of the Donnelly sons, who was killed in the massacre of 1880. The poem concerns the exploits of the Donnelly brothers when they ran their successful stage-coach line between London and Goderich. The first poem is narrated by William Porte, the postmaster and telegraph operator in Lucan whose diary provided much useful information on the Donnellys. Published seven years after Reaney had completed his trilogy of plays on the Donnellys and after he had visited County Tipperary in Ireland where the Donnellys originated, the poem shows how the Irish who emigrated to Biddulph brought the hostilities of the old country to the new land, just as 'The old crooked roads twist in the cage of the straight new.' The third poem, narrated by Mrs. Donnelly, paints a very different picture of her from the harridan image cherished by many Canadians 'bored by your Calvinist shoes.' In the poem, we see her as an ordinary woman longing to live an ordinary life while 'you project a more exciting me on me.' All three poems demonstrate a complexity in dealing with the Donnelly material that is rarely equalled even in the trilogy itself.

The puppet play *Sleigh without Bells* is one of three ghost plays Reaney is writing about the Donnellys. *Sleigh without Bells* has been performed in London, Ontario, by the Rag and Bone Puppet Theatre. Its large cast and multiple settings make it a special challenge for puppeteers. The play summarizes much of the story of the Donnellys, but its central conceit is the fictional character Ephraim Flummerfelt, who is rescued from a violent winter storm by the Donnellys in 1877 and returns to the site of their demolished home ten years later. The play is in fact his dream that the massacre of the Donnellys never took place, but at the end he must face the reality of the terrible events of their lives.

The excerpt from *Sleigh without Bells* is the last scene of the play, in which Flummerfelt drives Mrs. Donnelly to the station in St. Mary's and away from the fate that awaits her; he soon realizes that his rescue was only a dream. Nevertheless, his life has been changed by his dream of the Donnellys 'before they were set free from their bodies to wander into the wildernesses of our minds forever.' And he asserts, 'How loved they could be. Yet how betrayed, trusted yet deeply hated. My whole life was changed by my once — twice if you count this recent dream of mine — my whole life was changed forever.'

Reaney has shown again the pervasive power of the Donnelly story on his own imagination, and like an admiring biographer has reminded his readers and playgoers how their lives too may be 'changed forever' by a proper understanding of his subject.

James Noonan

Poems by James Reaney

Ballad

I'm sick of Biddulph,
Mrs Donnelly said.
If we stay here
We're going to be dead.

She ran out to the field
To stop them from sowing
The wheat in the ground
But already it was growing.

In the fall of '79
Down came the rain.
November!
Brown field turns to green.

Six shirts on her line
Till that night at Slaght's hotel
When a man stabbed Mike Donnelly
In the hope he'd go to Hell.

Down came the snow.
A clean shirt for his wake.
December!
Green field turns to white.

When they'd buried her son
There were five shirts left.
There used to be seven
But two are worn in death.

Take me in a sleigh
To Lucan Crossing.
It's away
To St Thomas I'm going.

Jim Carroll followed her
On the next train to St Thomas
And told her daughter
Her mother he'd arrest.

January 1880
Down came the snow:
'You set fire to Ryder's barns.
Back to Lucan you must go.'

We'll never leave Biddulph,
Mr Donnelly said.
We're sown here and we'll stay here
Till we are harvested.

And he said what was right
For February Fourth
A mob came in the night
With clubs and fire and death.

Now it's March, the snow has gone
Where they buried them,
But the wheat her sons sown
Is green in the sun.

Entire Horse

Poems Written to Assist the Renewal of the Townhall at Exeter, Highway #4. (Respectively, the three speakers of these poems are William
Porte, Tom Donnelly and Mrs. Donnelly.)

I

Around Borrisokane, in Eire, the roads twist
After cowherds with willow gads, after wise woman's spells,
After chariots and the widest go-around found in a mare's skin.

But in Biddulph, Canada, in Mount Carmel's brooder stove,
                                                    St Peter's fields,
The roads cross at right angles, a careful Euclidian net, roods, rods
Spun by surveyors out of Spider stars — Mirzak, Spicula, Thuban, Antares.

Like serpents, twitchgrass roots, dragons — the Irish roads twist,
The old crooked roads twist in the cage of the straight new.

II

We were horsemen, dressed well and from my brother's entire horse,
From his entire horse came the colt fast fleet hoofhand with which
We seized and held onto the path through Exeter down to London.

We lifted the hills, creeks, rivers, slaughterhouses, taverns,
We lifted their travellers and those who were asleep when we passed
And those who saw us rattle by as they plowed mud or whittled,

We lifted them like a graveldust pennant, we swung them up and out
Till they yelled about wheels falling off, unfair competition, yah!
And we lie here now — headless, still, dead, wagonless, horseless,

Sleighless, hitched, stalled.

III

As the dressmaker hems my muslin handkerchiefs,
The night the Vigilantes burnt down one of their own barns,
As I sit waiting for a cake to bake and my gentle niece with me,

I realize I am not doing what you want me to do.
You — bored with your Calvinist shoes chewed to pieces
By street of insurance, streets of cakemix, packages, soap, sermonettes,

You want me to — you project a more exciting me on me.
She should be burning! Clip! Ax! Giantess! Coarse, I should curse!
Why should I accept these handcuffs from you?

Excerpt From *Sleigh without Bells*

We get one last mesmerizing shot of Ephraim coming towards us thro' snow white-out with Mrs. Donnelly. Then lantern and lamp spark, blink, go out.

Suddenly, loud bird song, summer light, old woman in ditch picking strawberries, sleigh fades. Instead a wagon and horses are feeding under the shade of trees not there in 1880. But sleigh-bells take a while to fade. We see that there is also an old man sitting watching the old woman. After a while, we recognize the ghosts of Mr. and Mrs. Donnelly.

Real live men now appear, and they walk without the 'float' quality of the ghosts, who often fade away as their viewers' minds gutter like candles. The two men are undertaker Mudie, who buried the Donnellys, and McDiarmid, their Lawyer.

McDiarmid: Good morning, young fellow, whoever you are.

Ephraim: I was just helping Mrs. Donnelly into the sleigh when —
it was a bright morning with white clouds and blue sky and a fresh breeze — I could see an old woman picking strawberries in the ditch — strangely familiar. *[Pause]* And tying their horses to a fencepost — Mr. McDiarmid, the Donnellys' lawyer whom I had met at Lucan and Granton accompanied by a very sombrely-clad gentleman just a shade too smooth in his manners.

Good morning, Mr. McDiarmid. Mrs. Donnelly and myself are going to the railway station at St. Marys. Mrs. Donnelly, we'll be late for the London train. Please get into the.... *[He is puzzled by the wagon. He starts as the Donnelly ghosts appear.]*

McDiarmid: You're not from these parts, lad. Where did you stay last night, if I might ask?

Ephraim: With Mr. and Mrs. Donnelly. They very kindly took me in when it snowed so hard on January thirteenth. Oh, I was lost in the snowstorm coming south from Perth County. We met at their trial for incendiarism, Mr. McDiarmid.

McDiarmid: I have never met you before in my life!

Ephraim: Yes, you have. You asked me to witness on Mr. Donnelly's behalf before I made an errand to Southwold and once when I came back from there — why, yesterday.

McDiarmid: Nonsense! Where did you sleep last night?

Ephraim: Why, at the Donnellys' house over there. Where else? *[Music. House has gone. Screams as he turns and sees nothing but the enclosure of four stones that mark where the Donnellys' house used to be seven years ago.]* Where have they gone? Mrs. Donnelly! Come back, please. Where are you?

Mudie: Young man, get hold of yourself. You may be driven mad by what I have to tell you, so powerful and dangerous has been the illusion or spell someone has cast upon you. *[Music.]* Young man, seven years ago, I received a box of burnt bones and tortured flesh already picked over by souvenir hunters.

Ephraim: Who are you, sir? I'm . . . I'm Ephraim Flummerfelt, mein gott willen, from Perth County. My sleigh's turned into a wagon!

Mudie: I am Undertaker Mudie of Lucan.

Ephraim: Whose bones?

Mudie: Battered and smashed by a mob of forty vigilantes who broke into their house at one a.m., early in the morning of February fourth, 1880, murdered Tom, Bridget, their mother, their father. Burned the house over their heads. Ran to Whalen's Corners, called out Will Donnelly, got John Donnelly instead and shot him.

[Big death portrait of John Donnelly in coffin projected above. Ephraim cries out, runs to the enclosure of four stones. Picks them up, kisses them, rolls about the site of his dream visit in howls of grief.]

Ephraim: Then I did not help her escape. My Donnellys. My wonderful, lovely Donnellys. How could they have made so many hate you when — you weren't like that! I know. I met you. I want to die with them! *[Pulls out knife. The two older men lift him up and comfort him.]*

McDiarmid: There, Mr. Flummerfelt. It was only a dream. But many in these parts have seen them walking, in broad daylight, at twilight. They died unshriven.

Ephraim: But, Mr. McDiarmid, it was not a dream. They invited me to stay the night, and they fed me.

Mudie: Generally speaking, Ephraim Flummerfelt, it's not wise to accept food from the shades of the departed. Occasionally, in a professional way, I am afflicted with a supernatural visitant at my undertaking parlour. I never accept food or gifts or conversational sallies. *[Pause]* There was a sleighing party of five O'Hallorans who were singing a song about how horrible the Donnellys were — and 'tis said the reason a freight train ran over them at a level crossing was that the ghosts of your recent hosts — came up out of the ditch and held the hooves of their horses.

Ephraim: Why, there's the impression of my body in the grass between the four stones. That's *[pause]* where I fell asleep.

McDiarmid: Yes, Mr. Flummerfelt. Aye, yes, whoever slept between those four stones might dream of the Donnellys.

Mudie: Neighbours here, customers *[pause]* tell me that, at night, suddenly the house appears all lit up, but they run across the road to have a closer look and — it vanishes in a puff of smoke. *[Takes out scissors, gives them to Ephraim.]*

Ephraim: Where was I really, then? Why are you giving me these scissors?

McDiarmid: Your hair and your nails have grown long, wherever you have been, sir, down among the restless dead. Let Mr. Mudie tonsure you. He's good at it.

Ephraim: I let him, though the thought occurred to me that I had died and was being prepared for burial.

McDiarmid: There are certain things we must now tell you. *[Pause]* Mudie?

Mudie: Information reached me through the relatives of a recent customer that someone had parked their wagon in the Donnelly yard and had fallen asleep two nights back inside the four stones.

McDiarmid: When Mr. Mudie passed this on to me, I telegraphed Constable William Donnelly in Glencoe, and asked for procedural advice.

Mudie: He told us that any trespasser on his parents' farm should be told to leave, but when we came yesterday you looked so innocent and to be enjoying yourself so much that we threw an old blanket over you, told the neighbours to feed and water your horses, and — decided to evict you today.

Ephraim: Which is?

McDiarmid: You tell me.

Ephraim: February the third, 1880.

[The older men laugh.]

McDiarmid: June twenty-first, 1887.

Ephraim: But it was so real!

Mudie: If it was real, then perhaps you have some memento of your visit.

Ephraim: John Donnelly gave me some sleigh bells. One, a tiny one, I kept back in my pocket. *[He produces it, rings, but it fades away.]*

McDiarmid: Ah, fairy bells melt like dewdrops in the sun.

Ephraim: Wait! Mrs. Donnelly, in gratitude for my financial help with the bail, gave me a handkerchief edged in black, sewn in remembrance of her son Michael's death. *[He produces the handkerchief. The Donnelly ghosts reappear.]* Look. There they are now. Picking wild strawberries. Look! They beckon me to accept some berries.

McDiarmid: Do not go over. Ghosts kill friends too, you know. Anything to have some company in Limbo. They're lonely, are the dead.

Mudie: We can't see the ghosts, by the way, Mr. Flummerfelt. Or can you, Mr. McDiarmid?

McDiarmid: No, no. Now this handkerchief is a marvel. It has 'Judith Donnelly' sewn upon it, and should not exist because all the household linen was destroyed in the fire.

Ephraim: I wanted so much to taste the strawberries.

[*The ghosts show their faces, which are horrifying skulls. Laughing shrilly, they throw the berries at Ephraim and vanish. He screams at their skull faces. Pause. Mudie and McDiarmid walk Ephraim over to his wagon. Help him up.*]

Ephraim: I drove out of the yard. I knew my life would never be the same again. They warned me that, at the river, the ghosts might cause me trouble again.

[*He comes to a bridge at twilight. Owl. Moon. From the water, four hands reach up and grasp the ankles of the horses who panic.*]

Ephraim: [*Aloud*] Whoa, Wilhelmina! Quiet, Golden!

[*A young girl — Theresa — steps up from the ditch.*]

Theresa: Cross yourself, Ephraim Flummerfelt. It was myself sewed that handkerchief. Cross yourself.

Ephraim: No, Theresa. I'm not in the habit of . . .

Theresa: Like this. [*She crosses herself. Vanishes as he does cross himself. Music as he drives on out of sight.*]

Ephraim: You know, in 1877 — three years ago, before the murder of the Donnellys, I had visited them before — in the depth of winter. And returned up to my parents' home in Fullarton. Even up there we heard in fear and trembling of their terrible fate. For years, I kept thinking that I would drive down again just to see if anything was left of my old friends' house where I had spent such an evening. And this summer I did, in a waggon, only — when I fell asleep within the enclosure of the four stones where there once was a house — I fell asleep and dreamed — as you have seen and heard — that Mr. and Mrs. Donnelly were still alive — and it was winter — the last few days of their life — before they were set free from their bodies to wander into the wildernesses of our minds forever. How loved they could be. Yet how betrayed, trusted yet deeply hated. My whole life was changed by my once — twice if you count this recent dream of mine — my whole life was changed forever. [*Pause*] Crossing the river, crossing the river broke the spell I had been under.

[*End of the play.*]

Between the Lines

Biography, Drama and N.F. Davin

Ken Mitchell

There is a long and cantankerous relationship between history and story, and between biography and drama. The historian must give his or her account using only the proven, that is, publicly documented, historical facts. The storyteller must rearrange, sometimes even alter, those 'facts' to convey the story to its audience. The historian resents the storyteller's loose way with 'the truth,' while the storyteller registers contempt for the way 'superficial detail' hinders the most powerful expression of a story.

I speak from the point of view of the storyteller, the dramatist. Clearly, some selection of fact is necessary in the average two-hour telling of a life story, one that ranges over more than sixty or seventy or eighty years. It is no greater or lesser a problem than the biographer faces, trying to decide whether the subject's performance in primary school spelling must be included in the definitive biography.

The difference is this. Faced with a choice in determining inclusion, the biographer will exclude the intuitive, the suspected, and the unprovable—that is, the undocumented. Yet that's the very material the storyteller is going to seize on when breaking through to the character's 'inner story,' that territory of unlimited fascination to twentieth-century Western civilization.

For the purpose of this discussion, I intend to draw a distinction between historical truth, and an inner or 'essential' truth. Indeed it's this dialectic which often drives the plot of historical dramas, as was the case with James Reaney's Donnelly plays.

As an illustration of the divergence between forms, most biographies make very limited use of verbal dialogue, and the purest don't even engage in speculation on what the subject 'might have said' or 'was likely to have said'. Quotation will be restricted to interviews or published statements. And even in using direct quotations, the biographer must decide whether to correct the syntax, grammar or punctuation of the subject.

It would be foolish for the dramatist to attempt to obey such scruples while still remaining true to his craft. History allows selection—but historical drama requires it. And not only selection, but invention. Paradoxically, this is because the dramatic genre has a much more rigid form and structure than history.

There are many disciplines of history—military history, social history, political history, geological history, biography—more or less defined by subject, not by form. What structure there is is usually defined by chronology. But drama *must* adhere to certain organic principles—the presentation of a conflict (or series of conflicts) resolved through climactic struggle—or it is not dramatic, and will not work on stage, on a screen, or on radio. Without conflict there can be no drama. Thus a dramatist must find a subject already invested with conflict, or take a subject and invent the conflict. A story without conflict, and a character without deep internal conflict, cannot be dramatized.

Doctors Banting and Bethune are two well-known figures in Canadian medical history. No doubt there have been several biographies of each. And I think it's fair to say that of these two fellow students at the University of Toronto in 1921, Frederick Banting, as the Nobel Prize-winning discoverer of insulin, made by far the greatest contribution to medical science. His life and his work had international stature, and were the subject of a recent CBC film. But as a dramatic subject, Banting will forever pale in comparison to Dr. Norman Bethune, his unconventional, self-destructive and egocentric colleague. Bethune had been effectively written out of history, despite several medical contributions, until the Chinese put him at the centre of their political mythology after he died there in 1939. For complicated political and cultural reasons I will discuss later, Bethune's ghost fought his way back into Canadian history. The Chinese biographies, incidentally, are extremely selective of facts, virtually silent on his life before he went to China.

Thus Bethune may turn out to be the much more significant figure, in part because he transcended standard historical evaluation. He was a fascinating character, a rebel and a misfit whose character was shaped in the crucible of the history of a third-world country, who became an archetypal hero. Bethune's uncanny ability to position himself at the centre of social struggle made him—at least for Mao Zedong—the ideal twentieth century man, an 'internationalist'. It was his interrelation with historical forces that gave his story shape, and made Bethune the ideal subject for biographical drama.

A subject without conflict, a character without deep internal divisions, will not work in dramatic form—at least if the dramatist adheres to the historical facts. The writer of the Banting film could have invented a love affair, or two or three, or had Banting miraculously curing the King of England with insulin in a dramatic race against time, but there are real limits to public acceptance of historical inventions. Hollywood kept making this mistake in the early years of feature film — film biographies were very popular in the 1930s, but few of these romanticized histories will survive. But *Gandhi* and *Patton*, and Abel Gance's *Napoleon*, have entered the literature.

This limit of acceptable invention expands in direct ratio to distance in time. Look at what Shakespeare did to the great Scottish hero Macbeth to make his story acceptable to the aesthetes of Jacobean England — some 500 years after the events at Birnam Wood. Ah well, you may say, Macbeth is a tragedy, not a history. But the same problems arise in Shakespeare's history plays, if we examine his embroideries of the reigns of Richard III and Henry VIII.

In fact, a play can only alter history to the degree the audience will allow it, and this is why any dramatization of great historical figures of recent times — say Roosevelt, or Mackenzie King, or Sarah Bernhardt — that strayed from the known facts of dates and historical events would be laughed off the stage. It's a tricky area for dramatists, and the reason why many playwrights, not to say audiences, avoid the form altogether. Legendary minor figures are often safer, which is one reason why the Western film boomed in American culture, with its bogus accounts of Jesse James and Butch Cassidy, or even the treatment of train robber Jack Miner in the successful Canadian film *The Grey Fox*. These characters are not expected to be historically accurate, and indeed would fail dramatically if they were.

There are three basic questions to be explored here:

1. Why are historical dramas written at all?
2. How much invention can be tolerated?
3. Who is an appropriate subject?

1. Historians write books to share the result of their years of research in the dusty archives of the world. They seek to publicize, to make public, their work. A biographer offers for public scrutiny a life worth examining, either because the subject has intrinsic historical importance, or because the life is a model, either positive or negative, for our times. (One of the only predictable results of the Gulf War was an outburst of biographies of Saddam Hussein and General Norman Schwartzkopf.) So historical dramas also become Rorschach tests of our social psyche: in one period, a film of Lawrence of Arabia will win critical acclaim; in another decade, a film like *Gandhi*. Such

characters provide models of human behaviour, almost as culturally powerful as dramatizations of the crucifixion, the mass being a ritualized dramatic biography of Christ's last day.

2. The invention or imaginative reconstruction can take place only at the personal level, not the public one. That is, the dramatist is allowed to imagine private scenes, conversations and actions if they are consistent with public utterance — but generally must adhere to the times, places, events recorded. The audience must believe itself to be perceiving historical truth as well as essential truth.

3. The best subject is not the successful entrepreneur, the balanced individual, or the most admirable person, but the tragic failure, or at least the fatally flawed victor. In drama, the eccentric will prevail over the well-rounded conformist.

To illustrate, I offer the case Nicholas Flood Davin. To those who have never heard of Davin, I recommend the biography by Dr. C.B. Koester, *Mr. Davin, M.P.* Davin, after Thomas D'Arcy McGee, may be the most outstanding Irish immigrant to Canada. He was a poet, a journalist, and a politician, virtually from the time of his arrival in Toronto in 1872 until his death in 1901. He was the original M.P. from Regina when the Northwest Territories were enfranchised, published several books, and established *The Regina Leader*, the most powerful journal in the territories, forerunner of today's *Leader-Post*.

Davin was a colourful, highly quoted public figure of his day but, until Dr. Koester's research and my two dramas in the 1970s, almost unknown in modern Canada, even in Regina, where only a school bears his name. Local history is often unkind to people who disturb community values, as Nicholas Davin did with his bravado, his reckless consumption of whiskey, his scandalous public affair with the West's first feminist and poet, Kate Simpson Hayes, and his various assaults on the North West Mounted Police and John A. Macdonald's Conservative government, of which he was a professed member.

Though my children attended Davin School, and I once worked three years for *The Leader-Post*, I was barely conscious of his name until I read Dr. Koester's 1971 Ph.D. dissertation, *Nicholas Flood Davin, A Biography*. Though couched in academic language and bristling with footnotes, that document was a riveting account of an archetypal hero: an Irishman born in dire poverty who educates himself, goes to London to study law, becomes a journalist during the Franco-Prussian War, decides to create a new identity in the Canadian colonies, and hurls himself at the windmills of life with the feverish abandon of a prophet creating a new utopia in the wilderness. The theme is one of change, of willed metamorphosis, in which Davin sheds more skins than a Western rattlesnake.

Here is a new Canadian who defends the assassin of George Brown in the decade's most sensational murder trial, who nearly wins an impossible Orange seat for John A. Macdonald in Ontario, falls from grace once more, and sets out for the Great Lone Land on his fourth attempt (after Cork, London and Toronto) to reinvent himself. He arrives at the end of the railroad, the unpromising Pile of Bones, establishes a newspaper and founds the Western wing of the Conservative party. Davin's ambition was nothing less than creating a new civilization for all that were to follow, a utopia of prosperity and cultural intensity he literally envisioned in his various speeches and publications. He was every bit as much a pioneer as the sod-busters and cowboys, with a fundamental belief in the power of the word.

Alas, he died in disgrace, a political outcast and a suicide, betrayed by the apprentice he had taken in hand, Walter Scott, who took over *The Leader*, then defeated Davin in his final election battle. Scott later became the founding premier of Saskatchewan before dying, some accounts say, in an insane asylum.

To squeeze such a life, with its many secondary characters, into a two-hour drama is a challenge. Even the most orthodox historian would concede that events must be compressed, secondary players liquidated, and a few conversations invented. It is technically possible to illustrate a life using only historical documentation — the so-called documentary dramas, such as historical pageants — but while interesting in their own right, they are theatrically inert, and do not outlast their first production.

On the other hand, to invent a play about Davin, say a recreation of his final day of life at the Clarendon Hotel in Winnipeg, would do the subject a disservice, because it would exclude the epic sweep of Canadian history, and Davin's relationship to it.

The need for historical accuracy becomes critical because dramas — unlike comic books and television shows — are generally created for a university-educated elite, that small but significant ten per cent of the Canadian population which attends theatre, views Canadian films, and reads Canadian books. These are the people sometimes called opinion-moulders, who determine cultural values — the people who attend conferences such as this.

Nonetheless, the power of drama lies at the centre, within the character, not at the periphery. It is the playwright's challenge to understand the historical character so thoroughly, and intuitively, that the surface details — place, date, season — become material that focus on the discovery of character, the essential truth, and are not the centre of attention themselves. Character is revealed and understood through conflict, and that's why, out of the thousands of 'important' men and women in Canadian history, only a handful will ever become the subject of good dramas. Davin, like Norman Bethune, Archie Belaney, Tommy Douglas, Gabriel Dumont, and Père Athol Murray—other characters of dramas I've written—was an eccentric, a person who stood out like a sports car in a used car lot.

Now I must confess that my attraction to historical subjects is essentially political. I'm not known as a political writer—I have no 'ism' to promote. My heroes range from Norman the Red to Athol Murray, the right-wing Catholic priest who led the Saskatchewan doctors' strike against medicare. But personally and professionally I am committed to the development of an indigenous Canadian culture, that fragile cement which in the final analysis is the only defence for our national sovereignty. And one of the reasons Davin appealed to me was that this was one of his visions as well.

In his prophetic article, 'A National Literature,' written 100 years ago, he acknowledges a debt to the culture of Shakespeare and says, 'But this cannot supply all our needs. We have a national existence of our own. There is a Canada to be expressed; an eminence to be sought which we cannot reach without that which is to a people what the higher faculties of the mind are to a man.'[1]

In the conclusion, he proclaimed, 'Only a national literature can raise a nation to perfect unity and single ardour and make possible a generous statesmanship independent of petty clamps, ignoble props, rising in grandeur above clouds of faction and even the storms of party, broad based upon a people's will and crowned by the clear approval of an enlightened opinion, whose purity and splendour are drawn not only from the past, but from the future as well—that future for which foresight works and whence genius draws its best inspiration.'

Or as the character Davin says, entering in Act One, 'Small talk! Endo my boy, if you are goin' to stick by me in this venture, you'll leave small talk to small people! Small talk has no place in a big land! Words are like coins—they get thin from overuse! If we ever hope to change the face of this vast wilderness, we must become poets! We will inspire the public imagination!'[2]

So it is no doubt partly due to Davin's political and philosophical exhortation that I have taken up the vocation of locating heroes in our past, usually those peculiar men and women whose accomplishments are rarely recognized at the time, and are more often

enemies of the state than great statesmen. Such heroes are fundamental necessities in a healthy society, people who serve as models
for survival, if not success. In a contemporary world where there
seem to be no heroes, only various degrees of incompetence and
villainy, among our business, political and religious leaders, this
becomes a vital necessity. The Americans don't have this problem
because they have their sports heroes, comic book characters, and
movie stars, but we don't have the same access to popular culture
as represented in the mass media. All the better reason to look to
history as a source, to find those buried treasures.

So as soon as I read Professor Koester's account of Davin I began immediately sketching the form of the drama. It would begin
with his arrival in Regina, trace his meteor-like blaze across the
prairie sky and his tragic conclusion. A tragedy, then, but like all
good tragedies, leavened with comic scenes and verbal wit. The plot
would trace his parallel and intersecting vocations as poet, journalist, politician and lover.

All the characters but one in the premiere production (at Regina's
Globe Theatre in 1978) were historical entitities: Kate Simpson
Hayes, Walter Scott, Endo Saunders, John A. Macdonald, Louis
Riel, and John Thompson, the Conservative Minister of Justice. The
exception was a figure labelled 'The Man From Moose Jaw,' who
forms the political opposition at rallies, and in parliament.

I made one change for subsequent productions and publication, changing the Hon. John Thompson into the fictitious Stanley
Burroughs. The reason was simple: Thompson serves as Davin's
confidante throughout the play but he died in 1894, so to keep him
alive to 1900 required too much distortion. And even though very
few students of history know that John Thompson was our fifth
prime minister, and a fairly good one, my fidelity to historical truth
wouldn't allow me to stretch his role beyond the date of mortality.

This example indicates the kind of barriers one must be willing,
or unwilling to cross, to write both biography and drama. History
may provide two, or more, a dozen if need be, confidantes for the
hero, but dramatic convention only allows one.

Another character appeared in the first, earliest script, an old
woman who has no name. She opens the play by appearing with an
old ledger book and saying to the audience:

'My father's life was full of trains. Like so much of our history.
You might think history is dull, but it's not. A famous person once
said that those who don't learn from history are doomed to repeat
it. And it became my life's work. This is called, "A Search for My
Father." We never met. But I came to know him well. The story begins here — in Regina. You could argue that it starts in Toronto. Or

Ireland. But here in 1883—when trains began to play their part—this city was a village of tents. . . . '[3]

As Davin's apparent daughter, she illustrates the dilemma I've posed here. Is she a figment of imagination, or did Davin have a daughter, contrary to historical documentation? The archives say Davin was childless. But the historian, Bev Koester, told me—unofficially as it were—that, during his research, he interviewed a legal firm in Winnipeg which handled the estate of Kate Simpson Hayes. One of the lawyers had told him of a bizarre visit in the 1940s from a middle-aged woman claiming to be the illegitimate daughter of Davin and Kate. She had been raised in a convent orphanage, and knew Kate as her aunt. She had indeed compiled a scrapbook on the father she'd never met, Nicholas Flood Davin.

Dr. Koester had no factual evidence to prove the connection, so she was not referred to in the dissertation. I, however, seeing in this figure the persona I needed to frame the story, seized on her at once. For a time I was considering titling the drama, 'A Search for My Father,' counterpointing Davin's lifelong search for fame and glory, and his daughter's struggle to find out who he was.

After the first production, however, I became concerned that, supposing she might still be alive, without being historically documented, I would be abusing her privacy. The character was struck from the play. I was surprised, therefore, when Dr. Koester's book was published in 1980, to find that Davin discovered her existence following his marriage to another woman, but was unable to locate her, even with the help of a private detective. She was still unnamed, but cited in a footnote through 'private correspondence in possession of the author.'[4] Thus, in a new version of the drama now in preparation for publication, the mysterious daughter will be reincorporated.

This wilful creation and destruction of characters is relatively simple, however, compared with the complexity of dramatizing political issues central to Davin's parliamentary career: the Second Homesteads Act and the infamous Manitoba Schools debate. Both of these were long and complex issues that consumed thousands of hours of debate in the House of Commons, and preoccupied Davin and his colleagues for several years. I won't attempt to explain them here, but, inasmuch as both characterized Davin's eternal struggle between party loyalty and loyalty to his constituency, they need reference.

Davin was one of the first Western regionalists, and his electoral successes in three federal campaigns depended entirely on his vow to represent the interests of the West in Ottawa. Unfortunately, this led him into direct conflict with his own Conservative party—

and resulted in Davin cooling his heels on the back benches of Parliament for fourteen years.

This central conflict drives the second act, and rather than invent more, let's say, colourful issues, such as capital punishment or women's emancipation, I decided to simplify his issues into easily understood and dramatic lines of action.

The Manitoba Schools Question was the Meech Lake debate of the 1890s, dividing the country along religious and linguistic lines. The West, led by Manitoba, wanted to disallow French schools, which had been guaranteed under the constitution. The Conservative government was determined to resist, on constitutional grounds. Caught between his supporters and his leaders, between common sense and principle, Davin opted finally to go with his party on the crucial vote, and was pilloried by the opposition. He was labelled a traitor to the Northwest, and his last-minute loyalty to the government still failed to get him into the cabinet.

The Second Homestead Issue was a much less turbulent debate, but again typified Davin's political dilemma. Basically, the government had begun offering free second homesteads in the territories to certain immigrants, and had then abandoned the program. Davin took it on himself to fight Macdonald's reversal, promising second homesteads to his voters, and initiating not one but two private member's bills in his foolhardy campaign. He eventually won the case for certain groups of immigrants, but in the process alienated John A. and most of the cabinet over an issue the voters had already forgotten before the next federal election.

In short, Davin had a strong if not always palatable set of principles. He was a disturber of the excrement, to be blunt about it, and it's easy to imagine Davin leading a group like the Western Reform Party.

I could be wrong about the kind of hero that our culture needs or deserves, but I am fascinated by this archetypal character: the rebel, the misfit, the Socratic bone who sticks in the craw of the establishment, a flamboyant eccentric radical who chooses to go down in flames, defying the Canadian blandness which normally prevails.

I believe these characters are beginning to define our cultural mythology. Note the success of *Billy Bishop Goes to War*, of the various Bethune dramatizations, the enduring dramatic legacy of Louis Riel and Gabriel Dumont, of William Lyon Mackenzie, Emily Carr and Père Murray of Notre Dame. These figures, mostly failures or outcasts in their own lifetime, have become our enduring icons, and it's not just because plays about them are better *written* than pieces about Mackenzie King, Frederick Banting, or John

Diefenbaker. It's because their lives epitomize something we admire: the little person standing up to the mob, the nonconformist
who chooses to carve his or her life out of the Precambrian rock
rather than proceed along the well-followed path.

Without question, Davin was of limited historical interest — at
least in the realm of politics. He never did make it to the cabinet.
But more than any other public figure of his time and place he was
able to articulate the dream of the Canadian West, the belief that
this empty, barren-looking landscape would someday be home to
symphony orchestras and French restaurants, that a thriving literature might be born and bear fruit. He was a visionary and, like
most of that rare breed, was bad-tempered, mercurial and contrary.
He died disappointed, and no one understood the significance of
Davin's life in the nineteenth century. Only now do we see that his
destiny was not in politics as he had dreamed, and only marginally
in literature and journalism, certainly not as a lover. Davin's contribution was his life, that ball of flame that blazed out of Kilfinane
to Cork, Dublin and London, and finally to Canada where it crashed
to ground once again.

It wasn't Davin's substance that counted finally, it was his style.

Notes

1 N.F. Davin, A National Literature, unpublished MS, Saskatchewan
  Archives (#SHS 14).
2 Ken Mitchell, *Davin, The Politician* (Edmonton: NeWest Press, 1979),
  p. 14.
3 Ken Mitchell, unpublished MS.
4 C.B. Koester, *Mr. Davin, M.P.* (Saskatoon: Prairie Books, 1980),
  p. 217.

Tracking Down
the Irish 'Entertainers'
in the Ottawa Valley

Joan Finnigan

This audience is sprinkled with academics who can give you the history, politics, and demography of the Irish in the Ottawa Valley, with experts who can tell you why, and how, and when, and in what numbers they came to the Valley.

But I am here tonight to tell you about some very special Irish old-timers of the Valley, Irish old-timers I am pleased to call 'The Entertainers.'

For the past ten or twelve years I have been on 'The Moving Staircase' up and down the Valley, over thousands of miles, taping the old-timers of the Valley—the majority of them Irish. I have been privileged to collect over 400 life stories or autobiographies. Some of the best of these have been moved to the written tradition in *Some of the Stories I Told You Were True*; *Laughing All The Way Home*; *Legacies, Legends and Lies*; and *Tell Me Another Story*, my four oral-social histories of the Valley. Another thirty or so await publication in my fifth oral history, *Tallying the Tales of the Old-Timers*. The majority of my tapes have been used in Carleton University's five-year linguistic study of the Valley and I am in the process of depositing the tapes in the National Archives in Ottawa.

Contrary to all misconceptions held by Torontonians — and even by some Ottawa broadcasters—the Ottawa Valley is not the little stretch from Carp to Carleton Place. It is a huge area, larger than England, the watershed of a mighty continental river and its twenty-seven tributaries. The Valley reaches from Hawkesbury to Algonquin Park and from Brockville to Kirkland Lake and Timmins.

The late Professor A.R.M. Lower of Queen's University was the first historian of national status to immerse himself in the history of the Ottawa Valley. His classics, *Great Britain's Woodyard* and the *North American Assault on the Canadian Forest*, remain the academic cornerstones in the pyramid of writing and research directed toward the elucidation of the unique Ottawa Valley identity. As

Lower said to me once, 'The unique nature of the Ottawa Valley is hardly understood elsewhere in Canada.'

Lower also wrote some poetic 'colour' pieces on the Ottawa Valley which appeared over a number of years in *Queen's Quarterly*. In his article, 'Udawah's Stream', Lower defines for all Canadians, as well as for many people of the Valley itself, just how vast a territory is covered by the term, 'the Ottawa Valley.' Lower writes:

> If Montreal Island be taken as lying within the Ottawa Valley, the population of the whole Valley represents a respectable fraction of all Canada, in rough approximation about twelve percent. Most of this is concentrated around Montreal and Ottawa, but there are substantial towns all the way up, such as Hawkesbury, Arnprior, Pembroke, the towns on Lake Temiskaming and the mining towns of the upper waters. Apart from hydro-electricity, the mining region represents the most recent contribution of the Ottawa Valley to Canadian life; within it lie the Kirkland Lake gold mines, the Noranda cluster of copper mines, and lesser centres.[1]

In the nineteenth and early twentieth century in the Ottawa Valley, each hamlet, village, town and district had an outstanding character functioning as its strongman, chief brawler, peacemaker, champion or hero: Big John Horner of Radford, Quebec; the Seven Frost Brothers of Pembroke: Finnan the Buffalo of Glengarry; Bunker Joe Helferty of Barry's Bay; Big Lal Box and Wild Bob Ferguson of Calabogie; Big Michael Jennings of Sheenboro, Quebec; Cockeye George McNee of Arnprior; the Mulvihills, Culhanes and Maloneys from Mount St. Patrick; Big Bob Foy of Eganville; Le Prad of Temiskaming; and Mountain Jack Thomson of Portage-du-Fort.

As well as having its revered protector, every hamlet, village and town had its recognized resident 'entertainer,' the acknowledged storyteller, a man of wit and repartee, an originator of humour, a source of laughter, a creator of great one-liners, a man to leaven with his gift what was so often a hard life in pioneer Canada.

When this man appeared on the scene at the general store, it was like the sun coming out; all life gravitated towards him as every customer, every counter-lounger, every 'regular,' every talk-starved lonely farmer into town for supplies turned in his direction to absorb his words. When this man entered the scene in the farm kitchen, sometimes even the farm wife dried her hands on her apron and took a break for laughter. Or, as it was with Taddy Haggerty, Champion Wit of the Opeongo Line, everyone gathered around him on the church steps in Brudenell for Sunday entertainment and laughed together until the priest had to come and break up the crowd.

Very early on my 'incredible journey' doing the oral-social histories of the Ottawa Valley — I think it was 1978 — Lloyd Gavan, one of the Singing Gavans of the Nickabeau and Quyon, Quebec took me to the kitchen of his cousin Carl Jennings at Sheenboro, a 100% Irish enclave on the edge of the Quebec wilderness.

Continuously, for the twenty-five years *prior* to my arrival, Carl's Kitchen had been the meeting-place of the yarners and liars, the storytellers and myth-makers, the singers and dancers and drinkers who dropped in from everywhere in the Ottawa Valley.

From my first moment there, as I turned on the tape recorder, I knew by instinct that I was about to stake a gold mine. And it didn't take me much longer to realize that I had discovered 'The Celtic Twilight' of the oral tradition in the Valley. I have not yet tallied how many hours or how many people I taped in Carl's kitchen but I can tell you that the tapes are still so precious to me that I have not yet been able to turn them over to the National Archives.

Carl was not only host in his huge kitchen but he was also the lead 'entertainer.' Some of the material collected in Carl's kitchen appeared in *Laughing All the Way Home*, my first oral history collection of the humour of the Valley. When Gina Mallett reviewed the book in *Maclean's* magazine she described Jennings as 'a wit, a sage, and a master of imagery.' Here are some of his one-liners — those that would pass the censor:

Of his confirmed bachelorhood: 'Never tie a knot with your tongue you can't undo with your teeth.'

'He was the kind of a man who was too heavy for light work and too light for heavy work; so he did nothing.'

'There was enough wrinkles in his face to hold a week's rain anytime.'

'If you walk your horses when you're young, they'll trot at seventy-two.'

'She was a nice quiet girl; you could put your hand on her anywhere.'

'The difference between the Indian and white man is that the Indian builds a small fire and huddles over it. But the white man builds a huge fire and has to back off from it.'

'The last thing an Irishman says is "By Golly! I'm dead!" '

The recordings in the 'Celtic Twilight' of Carl's kitchen provided examples of every kind of humour from low-life slapstick to original wit, repartee and one-liners, from the raunchy, racy, irreverent story to the blackest of humour, from the characteristic Valley tall tales, legends and folklore through to the highest form — the indigenous humour arising out of the real event, the real character or the legitimate combination of both.

There are a thousand great stories from Carl's kitchen, but I have to choose one:

> 'There was once a famous lady of Chapeau who had been a widow for a very long time but she had remained active. She had six boyfriends. So finally she died. And Father Harrington knew all about her so he decided that he would commandeer all her lovers to be her pallbearers. They all agreed. But it was a cold icy January day and some of the pallbearers slipped when they were carrying her down the steps of the Chapeau church. And Father Harrington slipped up behind them and hissed out, "Hold on to her, boys! You did it before and you can damn well do it now"!'

I suspect Carl Jennings was one of the pallbearers.

One summer's day in 1981, I was returning to base from Carl's kitchen after an afternoon's recording session with storytellers, the late Jim Lampkin, the late Len Doyle and Carl Jennings himself. I found myself laughing like a madwoman in the car recalling the stories they had told. Then in one of those 'eureka!' moments that makes the life of the creative writer sometimes abundantly worthwhile, I suddenly realized that so often after taping the old-timers I was laughing all the way home. There and then I decided that I should be doing an oral history collection of that humour of the Valley — again, before it was too late.

The more I considered this new book idea, the more I realized that, for most of my life, as I had moved in and out of the Valley, I had been exposed to different forms of Valley humour. And I started tallying up all the great 'entertainers' I already knew or knew of, not only from among the people I had met and taped in Carl's kitchen, but people much further back in my 'remembering place': my uncle Bert Horner, who told stories of Jim Doherty of Quyon and Ragged Chute, Quebec; an old-timer in Quinn's Hotel in Killaloe telling stories of Taddy Haggerty of the Opeongo Line; and Bernie Bedore of Arnprior back in 1975 telling on tape that first couple of stories of Dinny O'Brien of the Burnt Lands of Huntley.

As well as an ancestral root in the Valley, there is also a 'laughing root.' The laughing root is ticklish, tender and unpredictable in growth. It does not perhaps go down as deep as some of the other roots, but it nevertheless nourishes the spirit. It is multiform, elusive and often invisible to the naked eye. One of its most priceless human qualities is that it dwells most often in the imagination. It is frequently symbiotic with the tragic root and, in its highest form, an integral part of the philosophy root.

And so, a self-designated 'laugh detective,' I set off in pursuit of the legendary 'entertainers.' That sleuthing trail was by both co-incidence and divine direction to lead me to so many others, like Vi Dooling of Douglas and Renfrew with her heart-warmingly hilarious stories of Wyman Towns; to Tex Maves of Pembroke who lived out part of his life of slapstick humour on a houseboat on the Ottawa River; to the nicely pseudonymed Nellie Finnuken, that very naughty nurse-in-training whose stories have been devoured now by a whole network of nurses who empathize, cry and laugh with her; to the younger generation carrying on the tradition of raunchy humour in the Valley, like Pierre, Jean-Paul and Hank in their chapter in *Legacies, Legends and Lies.*

As writer Edmund Lenihan went in search of healer Biddy Early throughout Ireland, so I have tracked down the 'entertainers' of the Ottawa Valley, travelling hundreds of miles up and down back Valley roads, coming to dead ends, finding treasures. If need be, to help the story along, I've taken my tot of grog to Doyle and Boyle alike. I've danced to Johnny Kiely's mouth organ in his little log house on the Whelan road, and I've traded story to beget story. I've driven up trails on the mountainsides, gone through flooded fields back of Rockingham, and walked in through the snows up to my knees at Mayo.

I've tracked people down in old folks' homes, in Ottawa high-rises, yes, once even in a log house with a mud floor and no electricity for my tape recorder. The old lad — an Irish bachelor — ran his TV off his tractor and offered to do the same for my recorder. Another old Irish bachelor, descended from Irish kings he was, apologizing for his lack of technology, said he had plenty of money to afford 'the lights' but felt that, at 90, it was just too late to be bothered with them.

I had come to know some of these 'entertainers,' like Jim Doherty of Ragged Chute and G.A. Howard of Shawville, by eavesdropping on my Shawville clan's kitchen talk when, as a child, I visited them from Ottawa. Jim Doherty, as it turned out, was an itinerant worker on the farms and in the lumber camps on both sides of the Valley from Quyon to Chapeau and from Killaloe to Rolphton. He had a harelip, and many of the people I later taped used to imitate his lisp when they were relating his stories. Today this might be construed unkind but, as it turned out, Jim Doherty was a man who knew his physical defects all too well and could laugh at them.

On Doherty's Trail I taped Dominic Curley, one of the Seven Quyon Fiddlers, at his home in Quyon, Quebec, in company with his then ninety-seven-year-old father, Frank, who said of Doherty,

'Ah, yes, Jim Doherty. Everything he said was funny. He never was around but you had a laugh.'

But it was Dominic Curley who gave proof of Jim Doherty's ability *to laugh at himself.*

> Jim had a harelip, you know, and he lisped because of it. But none of that ever held him down. I can tell you about the first time Jim Doherty met Joe Vachon. Jim had one harelip, but Joe Vachon had two of them. He had one on each side. So Jim Doherty looked at Joe Vachon a bit and then he said, "I thought the Lord made an awful mess of me. But he made a holy show of you!" And they both laughed together.

In his book *Laughter and Liberation,* when Harvey Mindess, an American psychologist, enunciates his theories of humour, he says that in its maturest form humour eventually ranges beyond jokes, beyond wit, beyond pun, beyond laughter itself, and should be fed with an awareness of the human comedy and its paradoxes. Humour, he believes, like love, courage, understanding, is one of the attributes that can sustain us through the worst, and includes the ability to laugh at oneself. Although Jim Doherty has been dead for some twenty-five years, I have followed his trail, collecting stories from the late Ken Hodgins of Thorne and Sudbury (retired to Renfrew when I taped him), from Carl Jennings of Sheenboro, the Curleys of Quyon, the Quinns of Aylmer and some anonymously collected in Ottawa.

One of my favourite Jim Doherty stories comes from Jennings' chapters in *Laughing All The Way Home:*

> One time Father Harrington at Chapeau hired Jim Doherty to help clean up the cellar in the priest's house there. Anyhow, there was a lot of wine bottles in the cleanup. And Father Harrington said to Jim:
> "Lots of 'dead soldiers,' eh, Jim?"
> And Jim snapped back, "Yes, father, and they all had the priest, too, before they died."

G.A. Howard of Shawville, like Jim Doherty of Quyon, was part of my childhood lore. G.A. was a highly respected local politician and businessman who ran one of the first Ford dealerships in the Valley and who, as a master of spoonerisms, really did sell cars with 'baboon tires,' 'automatic cutoffs,' 'rubber-bunters' and 'self-commencers.' His one-liners, malapropisms, stories and stories about him, were — and still are — woven into the web of Western Quebec lore.

In readings and lectures from Vinton to Vancouver I have told this G.A. original.

> 'G.A. moved up in the world and decided to take his wife on a holiday to Atlantic City, the fashionable watering place of the '20s, attracting even the affluent from the Ottawa Valley. G.A.'s wife became enamoured of the Atlantic Ocean, swam out beyond her depth and was hauled up on shore, half-drowned, by some onlookers.
>
> While she was lying on the beach at G.A.'s feet, someone in the crowd yelled out, "Give her artificial respiration!"
>
> "Artificial respiration be damned!" G.A. yelled back. "Give her the real thing! I can afford it!"

In 1986, after I spoke to the Gatineau Historical Society, Norris Brough of Ottawa, formerly of Shawville, came up to me and said, 'I have more Ned Finnigan and G.A. Howard stories for you.' You can imagine how quickly I got to his house with my tape recorder! Here is one of Mr. Brough's G.A. Howard stories to add to the repertoire of a man dead these twenty-five years:

> Back in the 1920's, A.G. Brough, Dougal McCredie, G.A. Howard and various other Shawville lads used to hunt at Lake Dumont, fifty miles northeast of Shawville. There were numerous stops on the way up to quench a growing thirst; at Ladysmith, Otter Lake, Bend in the River, John Cowan's Spring. At one point the old Ford had to be parked and left because the last three miles had to be concluded on foot. At this point G.A. opened the car trunk to get his liquor supply and discovered he had forgotten his gun. They were beyond the end of the Pontiac Telephone Line so they went to the nearest fire ranger and got him to key into the Pontiac system. G.A.'s son Dean answered the phone at home, but the line was very fuzzy.
>
> "Dean, Dean," G.A. yelled. "It's G.A. Howard."
>
> "Yes, father."
>
> "I left my gun. I want you to bring up my gun."
>
> "Bring up your what?"
>
> "Gun, gun," G.A. yelled back. But still Dean couldn't make out the message. So in exasperation G.A. yelled into the ranger's phone:
>
> *"Gun! Gun! 'G' FOR JESUS, 'U' FOR EUROPE, 'N' FOR PNEUMONIA."*

I had not been long taping in the Valley, and particularly along the Opeongo Line, when I realized that stories of a character named Taddy Haggerty were turning up in the taped interviews. Someone would be telling me tales of the lice in the lumber camps on the Schyan that were 'so big they left their bark-marks on your body,' and then they would suddenly smile to themselves, do a switch-over and say, 'Did I ever tell you this Taddy Haggerty story?' Or they'd be going on about Philomene Bergeron the 'he-lady' (or the 'she-man') of the Opeongo, and they'd change over and say, 'Now I'll tell you a story about Taddy Haggerty.'

Well, Taddy Haggerty, champion wit of the Opeongo Line, has been dead for 30 years, but he still haunts the minds and imaginings of the storytellers of the Valley long past the point of his leave-taking from this earth.

Again, over a goodly number of years and many more miles I collected the stories of Taddy Haggerty from people along the Opeongo Line: the Sheridans, the Jessops, the Heinemans, the Walthers, Father John Haas of Eganville, Mrs. June Winiarski of Quadville, Father Tom May of Vinton.

Here's a Taddy Haggerty story from Father Haas of Eganville:

> One year there was a terrible potato famine on the Opeongo Line. And after the bad crop was in in the fall the lads were sitting in the hotel at Killaloe having a quart or two and talking over the bad situation about potatoes.
>
> "Yes, siree," said Taddy. "When you have a year with a good crop of potatoes, when you put them on to boil you can hear them saying to each other, 'Move over. Move over.' But this year was the worst I've ever seen."
>
> "Tell us, Taddy, how bad was it this year?" asked some of the lads around the table.
>
> "Well, I'll tell ye," said Taddy. "In this year's crop of potatoes there were ones the size of marbles. And then there were the ones the size of peas. And then there were the really really small ones!"

In August 1983 I received a phone call from Father Tom May of Vinton, Quebec, who had grown up on the Opeongo Line in Taddy Haggerty's country. He was calling to tell me that he had heard me on Lowell Green's open-line radio program from Ottawa and that he had collected some Taddy Haggerty stories from his childhood. When I got to Vinton not only had Father May collected the stories, but he had written them out as though they were being told by Taddy Haggerty himself in his very own Irish!

Through Father May's reminiscences, Taddy Haggerty tells some stories of one of his favourite Brudenell priests, Father Frank Hogan.

> Father Hogan knew human nature pretty well. He always used to say, "Ten o'clock mass always starts sharp at ten minutes after ten."

He was also a great deer hunter. One Sunday in the hunting season he said mass real early for a few of the hunters. He told them to go down to Hartney's Lake and start a chase to pass by Brudenell church just as he would be finishing up with ten o'clock mass. So they did. And just about three minutes after ten, everyone in the church heard the deer hounds coming close. Father Hogan put his hand to his ear and said, "There will be no sermon today."

We all cried when he left Brudenell.

But of all the wonderful stories Father May converted from oral to written tradition using Taddy Haggerty as the mouthpiece, I treasure this one particularly because it is an example of my favourite kind of humour, the original indigenous humour that arises out of a real character.

There was a great tailor in Killaloe. As a young man he had lost his leg in a lumber camp, by a falling tree. Instead of getting a wood leg, he got a cork one. It was real handy in his tailor work. He would stick the needles, pins, awls, jackknife and so on in his cork leg where they were handy to reach. But strangers and children were goggle-eyed when they first saw him do it.

I'm forgetting to tell you his name. John D. Fleming. He was also an expert horseman. He made lots of money breaking in hard-to-handle horses. Once he was taking a horse-and-buggy ride up by Brudenell and Rockingham. He bought a calf there and tied it in the back of the buggy with a good strong rope. He stopped at the store at Brudenell corners, and while he was in the store, some wags cut the rope. He never found the calf. But he kept his ears open and formed a good idea about who had done the trick.

A few years later a man brought in a tanned deerskin to be made into moccasins and mitts, which John D. Fleming did. When the man came to get his fine mitts and moccasins and pay for them, John D. said to him, "Here is the scraps left over from your deerskin. I have made them into one small pair of mitts. There was not enough to put thumbs in them. But they might be real good to wear when cutting rope off a calf."

Mrs. June Winiarski of Quadville also answered my plea, on radio, for help in tracking down Taddy Haggerty stories before they were all lost in time. I can honestly say that the afternoon I spent listening to Mrs. Winiarski was one of the most enjoyable I have ever spent in all my oral history career. I did, indeed, find myself 'laughing all the way home.' From her interview:

Up in Brudenell, old Mr. Wingle got married for the second time. He got hold of another old lady and married her, and he was really blowing about the second woman he'd got. Oh, she was a good worker! And she could keep a fire on. And work in the barn. And milk the cows. But mostly he was telling everybody what a good cook she was. Oh, she was a good cook!

And one time he was talking to Taddy there at Brudenell at the church and he says, "I tell you, Taddy, I got a fine woman this time. She's a great cook. I tell you, Taddy, she can make a meal out of *nothing*."

And Taddy looks at old Wingle a moment and says, "And by god! she'd often have to do that!"

In 1975 on a CBC commission I taped Bernie Bedore, Arnprior storyteller, for the first in-depth documentary on radio ever done on the Ottawa Valley. *There's No Good Times Left—None at All* was aired twice on CBC Anthology.

It was in Bedore's interview that I first heard of Dinny O'Brien of the Burnt Lands of Huntley. My interest was piqued by this character, but it was not until I decided to do the oral history collection of the humour of the Valley that I went in serious search of him throughout the Almonte area.

Someone in Almonte told me that I should go to Concession 14 of Huntley off Highway 44 and there I might find him. That in itself was somewhat of a wry joke for, when I talked to the Lynches, Flynns, Graces and O'Briens along the concession, all descendants of Potato Famine Irish, I discovered that, although I was indeed in Dinny's territory, that legend-in-his-lifetime had been dead for forty years. I tracked down the farms on which he had lived only to discover that all that then remained of the O'Brien buildings was a roothouse on the side of a hill.

I went down a goodly number of dead ends in the Almonte area, visiting Vaughans, Morrows and Flynns. Some of them were 'beyond the pale' already, and one of them at least said to me, 'I cannot speak of the dead,' and closed the door. I was really despairing of ever truly fleshing out this incredible character.

Finally, an Almonte lawyer, a friend of mine, sent me to the then eighty-seven-year-old Ray Jamieson, a fourth-generation Ulster Irishman who had practised law in Almonte for over fifty years.

Jamieson immediately hung flesh on Dinny's legendary bones. 'I wouldn't say that Dinny drank a lot,' said Jamieson, 'but he was addicted to alcohol.

'Dinny was litigious. He was a good talker who could explain anything. He spoke pretty good grammar with a real lilt. Dinny was remarkable and unforgettable. If he had been educated, he would have done something. He was full of brains.'

Greedy to hear more about this amazing Valley 'entertainer,' I sent a letter to the editor of the *Almonte Gazette* and heard back from W.J. James of Carleton Place who, when I visited him, added more Dinny O'Brien stories to the collection.

It was finally a Vaughan who sent me to Basil O'Keefe, on Concession 11 at Almonte, who for several generations had had his ancestral farm adjacent to land that belonged to Dinny. Mr. O'Keefe, then aged seventy-nine, with genuine affection and caring, further reclaimed for posterity the character of Dinny, his friend and neighbour for so many years.

> Dinny always had a home for somebody. His only fault was that he used to like to drink a bit. He wasn't an Irishman if he didn't drink a little. But here at my place I could hear him coming away to hell out the road there, singing in the dark. He'd go to town and he'd come home singing at the top of his voice in the black night. I can hear him coming singing yet along that road there in the pitch black.

The trail then led to Judge C.J. Newton of Almonte, whom I taped in the Newton Room of Patterson's restaurant in Perth.

He not only told old and new Dinny O'Brien stories, but he also told great stories of some of the other wonderfully funny characters of Carleton Place, Perth and Almonte: George Comba, the Carleton Place funeral director cum practical joker; Straight-Back Maloney; Paddy Moynihan, 'The Mayor of Dacre'; Pat Murphy of Stanleyville; Tommy Hunt of Blakeney; Mrs. O'Flaherty of Carleton Place, who charged her lodger Lannigan with 'indecent assault'; Con Mahoney who ran the hotel out on the Burnt Lands.

Judge Newton added many treasures to the Dinny O'Brien collection:

> While they were building the new Roman Catholic church in the Burnt Lands of Huntley at Corkery, the priest came to collect from Dinny. He was collecting from each parishioner according to his means.
> "Now, Mr. O'Brien," said the holy father, "you have a fine farm here. You should be able to give fifty dollars."
> "Aha God!" Dinny said (he always said "Aha God!"). "Not from me. Sure I'd far rather join the Protestants first and go to hell. They're pretty near as good — and a damn sight cheaper!"

Of course, when I visited W.T. (Billy) James in Carleton Place to get his Dinny O'Brien stories, I realized while I was there that Billy James was himself one of the great characters of the Valley; he was ready to contribute not only to the humour collection but also to the lumbering saga and to the annals of farming lore through his experiences working in the bush for Gillies and from his many years at Appleton as one of the outstanding farmers in Canada, a breeder of prize Herefords and a pioneer in the fight for the elimination of the barberry bush.

It is so difficult to choose a story from the diversity of the James repertoire illuminating the social history of every place he ever lived and every field he ever worked in. But I think I would choose here his J.R. Booth stories because they are so rare.

I worked for Gillies, but I remember stories about lumber baron J.R. Booth who was the greatest of them all, I guess. The first one is about J.R. Booth and the Young Upstart.

This young fellow had got through college from up the line, probably somewhere at Pembroke or Renfrew, and after he graduated he seen that there was an opening advertised for a clerk at J.R. Booth's mill in Hull. So he got on the train this Monday morning and he went down to Ottawa. Everything was very quiet around Union Station there. As a matter of fact, when he got off the train at the station there was only this one old man around there at all. So the young fellow sat around for a while and waited. But still no one else appeared. So finally he went over to the old lad and he says to him,

"What would you take, old fellow, to carry my grips over to J.R. Booth's office?"

And the old lad says, "Oh, anything at all, young fellow, that you'd like to give me."

So the old lad carried the young fellow's grips over to J.R. Booth's office, and the young fellow threw the old lad fifty cents for his trouble. Then he noticed that the old lad was still hanging around, so he said to him, "Say, you couldn't tell me where I could find J.R. Booth, could you?"

And the old lad pointed to himself, "Yes, right here," he said.

One time after dinner at the Chateau Laurier, J.R. Booth, king of the timber barons, gave the waiter a quarter tip. And the waiter says to J.R. Booth, "Your son always gives me a dollar tip."

"Yes," says J.R., "but he has a rich father."

Charlotte Whitton, a native of Renfrew, the late colourful, talented and temperamental mayor of Ottawa, was one of the legendary Valley 'entertainers' whose stories were constantly turning up in interviews. I might be collecting the life story or autobiography of an old McLachlin shanty man and he would say to me, 'Say, would you like to hear a Charlotte Whitton story?' From Lloyd Francis, who sat with her on city council, and from Hal Anthony and

Lowell Green, who covered her mayoralty, I have collected a repertoire of Whittonese which appears in *Tell Me Another Story*. Many
of the stories are unadorned slapstick, almost burlesque, but she
did have a quick sharp wit preserved in stories like these:

During one of her terms of office as Mayor of Ottawa Charlotte
Whitton was entertaining the Lord Mayor of London at a very formal banquet at the Chateau Laurier. She was all dressed up in a
black dinner gown with a corsage of red roses at her shoulder. Re-
splendent in all his chains of office, the Mayor of London was seated
beside her at the banquet table. Attempting to make conversation
with a somewhat enigmatic lady, he gallantly decided to try a bit
of flattery to break the ice. So he turned to her and whispered in
her ear, 'Miss Whitton, if I lean over and smell your roses, do you
blush?' Charlotte looked at him in surprise and then snapped back,
'If I pull your chain, do you flush?'

And then there is another story in which the inimitable Miss
Whitton was one-upmanshipped. Again the setting was a large civic
reception. Amongst the guests was Ovila Dionne, father of the famous quintuplets who had just been born and who had made the
Dionne family of North Bay famous overnight. Charlotte went up
to Mr. Dionne and said, 'I guess you don't realize who I am. I'm
the Mayor of Ottawa.'

But evidently Mr. Dionne had already learned to do fast foot-
work in the spotlight.

'I guess you don't realize who I am,' he retorted. 'I'm the Cock
of the North.'

Just as great loving eventually becomes a truly religious experience, so tracking down 'the entertainers' became a major spiritual
process in my life, spanning a period of ten years. Indeed, it had
some attributes of a pilgrimage, as a rite of passage with transformation as the desired effect. It was a further exploration of roots
in the Valley — the laughing root.

Occasionally, after leaving someone who had just given of himself or herself through the gift of laughter, I had that rare and
mystical feeling of unity with fellow human beings, that sublime
'belonging to the universe,' which is at the summit of human emotional experiences.

And for all of us, the listener, the teller and eventually the
reader, it was an experience of profound joy. The storytellers gave
to me the only gift you can truly give to someone else — yourself.
I was entrusted with that gift and received it in trust with a responsibility to discharge that story authentically into print. The
storytellers' rewards were pride of recognition, personal fulfilment

and an achieving of permanency for that part of their life story or autobiography when it was placed between the pages of a book.

This experience of joy and laughter that passed between the teller and the listener then fanned out to encompass other lives — the lives of the readers. One woman in Carleton Place told me that her husband laughed so hard when reading *Laughing All the Way Home* that he had to lie on the floor. And just recently a lawyer from Ottawa told me that when he has a hard day or is feeling down, he picks up Legacies, Legends and Lies and rereads his favourite stories from the Valley 'entertainers,' both living and dead.

The Canadian National Institute for the Blind has received permission to put the Valley humour from *Laughing All the Way Home* on audio tape for the blind, so that they may be able to laugh in the dark, perhaps even 'see' the world from the perspective of a 'God's Eye View.'

There is an old Armenian saying that three apples fell from heaven — one for the story, one for the teller and one for the listeners. From my experience recording the oral (social) history of the Valley and tracking down its 'entertainers,' I would have to say that I suspect these heavenly apples fell on the Ottawa Valley.

For the sake of your health and sanity, then, may you feast often on the apples of heaven.

Notes

1 A.R.M. Lower, "Udawah's Stream," *Queen's Quarterly*, 66 (1959–60): 213.
2 Harvey Mindess, *Laughter and Liberation* (Los Angeles: Nash, 1971).

Notes on Contributors

Don Akenson is Professor of History at Queen's University, Kingston, Ontario. The author of a dozen books on Irish history, he has also published a number of historical works blending fictional and historical elements, including *At Face Value: The Life and Times of Eliza McCormack/John White*, and *The Orangeman: The Life and Times of Ogle R. Gowan*. He has received a Guggenheim Fellowship and both the Landon and Chalmers prizes for his work on Irish migrants to Canada. His most recent book *God's People: Covenant and Land in South Africa, Israel and Ulster* was named one of the best books published in the U.S. in 1992 by the *Library Journal*.

Ronald Ayling is Professor of English at the University of Alberta, and Vacca Professor of Liberal Studies at the University of Montevallo, Alabama in 1992–93. He has also taught at universities in Africa, Australia and Britain. His publications include several books on Sean O'Casey's writings and articles on Nigerian and South African literature. Most recently (1992) he edited a casebook on J.M. Synge.

Ann Beer, who wrote a doctoral thesis on Samuel Beckett at Oxford, is a professor at the Centre for the Study and Teaching of Writing at McGill University. She has also contributed work on Beckett to the *Journal of Beckett Studies*, *The Southern Review*, and a forthcoming collection from Cambridge University Press.

D.M.R. Bentley is Professor of English at the University of Western Ontario. A founding editor of *Canadian Poetry: Studies, Documents, Reviews* (1977–), he has published widely on Canadian literature and on Victorian poetry and painting. He is the General Editor of the Canadian Poetry Press Series of Editions of Early Canadian Long Poems and a past president of the Canadian Institute for Historical Microreproductions.

Paul Bew is Professor in the Department of Politics, Queen's University, Belfast. He is the author of *Charles Stewart Parnell, The British State and the Ulster Crisis, Conflict and Conciliation in Ireland 1898–1910*, and *The Dynamics of Irish Politics*. He is also a commentator on Irish affairs on British and Irish radio and television.

Desmond Bowen is Research Professor at Carleton University, where he was Professor of History for many years. He divides his time between Canada and Ireland, where he holds a fellowship in the Institute of Irish Studies, Queen's University, Belfast, and assists in postgraduate work in the Department of Biblical Studies and Theology at Trinity College, Dublin. His publications include *The Idea of the Victorian Church, Protestant Crusade in Ireland*, and *Paul Cardinal Cullen and the Shaping of Modern Irish Catholicism*.

Robin B. Burns teaches Canadian history at Bishop's University in Lennoxville, Quebec. He completed a study of D'Arcy McGee's Canadian career for his M.A. thesis at Carleton University, and of McGee's careers in Ireland and the United States for his Ph.D. thesis at McGill. He has written several articles on D'Arcy McGee and other Canadian subjects.

Jane McLaughlin Côté is an economist by training and the author of several studies on the European Economic Community and inflationary trends in the Canadian economy. She is the author of *Fanny and Anna Parnell: Ireland's Patriot Sisters*, and is writing a biography of Helen Taylor, stepdaughter of John Stuart Mill.

Conor Cruise O'Brien is an author, journalist, former diplomat, and currently Pro-Chancellor of Dublin University. He has published many books including *A Concise History of Ireland, The Siege: The Saga of Israel and Zionism, God Land: Reflections on Religion and Nationalism*, and most recently (1992) *The Great Melody: A Thematic Biography of Edmund Burke*. He was a member of the Irish Parliament from 1969–77 and Minister of Communications from 1973–77. He was Editor-in-Chief of *The Observer* (London) from 1978–85, and currently writes a weekly column for *The Times* (London) and is a contributing editor of *The Atlantic* (Boston).

Joan Finnigan (MacKenzie) is an award-winning poet, playwright and oral historian, the author of twenty-four books. Some of these have elucidated the very special identity of the Ottawa Valley. They include *Some of the Stories I Told You Were True, Laughing All the Way Home,* and *Old Scores, New Goals: The Story of the Ottawa Senators, 1891–1992. Wintering Over,* her ninth collection of poetry, was on Ontario's Trillium short-list in 1993.

Garret FitzGerald was Minister for Foreign Affairs in Ireland from 1973 to 1977, and Prime Minister (*Taoiseach*) from 1981–87. He was Prime Minister when the Anglo-Irish Agreement was signed between Ireland and the United Kingdom in 1985. He published his memoirs in 1991.

S. Finn Gallagher teaches in the Department of English Literature, Trent University. He was president of the Canadian Association for Irish Studies (1990–93). He edited *Woman in Irish Legend, Life and Literature.* He chose and introduced plays by Hugh Leonard in volume 9 of the Irish Drama Selections series published by Colin Smythe/CUP of America. He has acted in and directed plays by Synge, Friel and Leonard.

Brenda Maddox is an American-born author and journalist living in London. She is the author of *Nora: A Biography of Nora Joyce,* which has been published in seven languages and nominated for the National Book Award It was winner of the Los Angeles Times Biography prize, the British Silver Pen Award for Non-Fiction, and the French Prix du Meilleur Livre Étranger. She writes a weekly column on media for the *London Daily Telegraph,* and for many years was Home Affairs Editor of *The Economist.* She is currently writing a biography of D.H. Lawrence.

Dominic Manganiello is Professor of English at the University of Ottawa. He completed a doctoral dissertation at Oxford University under the supervision of the late Richard Ellmann. It was later published as a book entitled *Joyce's Politics.* His recent book *T.S. Eliot and Dante* (1989) is a reflection of his larger interest in Dante's impact on the modern imagination. He is an advisory editor of the *James Joyce Quarterly.*

Roger Martin is a doctoral student at Queen's University, Kingston, Ontario. His Master's thesis at Queen's was entitled *Borderline Novels: Metafiction in the Historical Novels of Rudy Wiebe*. He is also an Assistant Editor at McGill-Queen's University Press.

Ken Mitchell is Professor of English at the University of Regina. One of Saskatchewan's best known writers, he has established an international reputation as a screenwriter (*The Hounds of Notre Dame*), poet (*Witches and Idiots*), novelist (*Wandering Rafferty*), and playwright (*Gond the Burning Sun, Cruel Tears*, and *Davin: The Politician*). A new novel, *The Stones of the Dalai Lama*, is being pubilshed in Canada and the United States in 1993.

Ira B. Nadel is Professor of English at the University of British Columbia. He is the author of *Biography: Fiction, Fact and Form* and *Joyce and the Jews: Culture and Texts*, and has co-edited *Gertrude Stein and the Making of Literature* and *George Orwell: A Reassessment*. He is on the editorial boards of the *Journal of Modern Literature*, *Joyce Studies Annual*, and *English Literature in Transition*.

James Noonan is Associate Professor of English at Carleton Univeristy, where he teaches Canadian Literature and the Literature of Modern Ireland. He has published many articles on Canadian drama and theatre in *Canadian Drama, Theatre History in Canada, The Oxford Companion to Canadian Literature*, and *The Oxford Companion to Canadian Theatre*. He is working on a study of the cultural acitivities of Canada's Governors General. He organized the 1991 conference of the Canadian Association for Irish Studies on which this book is based.

Laura O'Connor is a graduate student in the Department of English and Comparative Literature at Columbia University. She is writing her dissertation on the irruption of Celticity in Anglophone poetry. Her essay, "Slave Spirituals: Allegories of the Recovery from Pain," will appear in the forthcoming *Contemporary and Postmodern Approaches to Folklore*, edited by Cathy Lynn Preston.

Cathal G. Ó Háinle holds the Chair of Irish at Trinity College, Dublin. He was Professor of Irish at Maynooth from 1967–1977, and Registrar there from 1970–72. He became a Fellow of Trinity College in 1982. He has wide experience as a lecturer on Early Modern and Modern Irish literature, and in 1983 made a lecture tour of eight cities in the United States under the auspices of the Irish-American Cultural Institute. He is the author of two books, *Promhadh Pinn* and *Gearrscéalta an Phiarsaigh*, and of many articles on aspects of Irish literature.

James Olney is Voorhies Professor of English, French and Italian at Louisiana State University. He is the author of *Metaphors of Self: The Meaning of Autobiography, The Rhizome and the Flower: The Perennial Philosophy Yeats and Jung* and *The Language(s) of Poetry: Walt Whitman, Emily Dickinson, Gerard Manley Hopkins*, and editor of *Autobiography: Essays Theoretical and Critical* and *Studies in Autobiography*. He is also editor of *The Southern Review*.

James Reaney is a playwright, poet, and recently retired Professor in the English Department at the University of Western Ontario. One of Canada's best known playwrights, he has written for both children and adults. *Colours in the Dark* premiered at the Stratford Festival in Ontario under the direction of the late John Hirsch. *The Donnellys* trilogy, which premiered at Tarragon Theatre in Toronto, produced by Bill Glassco and directed by Keith Turnbull, toured across Canada with great success. He is presently working with composer John Beckwith on an opera libretto based on the Brontes' youthful writings.

Hereward Senior is Professor of History at McGill University. He has researched and written widely on Orangeism in Canada in books and journals, including the *Dictionary of Canadian Biography* and *The Untold Story: The Irish in Canada*. He is the author of *The Fenians and Canada* and most recently *The Last Invasion of Canada: The Fenian Raids, 1866-1870* (1992).

James White is Professor of the History of Art at the Royal Hibernian Academy. An art historian and author, he was formerly the Curator of the Municipal Gallery of Modern Art, Dublin, and the Director of the National Gallery of Ireland (1964–80). He has been Chairman of the Irish Arts Council, and an art critic for *The Standard*, *The Irish Press*, and *The Irish Times*. He is the author of *The National Gallery of Ireland*, *Jack B. Yeats John Butler Yeats and the Irish Renaissance*, and more recently *Pauline Bewick: Painting a Life* and *Gerard Dillon: A Biography*.

This book was set using
the TeX typesetting system.
The body was set in Pandora,
designed by Nina Billawala.
The Irish knotwork font is by
Jo Jaquina.